Far-Right Fantasy

Far-Right Fantasy is a straightforward, jargon-free study of contemporary American right-wing extremism. Accessible to both professional and lay audiences, it allows activists to speak for themselves in their own words. It takes the self-announced religious motivations of extremists seriously, and illustrates this by citing numerous cases of radical politics. The book addresses the strengths and weaknesses of the standard psycho-socio-cultural explanations of far-right activism. It shows how extremists are similar educationally and psychologically to their more conventional neighbors; that they get into the movement in the same way that others become peace activists or radical environmentalists, namely, through their ties with fellow workers and churchgoers, family members, and classmates; and that their views are given a patina of certainty by being repeatedly corroborated within closed, noncontaminated communication systems.

The book avoids being preachy or judgmental, but it does try to challenge readers morally by submitting far-right fantasy to a formal ideological critique. It does this by showing how the reforms it recommends—a marketplace free of regulation; draconian immigration restrictions; an end to the federal reserve bank and the income tax; a balanced budget amendment to the Constitution; antiunion right-to-work laws and a return to debt slavery; the privatization of schools, the post office, and the commons; and so on—contradict its ostensible goal, which is to protect and enhance middle-class interests. *Far-Right Fantasy* is suitable for adoption as a supplemental text in political psychology and sociology, sociologies of religion and knowledge, collective behavior, and American political history.

James Aho is Professor Emeritus at Idaho State University, Pocatello, Idaho.

Aho revisits the dark world of right-wing extremist 'Christian Patriots,' and readers benefit from his deep acquaintance with this movement, which he analyzes with penetrating sociological insights. Perhaps the most disturbing aspect of his account is the evidence he musters to indicate how the worldview of these 'far-right fantasists' has percolated into mainstream conservatism.

Peter Kivisto, *Richard A. Swanson Professor of Social Thought, Augustana College Research Fellow, University of Trento*

Aho's study of the right-wing fantasies of Christain Patriots and white supremicists is grounded in a lifetime's study of sociological methods, religious history, and first-hand encounters with extremists in his own home state of Idaho. As he dispels simple-minded explanations of these outliers on the American scene, he also offers us a deeper understanding of their ideologies and convictions. A delightful read as well as a profoundly informative work of scholarship.

Charles Guignon, *Emeritus Professor of Philosophy, University of South Florida and author of* On Being Authentic

Authoritatively written and masterfully analyzed, this penetrating study journeys into the dark world of America's Christian extremists and their dangerous political fantasies. It is as gripping as it is unsettling—a must read.

Mark Juergensmeyer, *author of* Terror in the Mind of God: The Global Rise of Religious Violence

Far-Right Fantasy
A Sociology of American Religion and Politics

James Aho

Routledge
Taylor & Francis Group

NEW YORK AND LONDON

First published 2016
by Routledge
711 Third Avenue, New York, NY 10017

and by Routledge
2 Park Square, Milton Park, Abingdon, Oxon OX14 4RN

Routledge is an imprint of the Taylor & Francis Group, an informa business

British Library Cataloguing in Publication Data
A catalogue record for this book is available from the British Library

Library of Congress Cataloging in Publication Data
Aho, James Alfred, 1942–
    Far-right fantasy : a sociology of American religion and politics /
    James Aho.
        pages cm
    Includes bibliographical references and index.
    1. Right-wing extremists--United States. 2. Religion and politics--United
    States. 3. United States--Politics and government. I. Title.
    HN90.R3A654 2016
    303.48'40973–dc23   2015023540

ISBN: 978-1-138-96241-5 (hbk)
ISBN: 978-1-138-96242-2 (pbk)
ISBN: 978-1-315-65944-2 (ebk)

Typeset in Times New Roman
by HWA Text and Data Management, London

Printed and bound in the United States of America by Publishers Graphics,
LLC on sustainably sourced paper.

I hate them with perfect hatred: I count them mine enemies.

(Psalms 139:22)

Contents

Acknowledgments

Were it not for the technical support, material resources, and encouragement of my colleagues at Idaho State University (ISU), most notably Gesine Hearn, Chair of the Department of Sociology, Social Work, and Criminal Justice, this book would never have been completed. For over four decades, ISU has given me the opportunity to indulge my whimsies; I hope what I have written here does not betray its trust.

Dean Birkenkamp is that rare editor who takes a personal interest in his authors, dispensing needed advice, good cheer, and timely responses to my manuscript drafts. I am thankful for having had the chance to work with him on this project.

I owe my three sons—Ken, Kevin, and Kyle—gratitude for exemplifying what it means to be a professional academician and artist. Their plodding devotion to their respective callings—biology, philosophy, and music—has been a constant source of inspiration and wonder.

Margaret Aho has been my personal in-house editor, critic, fellow intellectual adventurer, and loving companion for longer than even my stay at ISU. This book is inconceivable without her presence in my life, and is dedicated to her.

Large parts of Chapter 6 previously appeared in print as "Christian Heroism and the Reconstruction of America" in *Critical Sociology*, 39 (4): 345–60.

Prologue

The Battle of "Bunker Ville"

Cliven Bundy, a grizzled Mormon rancher, is said to have fifty-seven grand- and great-grandchildren. His family has grazed cattle on 600,000 acres of yucca- and mesquite-dotted desert near Bunkerville, Nevada, since 1877. In April 2014, federal agents rounded up Bundy's livestock for allegedly trespassing on Bureau of Land Management (BLM) property. During the ensuing scuffle, one of his sons was bloodied by a Taser gun, and a daughter was knocked to the ground.

Sensing a good story, Fox TV inflamed the situation by portraying Bundy as a "martyr" for freedom and liberty and theorized that the cattle seizure was part of "Agenda 21," a United Nations environmental conspiracy. Others on the far-right gossiped that Nevada Senator Harry Reid had orchestrated the BLM roundup so that a Chinese company he was invested in could build a solar power plant on the land and, still others, that Reid was trying to help a Canadian company access the land for a gold mine. Neither story was true (for a history of the dispute, see Fuller, 2014).

Responding to a call for supporters, an estimated 1,000 Patriot militiamen from across the country were "mobilized" and tweeted GPS coordinates so that they could negotiate their way to Bundy's homestead. On arriving, one of them, hefting a large pistol, told reporters, "I don't want no one to get hurt, but sometimes we have to stand up." A companion wagged his head in agreement and warned, "I'm ready to pull the trigger if fired upon." As if to underscore the seriousness of their threats, several weeks later two of the militia, Jerad and Amanda Miller, murdered a pair of Las Vegas policemen and a private citizen before killing themselves (see Appendix, June 8, 2014).

Wary of the danger the militia posed, a score of uniformed federal officers and growling K-9 dogs greeted the Patriots at Bundy's gate. They were then unceremoniously dispatched to their own holding pen, a fenced-off "first amendment area." There they posted a sign-up sheet ("Militia sign-in") and erected a banner reading, "Liberty and freedom for God we stand." There were placards: "End marshall [sic] law, now!"and "Utahans stands with Clive Bundy." Vows were made that if fired upon by the feds, they would use women and children as shields and record the massacre for posterity on their cell phones.

Bundy argued that on the basis of tenure rights recognized in common law, insofar as his family had worked the land for many years prior to the establishment of the BLM, "we own this land." He called on the local sheriff to disarm the federal interlopers and have them arrested for trespassing. Prudently, the sheriff demurred. (Bundy claims that when he arrived at his office, the sheriff was "hiding under a table.")

Fox News pundits praised Bundy, saying that the land under dispute "was not being used" and that, if anything, the Bundys should be given a medal for performing a "public service" by keeping the price of beef down and for "mowing the lawn."

The BLM maintains that the reason for the roundup in the first place was that Bundy had refused to pay grazing fees since 1993 and that his debt (at $1.35 monthly per animal unit [one cow and her calf]) × 240 months × 900 cows + interest, fines, and roundup expenses) equals more than $1 million. Bundy, they say, is a "million-dollar welfare deadbeat" and his actions are "unfair to the thousands of ranchers who graze livestock in compliance with federal laws and regulations." Besides this, Bundy's livestock threaten the habitat of the Mojave desert tortoise, an endangered species. Environmentalists add that Bundy's cattle hinder the ability of plants to recover from range fires and damage ancient Native American cultural sites and that Bundy's presence itself is a threat to recreationists.

Federal courts support the BLM complaint, arguing that the Nevada state constitution, written in 1863 by Civil War unionists a decade and a half prior to the arrival of the Bundy clan, grants the federal government "paramount allegiance" in land disputes. They ordered that Bundy remit the fees and fines, remove his herds from federal land, and cease interfering with the administration of law.

Bundy admits to being a citizen of the "sovereign state of Nevada" but does not recognize the authority of the United States, which he considers a "foreign country." He claims that federal agents illegally "seized Nevada statehood, and we're here to take it back ... . I'll do whatever it takes to gain our liberties and freedom back!" Bundy has said that the actions of the BLM confirm everything that the far-right has long supposed: This is "how the federal government feels about 'we the people'." They "pay to kill babies in the womb," and now they are "willing to kill an adult human being, Cliven Bundy, over a desert tortoise."

The militia issued an ominous forecast, saying that the impending "Battle of Bunker Ville" was "only the beginning," that "battlefield America" had become a reality and that a nationwide insurrection was imminent. As proof, they offered astronomical predictions of a "tetrad of blood moons," four total lunar eclipses, that would occur in the years 2014–15. This, they solemnly decreed, was an indisputable sign of the End Times.

As it turns out, the government siege ended peacefully. Cognizant that escalating tensions endangered people on both sides, the BLM quietly returned Bundy's cattle. (In the 1990s, as a protest against what locals said was "government over-reach," BLM and U.S. Forest Service offices in Nevada had been bombed.) Bundy's supporters erupted with joy, waved flags, and called him a hero. "The citizens of America," Bundy prated, had brought the standoff to an end by threatening force. The militia had "backed those bureaucrats down and they run out of this county into Utah."

What the BLM's concession portends remains to be seen. One Fox TV commentator interpreted it as a sign of President Barack Obama's seemingly inveterate weakness. Obama had "caved, as [he] did earlier with [Russian President] Vladimir Putin." And as was true for the Crimea and Ukraine, his frailty would only stir more resistance to tyranny. As if to confirm the point, the militia established armed checkpoints in the neighborhood of Bundy's ranch and demanded that drivers show proof of residency before being allowed to enter. Several dozen others traveled to nearby Blanding, Utah and, with their own children as shields, defied the government by driving ATVs (all-terrain vehicles) on roads the BLM had earlier closed to motorized travel to protect fragile Pueblo Indian burial sites.

Senator Reid has issued his own warning: "We can't have an American people that violate the law and then just walk away from it. So it's not over." He reminded voters of a series of armed encounters 30 years earlier that involved another Mormon government-hating rancher, Gordon Kahl, which resulted in several deaths, including Kahl's (Corcoran, 1996; see also Appendix, 1983).

Some recommend that the dispute be resolved by seizing Bundy's monetary assets, assuming he has any. Others suggest that his ranch house be foreclosed on, and still others that a lien be placed on his cattle so they can't be sold. One person even proposed that Patriots hold a fundraising drive to raise the million dollars or so that Bundy needs to pay off his debts. Much pro-Bundy sentiment faded away, however, after Bundy went on the air to "wonder" about "whether black people were better off as slaves," picking cotton and sitting on their porches watching over their chickens and gardens.

Introduction

This book concerns what a small but vociferous group of Americans believe has caused the loss of "their" country and the policies they recommend to get it back. It is a worldview so contrary to that of the average citizen as to warrant its own special designation: *far-right fantasy*. Far-right fantasists call themselves "Christian Patriots," a title that I will honor in these pages. Critics, however, say they are neither. Others are less charitable. Celebrated religious historian Karen Armstrong (2000: 361–2), for example, writes that far-right fantasy has "fascist potential," a judgment with which both Chris Hedges (2006) and Naomi Wolf (2007b) agree. The conservatively inclined Assembly of God Church speaks of it as displaying "unscriptural triumphalism," and Rick Perlstein (2007) condemns it as "Christian imperialism." Theologian Gregory Boyd (2007: 24) claims that far-right fantasy harbors a "demonic dimension," and Frank Schaeffer (2008) says, simply, that it is "anti-American." Schaeffer is the son of Francis Schaeffer, whose *Christian Manifesto* (1981) is discussed later.

As used here, *far-right fantasy* refers to an intellectual style with a belligerent tone, an exotic history of the world, and a concrete program of social reform. My argument is that its proponents are neither monsters, morons, nor madmen, but basically rational people of normal intelligence: good people with blind spots. Which is to say, they are superbly gifted at espying the "splinter" in their neighbor's eye, yet remain largely oblivious to the "log" in their own (Matt. 7:3–5; Luke 6:41–42). In this way they resemble the ancient Pharisees who are said to have thanked God "that I am not like the rest of men—extortionists, swindlers, adulterers, or even like this tax collector here" (Luke 18:9–14). It is this blind spot, this scotoma, that explains their sometimes flippant cruelty, their moral certitude and, above all, their unwillingness to compromise, even when the costs of inflexibility are exorbitant. The goal of this book is to aid the blind to recover their sight, so to say; to remind them, *and ourselves*, of the harm that can come from good intentions when untempered by wisdom, justice, and mercy.

My sojourn into the world of the radical right began in 1985 after learning about what has since become an all-too-familiar scene on the evening news: a shootout between federal marshals and a band of malcontents. They called themselves the *Brüders Schweigen*, a German phrase that means "brothers keep silent." Evidently, they had sworn an oath over the head of one of their infant children to reply, "I know nothing," if ever interrogated by the police (Flynn & Gerhardt, 1990).

The shootout had started when the *Brüders Schweigen* tried to shut down shipping lanes in Puget Sound, Washington, as a first step in what they hoped would grow into an all-out race war between themselves and what they called "ZOG," Zionist Occupation Government (i.e., the federal government) (Aho, 1990: 61–7). They maintained that ZOG was allied with Earth's "mud people"—blacks, Hispanics, Asians, and Indians, whose dark skins "proved" they have no souls—to rid Earth of spirit-inclined whites. Although it may be coincidental, ZOG bears an uncanny resemblance to Zod, the arch-villain of Superman's home planet of Krypton.

The mythology of the *Brüders Schweigen* derived from a heretical theology known as Christian Identity (CI), which holds that the ancient Israelites were not Jews at all but Aryans. Jews, CI teaches, are descended from Cain, history's first murderer, who is said to have been conceived by Eve after being impregnated by the Devil (the serpent of Genesis). After killing his brother Abel, so the story goes, Cain was exiled by God to "east of Eden," where he mated with the "witch women of Nod," giving his name to the Canaanites of the Old Testament. The Canaanites thenceforth evolved into the Jewish Zionists of our era. Meanwhile, the non-Jewish Israelites, after having been freed from Babylonian captivity, migrated over the Caucasus Mountains— hence, their racial type, Caucasian. According to CI, these Israelites settled in various European countries, some of which today presumably bear the titles of their founding tribes: Denmark, by the tribe of Dan, for example; Jutland, by the tribe of Judah; and so on. It is from the Aryan Israelites that Jesus Christ is said to have come. As evidenced by Sunday school paintings familiar to most readers, he was a movie-star chinned, brown-eyed brunette. And it is his blood that courses through the veins of Germans, Scandinavians, Finns, Russians, northern Italians, the British, and white Americans (for a comprehensive history of CI, see Barkun, 1996).

As it turned out, incendiary flares fired by the police ignited the cabin where the *Brüders Schweigen* were holed up, burning it to the ground. The body of its founder, a one-time John Birch Society activist, Robert Mathews, was found, roasted, in a bathtub (for his manifesto, see Aho, 1990: 246–50). In the ensuing months, scores of his followers were arrested and convicted of charges ranging from arson and armored car robbery—the largest at the time in American history—to counterfeiting, murder, and at least one teenage suicide.

The shootout might have passed me by unnoticed were it not for the fact that the *Brüders Schweigen* was hatched in the pine-forested lake country of northern Idaho, near the headquarters of a CI congregation known as the Church of Jesus Christ Christian (Aryan Nations). As a professor teaching at a university located within driving distance to the area, I undertook a several-year effort to comprehend what had transpired in my backyard. The findings of that research need not be reviewed here. It is important to note only that I renounced the entire project in April 1995 after a disaffected veteran of the first Iraq War, Timothy McVeigh, in the name of Christian Patriotism, blew the façade off the Murrah Federal Building in Oklahoma City, killing 168 mostly female clerks and children. Until Al Qaeda flew planes into the World Trade Center in New York City, September 11, 2001 (9/11), this was the bloodiest terrorist event ever witnessed on our shores.

By his own account, McVeigh was seeking revenge for an earlier armed encounter, also involving federal agents, with a right-wing extremist family who had occasionally attended services at the Church of Jesus Christ Christian (see Appendix, Aug. 21–31, 1992) and for another conflagration a year later, recorded for TV in real time, that incinerated over 25 children at the headquarters of the Branch Davidian sect outside Waco, Texas (Aho, 2006). McVeigh claimed to have been inspired by the same novel, *The Turner Diaries*, that had earlier served as the blueprint for the *Brüders Schweigen*. Reports are that he was so infatuated by the book that he was seen at gun shows giving away free copies.

Following the bombing, I began to have misgivings about my research, feeling that I was profiting from the misfortunes of others: g-men, the radicals themselves, and their wives and children. I came to believe that in a perverse way my fascination with political violence was adding to the seemingly voracious appetite for it in the public. In other words, I felt like a hypocrite. I was content with this stance until the late 2000s when I overheard the admonition, "Starve the Beast!" enunciated by a now-forgotten guest on a Fox TV talk show. Legend has it that the phrase had earlier been coined by an unnamed staffer with the Reagan administration; it first appeared in print in 1985 in the *Wall Street Journal*. I was introduced to it while attending an Aryan World Congress around that same time.

The Aryan World Congress was held each July at the barbed-wired compound of the Church of Jesus Christ Christian. Advertised as "bringing together the great minds of the Aryan movement," it attracted pretend SS officers in jodhpurs and black riding boots, garish-robed Klansmen, buttoned-down libertarian college students, and elderly Holocaust deniers from across the globe, including (the time I attended) a self-styled cowboy, Mormon polygamist. We have to "starve the Beast!" he told me, adding that his having multiple wives had nothing to do with sex. "That's a big misunderstanding." Rather, it is that by impregnating them he could produce many dependents, all of whom would live off the public dole. Since, he bragged, he paid no income taxes, this would help bankrupt the Beast described in Revelation 13:1–10.

Biblical exegetes claim that the Beast is an allegorical allusion to the Roman Empire, which CI insists worked with Jews to persecute the early Christian church. Today, however, it refers to the United States Government. *Ours*, the polygamist cowboy told me, are the Latter Days prophesied in the Book of Revelation, and the Battle of Armageddon between the sons of Darkness and the sons of Light is about to commence.

The Aryan World Congress was profoundly unsettling and, after having witnessed the lighting of a gigantic kerosene-soaked, rag-enshrouded cross (Aho, 1999), I drove back to my hotel room, giving thanks that I would never have to listen to such bile again. Imagine my dismay, then, to hear exactly the same expostulation—"Starve the Beast!"—and the strategy implied by it, promulgated by luminaries of the New Christian Right two and half decades later: first, by the Fox talk-show guest mentioned previously, then by the likes of Sarah Palin, Herman Cain, Michele Bachmann, and Rick Perry, all of whom would go on to participate in the Republican Party presidential primaries of 2010–11. Oratorical pronouncements that just a few years earlier were considered beyond the pale had, it seemed, been assimilated into the worldview of the Grand Old Party.

Palin, Cain, Bachmann, and Perry are not Aryans; Cain, for one, is black. Although a number of their followers do profess to racism, on the whole Palin and her fellows seem driven less by racial animus than by religious conviction. It is hard to envision them screaming, "The niggers are in! The niggers are in!" after learning of a local school being integrated, of decrying the machinations of the "Jews-media," or ruminating about "international Jewish bankers." Instead, they speechify about "equal opportunities, not equal outcomes," "reverse discrimination," "state's rights," "law and order," and "welfare queens" (a codeword for needy black women). While these are largely inaudible to the general public—in the sense of being heard yet not listened to—they encourage politically astute, prosperous older white males and their spouses to support politicians and policies that have the effect of disproportionally harming the poor, young minorities, and females (Lopéz, 2014). Eduardo Bonilla-Silva (2003) calls this rhetorical style "racism without racists." Lawrence Bobo, James Kluegel, and Ryan Smith (1997) speak of it as "laissez-faire racism," which they describe as a "kinder and gentler" variation of the same message once voiced by pre–civil rights era bigots.

If Palin, Bachmann, and the rest are not biological racists, neither are they conservatives in any conventional sense. Their stated intention is not to safeguard established authority through conciliatory means, a standard conservative goal, but to overthrow it altogether. They call for armed insurrection (Palin's so-called "Second Amendment remedies"), of state nullification of what they consider unconstitutional federal laws, of seceding from the country (Tea Party, 2012), and of voluntarily exiling themselves to armed enclosures within America's borders (Weyrich, 1999). They compare the U.S. government to Nazi Germany (GOP presidential aspirant Ben Carson, in Strauss, 2014), gleefully entertain the possibility of revolution, and liken themselves to the Founding Fathers, sometimes dressing the part. Above all, they take it as a compliment when real conservatives (in the sense just described) criticize them for being unwilling to compromise. "Thank you," says one, "for pointing out a quality I want the community to recognize ... Compromise is not in my nature" (Earl, 2014). They talk of the need to "shrink government down to the size where we can drown it in a bathtub" (Norquist, n.d.) and dabble in the politics of what conservative Michael Gerson characterizes as "apocalyptic utopianism." This is an outlook that gives little thought to the human costs of their policy proposals. Indeed, in some respects—absent his Judeophobia and racism—they remind one of Earl Turner, the central protagonist of the *Turner Diaries*, whose contempt for progressives is exceeded only by that for conservatives. Conservatives, says Turner, are not only the "world's biggest conspiracy mongers"; they are "also the world's greatest cowards." "Woe betide any whining conservative ... who gets in the way of our revolution." Rather than debating them, "I will simply reach for my pistol" (MacDonald, 1980: 63, 94). (For a less virulent, but equally contemptuous dismissal of conservatism by a typical far-right pundit, see Larsen, 2013b.)

The point is that while *I* may have disappeared after the bombing of the Murrah Building in 1995, the far-right did not. After initially suffering large-scale defections following the McVeigh bombing, the far-right returned with a vengeance when a "black man," Barack Obama, moved into the White House in 2009. Reports are that on the day of his inauguration three self-proclaimed Christian Patriots, one of whom had just compared him to Hitler and Stalin, snuck onto the walkway leading to the stage, anointed it with holy water, and prayed that it be cleansed of evil (Daily Kos, 2009). Less than a year later, a reputable poll reported that 35 percent of Republicans wanted to impeach Obama for "his actions so far" (Jensen, 2009). When, despite the GOP's best efforts to obstruct everything Obama proposed, the Patient Protection and Affordable Care Act (Obamacare) eked through Congress, extremist alarms were sounded. "The hour grows late!" shrieked one talk-show host. "The gates are open! The Nazis are here!" Libertarian Wisconsin Senator Ron Johnson called Obamacare "the greatest assault on freedom in our lifetime" (Johnson, 2013).

Rumors that Barack Obama had not been born in the United States and was thus ineligible to run for president persisted throughout the duration of his first term. Nevertheless, he was convincingly reelected in 2012. Attention on the far-right then shifted to how to subvert his signature legislation. Secret planning sessions are said to have been held and a "blueprint" devised on how to shut down the federal government if Obamacare was not defunded (Stolberg & McIntire, 2013). A "tool kit" was assembled to carry out the plan, underwritten by bequests of tens of millions of dollars from right-wing business elites. Elderly "sentinels" were paid to infiltrate town meetings and express their outrage at "socialized medicine"; fake "Obamacare cards" (to be burned on college campuses by "conscientious objectors" to health care for the poor) were printed; cliché-filled sample letters to the editor were composed; and a mass advertising campaign was mounted against those suspected of interfering with the anti-Obama campaign.

Soon thereafter, a national poll found that 29 percent of registered Republicans believed an "armed revolution" might be necessary to "protect our liberties" (Drudge, 2013) from a "tyrant," wrote one Patriot, who had "declared war" on the people (Earl, 2013a). Radio gossip repeated tales about President

Obama's hatred of the Constitution, his worship of Allah, his devotion to the Muslim Brotherhood, and his similarity to Hitler (Now the End Begins, 2009–2014). It told about how he had lost his license to practice law because of his criminality, how he had given away cell phones to poor people and free food to illegal immigrants in order to win their votes, and how he was secretly married to another man. He was, one Patriot concluded, "the most dangerous person that's ever walked in these United States" (quoted by Capehart, 2013).

Talk turned to the advisability of the "real" America—the old Confederacy, the Midwest, and the Rocky Mountain states—seceding from the country. And reminiscent of the so-called "Running Nigger" targets I first came across at the Aryan World Congress "nigger shoot" (Aho, 1990: 230), National Rifle Association (NRA) convention-goers in May 2013 were given the opportunity to purchase human-sized, plastic Obama targets that would, they were promised, bleed when shot. (After being displayed for two days, the vendor removed the target at the request of the NRA [Miller, 2013].) One activist, speaking to a Don't Tread on Me, Confederate flag-waving crowd, warned that President Obama "needs to leave town, get up off his knees, put the Qur'an down, and come out of the White House with his hands, figuratively, out—up" (Alman, 2013). Days earlier, that same speaker had set a date for Obama to resign if he wished to avoid being jailed for his "Muslim, socialist, anti-Christian, antiwhite, pro–illegal immigrant, pro–radical gay and lesbian agenda" (Brown, 2013).

Death threats against President Obama reached historic highs soon after he took office, averaging thirty a day, a rate four times higher than those directed at President George W. Bush (Harnden, 2009). In 2010, the Southern Poverty Law Center described the recent proliferation of right-wing paramilitary organizations nationwide as "astounding" (National Public Radio, 2010). Three days after Obama's reelection in 2012, a crazed Idahoan, announcing that he was a "modern Jesus Christ," took it upon himself to save the country from what he called "the Devil" by firing on the White House with a semiautomatic rifle. After leaving at least five bullet pockmarks on the building, he sped from the scene, crashed his car into a highway abutment and, to avoid life imprisonment for attempted assassination, pled guilty to illegal gun use.

In 2013, the self-anointed "founder" of the modern militia movement, one J.B. Campbell, emerged blinking into the sunlight in Teton Valley, Idaho, to announce that Obama was a "rabid dog" out "to enslave all of us and kill some of us" (Levy, 2013; cf. Campbell, 2011). Predictably, there followed a run on local firearms and ammunition. "Preppers" throughout the upper Rocky Mountain region began stocking up on nonperishable enzyme-rich vegetable juice extracts and water jugs. Plans were made to erect armed "redoubts with defensible perimeters" high in the mountains to fend off city-dwelling liberals who, it was said, would soon be fleeing chaos in the lowlands.

I could go on, but the point, I think, has been made: The time has come for me to re-engage the larger conversation about happenings on the far-right with the tools afforded by my professional training as a sociologist. My earlier reluctance to feed the hungry maw of American loathing has been superseded by a more urgent obligation—to understand and, if possible, temper the voices of hate.

I am well aware that there exists a virtual library of coverage about the contemporary extremist right. In fact, I draw on much of it in this book. The most recent and informative example is Leonard Zeskind's *Blood and Politics* (2009), a masterfully detailed account of how, since the 1970s, far-right ideology has gravitated from the margins of American political discourse to inform mainstream "conservative" thinking on a host of policy issues, domestic and foreign. There is a problem with Zeskind's account, however, at least from the standpoint of sociology: It lacks methodological rigor and theoretical grounding. Zeskind addresses the who, the when, the what, and the where of right-wing extremism, but overlooks the most pivotal question of all: why? Why is there such a phenomenon at all? And why are some people drawn to it? To address these questions, we need to approach the subject from a different angle. Instead of just ordering things temporally as Zeskind does, we must base our analysis on what social scientists have come to believe are some of the reasons behind hate groups, urban legends, and political violence.

Journalists are in the habit of spinning social conflicts in order to advance partisan ends. Sociology has a very different goal, namely, to learn what animates the disputants in the first place. The word for this is *Verstehen*, a German term that means literally to "stand there" (*stehen*) in the subjects' shoes. Instead of berating them from a distance, sociologists try to get up close to them, momentarily suspend judgments, and then empathetically "take their role": seeing, thinking, recalling, and feeling about the world as they do. Georg Simmel (1977) has argued that the ultimate test of whether *Verstehen* has been attained in a particular case is if the analyst in question can glimpse something of him- or herself in the subjects and aspects of the subjects in him- or herself. Exactly how one goes about doing this goes beyond our immediate concerns. All that needs to be emphasized here is that *Verstehen* can go a long way to help promote civil discourse. After all, it is hard to demonize another if you can see yourself in them (and them in yourself).

Having said this, it is important to note that no one is *just* a sociologist. Once they doff their professional spectacles, sociologists can be as censorious and mean-spirited as the next person. There is an advantage to being habituated to the discipline required for doing sociology, however. It is that its practitioners are instilled with warning bells that alert them when their parsing begins devolving into preaching and they risk becoming what they decry. It hardly needs to be added that no matter how dispassionate and fair-minded sociologists want and believe themselves to be, it is naïve for them to expect extremists of any sort to extend to them the same courtesy.

As readers probably already know, there are sociologies of pretty much anything: family life, economic behavior, youth culture, personal faith, crime, the body, and even time. This book falls under the category known as the sociology of knowledge. This is a specialty that seeks to describe, explain and, where appropriate, critique how such collectivities as classes, races, religions, and nations perceive, wonder about, remember, and emote toward the things around them (for an introduction to the sociology of knowledge as used here, see Aho, 1998). In regard to the subject of this book, my goal is first of all to understand the lived world of Christian Patriots, not from the viewpoint of their detractors but from the "inside," from the standpoint of the Patriots themselves. This requires that we drink deeply from their considered fountains of wisdom: their books and pamphlets, orations, Internet blogs, letters to the editor, radio commentary, videos, and so forth. I am especially interested in the Patriot theory of history, how it accounts for the events that disturb them and what it recommends by way of reform.

My second objective is to review what social scientists have determined are the causes of this way of experiencing the world, why Patriots believe as they do. Are they, as some claim, ill-educated or crazy? Are they drawn to the cultic elements of extremism because of their social alienation? Or is the opposite true: Are they fanatical because of who their friends and acquaintances are? Do they see themselves as innocent victims of a "war on whites," to quote an Alabama congressman (McCalmont, 2014)? And finally, what role does the peculiarity of their communication systems play in the generation and sustenance of their beliefs?

My third and final objective is to conduct what is technically known as an "ideology critique." Here, instead of imposing on Patriots moral standards with which they may disagree, I try to uncover internal inconsistencies between their professed goals and the means they advocate to achieve them.

Sociology has a well-deserved reputation for turgidity and obfuscation and for a propensity to turn active-voiced verbs into passive nouns. In fact, the very term *sociology* is a nineteenth-century neologism fabricated out of Greek and Latin. To avoid marginalizing myself from current debate about the far-right, this book seeks to break through the chatter, the tedious statistics and, wherever possible, the long words; to address the questions before us in a straightforward, simple, if not simple-minded, way. If this contributes in some small degree to a better understanding of right-wing extremism, momentarily disarming fearful, hate-filled voices on all sides, thereby lessening the likelihood of violence, I will be satisfied.

Chapter 1 discusses how I use the term *far-right* in these pages, and it places the contemporary movement in the wider context of American political history. My aim is to show that while outbreaks of right-wing fanaticism are typically experienced as unprecedented and novel by their enthusiasts and critics, there is rarely anything new or, for that matter, of lasting significance about them. This should disarm "catastro-freaks," as I like to call them, who see in the recent upsurge of extremism "The End of America."

Chapters 2 and 3 provide an overview of what social scientists consider to be the preconditions of right-wing radicalism. It is primarily for the benefit of readers unfamiliar with the vast research on hate and hate groups and provides them with some of the classic references to which they can go to further their knowledge of the subject. Chapter 2 examines theories relating to formal education, psychosis, authoritarianism, and social estrangement. My goal here is to normalize extremists by showing that by and large they are psychologically and socially indistinguishable from their less ideologically purposed neighbors. Chapter 3 refocuses the question of causality by taking into consideration what activists *themselves* say about their motives. This leads to discussion of the cultural memes of white male victimhood and heroic redemption.

Chapter 4 deals with how far-right fantasies are nurtured, namely, through self-referential "echo-chamber" systems of communication. I argue that such systems attract communicants who have a need for nonfalsifiable certainties, a yearning that increases when, among other things, official claims makers breach the public trust. Distrust is aggravated under conditions of secrecy.

In Chapters 5 and 6 we step into the shoes of Christian Patriots to get a close-up look at their fantasies. Chapter 5 deals with the Patriot claim that there is a plot afoot to "satanify" the nation. While this is advertised as a fresh revelation, in actuality it is a literary theme traceable to America's founding, if not far earlier. This suggests that the legend of a conspiracy is less a reflection of reality "out there" than a projection *onto* that reality of deep-seated, perhaps unconscious personal issues. The balance of Chapter 5 focuses on recent allegations of government plots to promote gun massacres and bombings, establish a collectivist educational curriculum, and dramatically alter the climate.

Chapter 6 delves into a second fantasy, that by "re-Christianizing" America, reconstructing it on the basis of (presumed) biblical/constitutional designs, the fate prophesied by conspiratologists[1] can be averted. Here I detail the political economic program advanced by Christian Dominionism, the considered vanguard of the far-right movement in the present era. In the liberal media, Dominionism is associated with "no!" No to equal rights for gays, no to abortion, no to undocumented immigrants, no to global warming, no to Darwinism, no to scientific geology, no to helio-centrism (the theory that Earth revolves around the Sun), no to artificial birth control, and sometimes even no to vaccinations against deadly diseases. But as Albert Camus (1956 [1947]) has shown in his study of the rebel, every no implies a yes, every rejection an affirmation. The point of chapter 6 is to spell out exactly what this yes is for Christian Patriots.

Chapter 7 offers a critique of Christian Dominionism, demonstrating how it is not only impious and hypocritical but, more important, how it is "ideologically false." That is, the policies it recommends are inconsistent with its ostensible goals. This once again underscores its fantastical nature.

Chapter 8 comments on a second kind of falsity emblematic of Dominionism: false consciousness. This refers to the unwillingness or inability of Patriots to acknowledge that the dragons they labor so tirelessly to slay are largely their own fabrications.

Following each chapter there is an Interlude that illustrates what Christian Patriotism means today: advocacy of secession, sovereign citizenship, racially pure townships, the shutting down of the government, and so on. The Epilogue describes one of the latest and most bizarre experiments on these lines: the effort to establish a radical Patriot communal theme park.

The number of Christian Patriots who resort to firearms and bombs to get their way is miniscule, but it is estimated that from 1980 through 2014 this tiny aggregate has been implicated in over 400 violent deaths: murders, suicides, and killings by police. The Appendix itemizes the dates, locations, names of the perpetrators, and body counts of the relevant encounters. Many of these are referred to in the course of the text.

Note

1 Neither "conspiratologist'"nor "conspiratology" (a term I introduce in Chapter 5) are in *Webster's*. Both terms, however, are widely invoked by far-right rhetoricians. I do not use terms like 'conspiracy-monger' or 'conspiracy-mongering' in this book, in order to avoid casting aspersions on this style of thinking. Conspiratologists, as they call themselves, consider what they do to be serious historical inquiry, not 'mongering.' There exists an Institute of Conspiratology, an International Conspiratological Association, and a Royal Institute for Conspiratology, all of which claim to conduct 'scientific' investigations into the alleged one-world plot.

Interlude 1

Sovereign Citizens

Following a four-month undercover investigation by the Las Vegas Metro Police, David Brutsche, 42, and Devon Newland (female), 67, were arrested in 2013 for plotting to torture, try, and then execute police officers found guilty of "treason" by a private citizens' court. Reportedly, the couple had rented a vacant house for use as a jail, rigged its crossbeams with ropes to bind the "defendants," and prepared a way to "arrest" them as they conducted routine traffic stops.

Brutsche is a convicted child predator and considers himself a "Sovereign Citizen," so named after the title of a leaderless radical movement that has been involved in several murders in the last few years (see Appendix, Feb. 18 and May 20, 2010, Jan. 26 and 30 and Aug. 16, 2012, June 6 and 8, 2014), including the bombing of the Murrah Federal Building in Oklahoma City. According to its on-line pronouncements, Sovereign Citizens believe that one can be either a "true American" or a "slave" of a corporation known as the United States, not both. The U.S. Corporation is said to have been established according to the strictures of British admiralty law, which itself presumably was written to facilitate colonialism, the plantation system, and the enslavement of both white Irish people and black Africans. The website says that at birth each child is given a corporate account that assigns him or her to a specific corporate bond holder and allots to the child a grant of money that can be accessed by filing appropriate papers. As reputed "Americans," Sovereign Citizens refuse to pay taxes, purchase license plates, or buy driver's licenses. (Timothy McVeigh initially was arrested for driving a car that had no plates.) They print their own currency and the legalistic papers they believe are sufficient to access their corporate accounts. Because they do not acknowledge the legitimacy of any law enforcement official but the "shire-reve"(sheriff), a pre-twelfth-century English rural magistrate that predates the existence of the modern police, urban police forces such as Las Vegas Metro are, by definition, seen as criminal enterprises.

1 The American Far-Right in Perspective

More than a half century ago, sociologist Seymour Martin Lipset (1960) postulated that each stratum of modern society—upper, middle, and lower—has a characteristic brand of demagogic extremism and an audience for it. "Working-class authoritarianism," for example, finds its core of support among the lower stratum of manual blue-collar laborers and peasants. Conservative authoritarianism, on the other hand, attracts the upper stratum of nontitled gentry, landed aristocrats, ordained clerics, and the general staff of the military. As for the middle stratum of small merchants and farmers, craftspeople, low-level clerks, and professionals, they gravitate toward what Lipset calls "classical fascism," an objectionable label that I will avoid in these pages (for a scathing critique of the rhetorical abuses of "fascism," see Gregor, 2006).

Lipset characterizes the authoritarianism of the middle ranks this way: It is hostile to both the lower and upper classes, although it can temporarily ally with either. It glorifies the "exceptionalism" of the middle ranks, whose values and interests it conflates with those of the nation. It calls for moral renewal, meaning the bourgeois ethos of small merchants that valorizes industriousness over idleness and luck, promotes deferred gratification, and advocates frugality. It is xenophobic, except when foreigners can be economically exploited, and jingoistic when not inward turning and isolationist. Most important, it utilizes "nondemocratic" means to achieve its ends. Updated to take into consideration recent American developments, without being exhaustive, these include:

- Denying or suppressing the civil rights of poor minority citizens, including their access to public accommodations and/or to certain occupations. Denying them the right to marry and/or adopt children; to express themselves and/or worship as they see fit; to bodily privacy; and/or the rights that would otherwise be granted them as criminal suspects (trial before a jury of their peers, competent counsel, protection from illegal search and seizure, immunity from torture or cruel and unusual punishment, and immunity from double jeopardy, etc.);
- Infringing on or denying the political rights of poor minority citizens, including the right to vote and/or to hold office or to peacefully petition civil authorities; this by geographically limiting their access to polls, setting

up onerous voting requirements, or outlawing same-day registration or Sunday voting;
- Denying the social rights of poor minority citizens, including their right to a reasonable public education, food surpluses, adequate shelter, and/or competent health care;
- State nullification of what are considered unconstitutional federal laws and mandates, such as those concerning racial desegregation, mandatory federal health insurance, and/or federal gun registration;
- Advocacy of secession from the United States;
- Politically motivated welfare fraud, robbery, counterfeiting, tax evasion, and/or the issuance of fraudulent liens;
- Criminalization of efforts by state and/or local officials to enforce considered-unconstitutional federal laws; the use of nonauthorized private "citizens' courts" to try such officials; and/or the execution of their judgments by means of private citizens' militias or posses;
- Establishment of private paramilitary encampments, engagement in combat training exercises, and/or the display of weapons in public for purposes of political intimidation;
- Vigilante monitoring of border crossings and/or the private lives of citizens; and
- Armed insurrection through nonfatal assaults on citizens, targeted assassination, and/or indiscriminate murder (for examples, see Appendix).

Lipset observes that whatever such "classical fascists" as Franco, Hitler, Tojo, Mussolini, Perón, Pinochet, or Poujade (an anti-Jewish French tax resister and advocate of the "Common Man") have in common, the flavor of a country's middle-class extremism always reflects its history and culture. Thus, insofar as the American far-right emerges from a middle stratum imbued with a fundamentalist Protestant outlook and with a mythos of constitutional republicanism, its authoritarianism marches under the Cross and Flag. That is, it exhibits a puritanical obsession with (female) body functions, dirty pictures, homosexuality, and erotic books, dance, and music. It is unfriendly toward non-Christians and nonfundamentalist Protestant Christianities, which it rebukes as "cults." It is suspicious of "nonproductive" mental activities such as science for itself, the fine arts, and poetry. Its republican antipathy toward royalty takes the form of distrust of "big government." And its antagonism toward the working class finds an outlet in hostility toward labor unions, which it equates with socialism or Communism.

A telling case of American-style ultra-right politics is the anti-intellectual, antipapist, anti–eastern European immigrant American Protective Association of the 1890s, whose rolls are said to have included 2.5 million members from 1893 to 1894. This was an era during which Jim Crow laws were introduced in the Confederate South and the Supreme Court (in *Plessey v. Ferguson*) ruled that racial segregation and the denial of voting rights to blacks were constitutional.

Another example is Louisiana "dictator" Huey Long who, in the 1930s, campaigned against the Bourbon gentry on behalf of the "Little Man." Still another is (Catholic) Father Charles Coughlin's National Union for Social Justice, the first right-wing movement in America to market itself through radio broadcasts, the audience for which was over 1 million by the late 1930s. Sinclair Lewis uses Coughlin as the model for Bishop Prang in his antifascist dystopia, *It Can't Happen Here* (1935). In Philip Roth's *The Plot against America,* based on the author's childhood traumas, Coughlin is portrayed as a particularly villainous figure. While at one time he supported Franklin Roosevelt's New Deal, Coughlin eventually turned against it (and him), claiming it favored New York banks over Main Street merchants. Wall Street, he said, was one of the "twin faces of Satan," the other being Bolshevism. Both, he contended, were Jewish plots.

Other, more recent, instances of right-wing extremism include Rev. Carl McIntire's Christian Anti-Communist Crusade of the late 1950s and Rev. Gerald L. K. Smith's *Cross and Flag*. Smith's one-time bodyguard, ex-Methodist minister and Ku Klux Klan chaplain Rev. Wesley Swift, founded the Church of Jesus Christ Christian (Aryan Nations) mentioned in the Introduction. A fourth instance is Rev. Gerald Winrod, the so-called "Jayhawk (Kansas) Nazi," who flourished in the Midwest in the 1930s and 1940s. The latest expression of comparable sentiments can be found in Christian Dominionism, an outgrowth of an even more radical movement known as Christian Reconstruction, both of which are discussed at length in Chapter 6.

Lipset points out that the American middle class has experienced many outbursts of ultra-right insurgency but, for the most part, its politics lean liberal. That is, it favors the extension of the voting franchise and civil rights to once-excluded minorities, supports universal access to education, parks, utilities, and medical care, and champions measures that encourage open competition and a culture of achievement over inheritance and titles. During times of economic distress and/or status insecurity, however, its politics can turn mean-spirited, reactionary, and "to some degree irrational" (Lipset, 1960: 136). This is the thesis of his encyclopedic social history of American extremism, co-authored with Earl Raab, *The Politics of Unreason* (1970). In it Lipset argues that all major American right-wing movements, beginning with the anti-Illuminatists of the early 1800s, have been composed of people who feel disempowered and displaced by industrialization, immigration, urbanization, and government bureaucratization. Besides the groups cited earlier, Lipset and Raab mention the Anti-Masonic Party (of the 1830s), the Southern secessionist movement (of the 1850s and 1860s), the "new" Ku Klux Klan, which came into control of municipal and state governments from Indiana to Oregon during the 1920s; McCarthyism and the John Birch Society of the 1950s and 1960s, George Wallace's American Independent Party in 1968, and (in Lipset & Raab, 1981) the New Christian Right of the 1980s, whose most rabid cadres were members of the Christian Coalition and the Moral Majority. (For a critique of Lipset and Raab's account of the New Christian Right, see Simpson, 1983.) There is evidence that one-time Klan leader David Duke's nearly successful campaign for Louisiana governor in 1991 also drew its most energetic support from the "dispossessed" middle class (Zeskind, 2009: 271–7).

To label these and related movements "fascistic" is, as I said earlier, unfortunate for a number of reasons, not the least of which is that the word was not even coined until the 1920s and then by Futurist Italians, whose probable nearest American cousins—absent Italian fascism's glorification of battle-torn flesh and the mystical communion of race and nation (very big absences indeed)—were the proponents of technocracy. Technocrats have little in common with the science-wary, backward-looking, profamily fundamentalist Protestants and Constitution fetishists who historically fill the ranks of American rightist insurgencies.

For all this, however, Lipset and Raab's historically grounded, measured tone is leagues ahead of what passes today as intelligent political commentary. "Femi-Nazi," "lesbo-fascist," and "food-Nazi" (as used by radio entertainer Rush Limbaugh to describe feminist "sluts" and officials at the Center for Disease Control, respectively) are routinely bandied about, often interchangeably, with "socialist," "liberal," "Fabian," and "Progressive," sometimes in the same sentence. Indeed, if we can believe recent punditry, left- and right-wing alike, we are awash in fascists. There are "eco-fascists" (Murray Bookchin's term), "Islamofascists" (a favorite phrase of the late Christopher Hitchens, and critically slammed by Sheehi [2011]), "body fascists" (Pronger, 2002), "technofascism" (a reference to mechanized music), "the merry band of [atheist] fascists" (Bill O'Reilly), and "homo-fascists" (Glenn Beck's term for gays and lesbians who are conspiring to "force" Americans to grant them "special rights"). And this is to name just a few. According to Jonah Goldberg (2007), there are even counterintuitive "liberal fascists." In sum, what George Orwell once observed is true: "The word 'fascism' … is almost entirely meaningless, except in so far as it signifies 'something not desirable'" (Orwell, 1944).

Take liberal fascism. Goldberg announces that, contrary to what readers might think, fascism is not a right-wing phenomenon at all. "Instead, it is, and always has been, a phenomenon of the left" (J. Goldberg, 2007: 7). Adolf Hitler, head of the National Socialist German Workers Party, for example, was a devoted "man of the left." So too, Goldberg insists, were the "Progressive fascists," Woodrow Wilson and Franklin Roosevelt. In fact, to Goldberg (2007: 8), American Progressivism was not just a relative of fascism; it was "in some respects the major source of the fascist ideas applied … by Mussolini and Hitler." He alleges that Progressivism, in turn, was in thrall to history's "first fascist movement, the French Revolution" (2007: 12). A more sober assessment of Roosevelt is that he was an easygoing, conservatively inclined, but otherwise ideologically blind pragmatist who borrowed his ideas ad hoc from virtually every conceivable source. "There was no master plan, no guiding philosophy, for the reforms that Roosevelt oversaw," according to David M. Kennedy in his Pulitzer Prize–winning biography, *Freedom from Fear* (quoted by Menand, 2013: 72).

Jonah Goldberg (2007) goes on to argue that in the present moment, Hillary Clinton is the most cunning and dangerous agent of the fascist conspiracy. (His book was composed before her presidential ambitions were crushed in 2008 by Barack Obama, whom Goldberg would view as an even more sinister character.) Included in Goldberg's itemization of so-called "crypto-fascist" sentiments are medical homeopathy, the animal rights movement, New Age spiritualism, vegetarianism, advocacy of artificial contraception, antismoking campaigns, the Civilian Conservation Corps (the harmless Boy Scout–like work project that built trails and shelters in national forests during the 1930s), and John F. Kennedy's Peace Corps. By all appearances, in Goldberg's imagination, "fascism" is his verbal substitute for the cultural orientation of modernity, with its embracement of difference, its scientific skepticism, and its toleration of moral ambiguity.

The Audience for American Right-Wing Extremism

Whatever we call it, and whatever its source, the American appetite for far-right ideology has always been small, and that remains true today. A 2013 survey finds that membership in its latest, most vocal iteration, the tea party, adds up to only a fraction of the American public: to be exact, 0.14 percent (or 14 for every 10,000 citizens) (Burghart, 2014). The count of tea party sympathizers is a bit larger than this. As indicated by "favorable" responses to polling queries about the tea party, this number fluctuates somewhere between 20 and 40 percent of the public, depending on the crisis of the moment. The percentage of active supporters, as operationalized by Facebook "likes," however, totals but 2 percent. As has been the case for far-right activism since at least the 1980s (cf. Aho, 1994: 153), about two-thirds of tea party members are men, with the largest per capita representation coming from the sparsely populated, rural states of Alaska (no. 1), Montana (2), Wyoming (3), Idaho (4), and Utah (5).

The results of more comprehensive surveys comport with this. One poll conducted by the Pew Center on the religious landscape of the United States (Pew Forum, 2008) found that no more than one-quarter of Americans are affiliated with an evangelical Protestant church (either liberal or reactionary).[1] George Barna (2008) argues that far fewer than half of these, perhaps 10 percent of all Americans, can rightly be considered political activists. These 10 percent are the subject of this book.

As tiny as the tea party or any other right-wing insurgency is or has been, it is a grave mistake to dismiss any of them as artificial fabrications of business elites or media executives (as claimed, for example, by Eric Zuesse, 2013). As we will see presently, right-wing movements burst from the grass roots as expressions of popular discontents and grow through face-to-face contact between ordinary people at the workplace, church, and school. Only after they have taken root are they set upon by profiteers, proselytizers, politicians, and pundits to enhance their own interests.

Cycles of Far-Right Enthusiasm

Many commentators are willing to concede that in the past the American far-right was able to mobilize only a small following, but today, they claim, the situation is different (cf. Wolf, 2007a). After all, Lipset, Raab, Hofstadter, and others such as Louis Hartz (1955) were writing during an era of buoyant postwar optimism, when prosperity was relatively widely shared and there was unanimity of national vision. But that reality no longer exists. America's erstwhile enemy, the Soviet Union, has faded into obscurity and been superseded by a succession of cartoon bogeymen such as "Panamanian Strongman Manuel Noriega," the "Communist outpost" of Grenada, the blustering Iranian traffic engineer, Mahmoud Ahmadenijad, and the pudgy North Korean despot, Kim Jong Un. Most important, to an extent not witnessed for over a century, America's surplus wealth has been expropriated by bankers and corporate CEOs, leaving the American middle stratum comparatively impoverished, its opportunities for upward mobility shattered, and its political prospects hollowed out. (For riveting documentation of this fact, see Packer, 2013, and Dyer, 1997.) Which is to say, any capacity American institutions once may have had to moderate the frothing rages of authoritarian demagogy from the right (or the left) has collapsed—some fear, forever. In other words, so the argument goes, ours is an unprecedented age, not one of temperance and magnanimity but of misery, bitterness, and despair, and a style of political thinking has arisen to mirror it: far-right fantasy. The 1995 Oklahoma bombing, warns Joel Dyer, was "only the beginning of [what he predicts will be] an unprecedented wave of terror" (Dyer, 1997: 2).

Before jumping to conclusions, however, let us pause for a moment to reconsider past periods of ultra-right insurgency, when equally dire warnings were aired, and a pattern becomes evident: While far-right fantasies are always afloat in the cultural atmosphere, and have been since the beginning (Stock, 1996), they seem to seize the public imagination only every third decade or so, as phases of a larger cycle of Democratic-revisionist vs. Republican-traditionalist ascendancies (Schlesinger Jr., 1986).

Take the anti-Illuminatist fervor of the early 1800s. After it barely left behind a footprint of its short existence, the Anti-Masonic movement arose in the 1830s to take its place. Then, three decades later, Southern secessionists placed Fort Sumter, South Carolina, under siege and ignited the Civil War. After Americans tired of killing each other over the question of slavery, in the 1890s political attention shifted again, this time to the perils of eastern European immigrants and Asians; the American Protective Association was born. This, in turn, was followed by a resuscitated Ku Klux Klan, which during the 1920s grew to 3 million members (Chalmers, 1981 [1965]: 291). The 1920s were a period of antiblack lynch mobs, anti-Asian riots, and passage of a National Prohibition Act, the first attempt in American history to outlaw a consumable substance associated in urban legend with foreign immigrants. Thirty years later came the grim, dark days of the 1950s, when "tail gunner Joe" McCarthy brought forth his anti-Communist tirades. Until the coattails of Ronald Reagan carried a newly awakened right-wing into Congress in 1980, the McCarthy era was the only period since the New Deal during which the GOP held a majority of either house of Congress. Finally, and with uncanny predictability, in 2010 (or more precisely, early 2009), a new incarnation of right-wing enthusiasm arose: the tea party. Stoked by "very conservative business elites" interested in lowering taxes, deregulating commerce, and ending "entitlements" to "freeloaders" (illegal immigrants, retirees, and college students), before a year had passed the tea party was staging massive protest rallies and running candidates for office. (For a detailed time line, see Williamson, Skocpol, and Coggin, 2011: 37–9.)

When their programs have not been watered down and assimilated into the platforms and policies of various political parties, each upsurge of right-wing extremism quickly burns itself out. Often, this is accompanied by prosecutions for embezzlement of movement funds, allegations of fraud and corruption, acts of armed intimidation, and/or rumors of sexual impropriety. Soon thereafter come finger pointing, schism, and public derision. The ultra-rightist mood slinks back into the recesses of the collective unconscious, where it festers like a cicada, until several years later when it noisily bursts again from its cocoon. This is when a younger generation of activists, just coming to political age and for whom rightist ideas are still novel and exciting, begins to reconstitute itself around a new demagogue. "Each generation," says Arthur Schlesinger Jr. (1986: 30), "spends its first fifteen years after coming of political age in challenging the generation already entrenched in power. Then the new generation comes to power itself for another fifteen years, after which its policies fail and the generation coming up behind claims the succession."

Schlesinger goes on to say that this 30-year cycle "has nothing to do" with business booms and busts. True, the anti-Catholic American Protective Association reached its high point during an economic recession, as did support for Ronald Reagan (although in Reagan's case, the downturn happened after he took office as a result of his own monetary policies). The same is true of the tea party, Father Coughlin, and Huey Long: Each appeared during periods of massive unemployment and widespread economic distress (Lipset & Raab, 1970: 194–7). But the anti-Catholic Know-Nothing movement of the 1840s gained its widest following during an era of economic expansion and full employment, as did the hooded hatred of the Klan, which rocketed to popularity during the Roaring Twenties. The John Birch Society emerged during a period of unprecedented postwar prosperity.

The point is that economic dislocation is not new to American history. It *is* American history. For every anchor store in a suburban mall put out of business today by an e-retail firm, a downtown general store went bust a century ago owing to the introduction of postal catalogue commerce. And for every family farm being bankrupted now by the nearby presence of an agribusiness, many more were victimized by debt a century ago. True, foreclosures are always accompanied by heartache and sometimes by addiction, domestic abuse, and suicide, but they are not always followed (as they were in the 1980s [Zeskind, 2009: 114–15]) by "wildfires" of right-wing rage. Occasionally, they spawn progressive reforms, as during the 1900s and 1930s.

As early as 1924, Schlesinger's father, Arthur Sr., was using a 33-year marker to forecast American political futures. With it he foretold an imminent end to the scrooge-like Coolidge era, when Congress debated whether postmen's bags should be painted white and blue or remain canvas gray (in order to save $50,000) (Mallon, 2013: 70). He also predicted that rightist extremism would reappear in 1947 and once more in 1978. We are not surprised to learn, then, that President Truman signed the National Security Act in 1947, which ignited the second "red scare" (the first having occurred in 1917), and that the Moral Majority was founded after a gigantic "Washington for Jesus" rally in 1980. Schlesinger Sr. subsequently invoked his 33-year formula to account for the disaster of Barry Goldwater's "ill-timed" venture into presidential politics in 1964, "since not twenty or thirty years but only ten had elapsed from the last eruption" (Schlesinger Sr., 1965). Goldwater became a favorite on the far right for voting against the Civil Rights Act in 1964 and for his assertion that "extremism in the defense of liberty is no vice." There is no little irony in the fact that his name was put into nomination by Ronald Reagan, who was just then honing his right-wing bona fides by denouncing "Hollywood Communists." It was Reagan's nominating speech that convinced ten California kingmakers to commit a fortune each to bankroll his future career, one in which the Christian Right of the 1980s would be a prime mover.

History, of course, is never a mindless, mechanical process, and this is especially true for political extremism. The truth is that in America there has never been a time without authoritarian personalities obsessed with secret cabals, erotic shenanigans in high office, and "un-American" activities. But there are also moments—again, they seem to occur about once every 30 years or so—when what lurks beneath the surface of civility explodes into widespread panic about the state of the republic, and a search for a new domestic enemy commences: 'spics, nips, krauts, wops, reds, micks, fags, niggers, sluts, hajjis, or chinks. This alters the terms of national political discourse, at least temporarily. It appears we are living in just such a time now.

Conclusion

Far-right fantasy provides harmless late-night entertainment for insomniacs, but it can also goad people to act. When this happens it can become dangerous, occasionally deadly, and, to use a term from critical social theory, "contradictory." That is, it can end up promoting policies inimical to the interests of its proponents. But when this happens, it is incumbent on us to resist the temptation to catastrophize, to mistake what is likely to be of short duration and minimal significance as a sign of the End Times. Americans are not likely to see secret police marching down Main Street, at least any time soon, putting innocent pedestrians in handcuffs, erecting gas chambers on the local fair ground, and gassing people to death.

Yet the situation begs the question, Why? What would cause people to pursue their ends through far-right means? We may never be able to answer this question definitively but, with the help of social science, we can at least shed some light on it.

Note

1 By this, Barna means "born-again" Christians who feel obligated to spread the faith and who believe that Satan exists, that salvation comes from grace alone, that the Bible is inerrant, and that God is all-good and all-powerful.

Interlude 2

The Secessionist State of Jefferson

In 2013, the supervisors of Siskiyou County, a place ordinarily known for high-quality marijuana and an aging hippie populace, voted 4–1 to secede from California after learning that five Colorado counties had just done the same (Activist Post, Sept. 4, 2013). They dubbed their new state "Jefferson," proudly erected its forest-green flag, and invited other rural counties in California and southern Oregon to join them. Reportedly they were angry at being "denied access" to local logging resources by a proposed dam removal project intended to save migrating salmon, by new gun registration laws, and by a $150 annual rural fire abatement fee that had just been passed in Sacramento. "Many proposed laws are unconstitutional and deny us our God-given rights," said one secessionist. A local blogger named "Anonymous" agreed, writing that Jeffersonians should secede from the "United States of Israel, before they start tyrannically imprisoning us in their FEMA camps." A third blogger, Hide Behind, recommended taking back "the Oregon Territoys [*sic*] as well, to protect the new state from federal theft." Still a fourth, Snakebelly, wrote, simply: "I just love the sound of this word, "sucession" [*sic*].

Right-wing separatism is not new, even in California. In 2011, Riverside County activists proposed setting up a state they called "South California." And students of right-wing extremism are familiar with plans to establish a five-state Pacific Northwest "White Aryan Bastion," of which the township of Nehemiah in northern Idaho was to be capitol. A Christian Patriot Defense League was established in Licking, Missouri, in the 1980s, about the same time that Europolis, "an armed reservation for the dwindling Aryan species," was founded. What proponents fail to realize is that legal secession requires the majority support of a popular referendum, both by secessionists and by host state citizens, the approval of the U.S. Congress, and a presidential signature.

2   Explaining the Far-Right

There are two ways to account for extremism. There are narratives supplied by professionally trained outsiders, psychologists, and sociologists. Then there are stories provided by insurgents themselves, how *they* understand their involvement in the movement, the reasons *they* give. Each type of account makes some elements of the phenomenon visible while at the same time veiling others. (For an elucidating discussion of the merits of each approach, see Fay, 1996.)

It might be supposed that because they originate closer to the subjects, insider accounts are more accurate or valid than those issued from the outside, but this is not always true. Certainly, insiders are better positioned to reflect on their own mental states, but often they are in denial about them or they are ashamed to openly express them because they might be judged politically incorrect. Furthermore, even when they do attempt to be "honest"—as in, "I don't want to hurt your feelings, but I'm going to speak the truth"—insiders typically do so by echoing what are known as "vocabularies of motive" (Mills, 1940). These are readymade verbal scripts provided to them by the movement that disown, excuse, or justify what the public views as offensive. In their enumeration of the motives voiced by multiple-victim murderers to explain their behavior, James Fox and Jack Levin (2005: 19–25) cite thrill seeking, a craving for revenge, misguided loyalty, expediency, and ethical principle (i.e., mass killing undertaken to rid the world of a putative evil). What they fail to note is that such vocabularies often have little, if anything, to say about the actual *causes* of extreme violence. By this I mean the bio-psycho-social conditions prior to and independent of it and with which it is highly correlated, even when the effects of other possible causes are eliminated or, as it is said, "controlled" for.

To illustrate the difference between motives and causes (or, as Mills [1940] would say, motives and motivations), reflect for a moment on the hypothetical case of an outwardly well-adjusted American middle-class family. Its causal dynamics may be so familiar to its members that, like sunlight to desert inhabitants, they may not be fully aware of what is painfully obvious to their next-door neighbors or, as sometimes happens, their family counselor: the tacit judgments and snide comments made over dinner, the scowls and slumped shoulders of the children, the stomping outs and cupboard slams and, above all, the excruciating double, triple, and quadruple binds that parents thoughtlessly inflict on their kids: "Is your homework finished yet?" "I just heard from Mary that her daughter got straight As in her accelerated math courses." "Have you gone jogging today? If you don't exercise, you're going to end up just like Aunt Faye, f-a-t!" "And what about your piano lessons?" "By the way, that college application has to be in the mail by tomorrow morning." "Did you know that Johnny's Fashions is looking for a new part-time salesgirl?" "And how are you, dear? Are you getting enough sleep? We're worried about you. Here, have another slice of pie."

This chapter and the next deal with what social psychologists and historians have concluded are some of the major causes of right-wing extremism. Loosely, these can be divided into micro-, middle-range, and macro-level accounts. Although we touch on some of the evidence in support of each type of cause, no suggestion is made that any of them is unequivocally superior to the others. Instead, like the insider-vs.-outsider accounts, they are merely alternative ways to understand the same thing. Micro-level accounts focus on the mental states of right-wing radicals, particularly as these relate to their immediate social milieus, their familial and classroom experiences. Middle-range explanations attend primarily to how people in these states of mind are "channeled," so to speak, into extremist groups, how they are recruited to or, as political sociologists like to say, "mobilized" into activism. Finally, there are macro-level accounts that address how and why the groups themselves exist. I address the major macro theory of right-wing extremism in the next chapter.

Micro-Level Theories

Are They Stupid?

It is well-known that voters from rural districts are more right-wing than those residing in cities. This is true regardless of what part of the country they come from. In several sparsely populated precincts in Idaho, for example, Bo Gritz (who at the time was platting acreage for his survivalist subdivision, Almost Heaven) received more votes than Bill Clinton for President. Gritz, who claimed to be the most decorated veteran of the Vietnam War, is alleged (falsely) to have been the model for the Rambo movie franchise; earlier in 1992 he had helped bring an end to a deadly shootout between g-men and self-proclaimed Aryans on Ruby Ridge, Idaho (Aho, 1994: 50–67; Zeskind, 2009: 294–300).

Some analysts attribute the varying rates of conservative and liberal voting patterns to different levels of formal education, city-slickers spending on average more years in school than their presumably dimmer country cousins. Of course, some of this is just stereotyping, yet there is also sound theory behind it. Public schools are charged with instilling students with the democratic ethos of tolerance, civility, and respect for science. They are also noted (or reviled, as the case may be) for inculcating empathy for the less fortunate. This being so, it is reasonable to expect that children who dwell in public schools the longest will be more liberal.

In a still classic study conducted during the frenzy of the McCarthy era, using data gathered by the National Opinion Research Center, noted pollster Samuel Stouffer (1966) found that one of the best predictors of tolerance (of Communists) was the highest grade level attained by the respondents. The correlation persisted after Stouffer controlled for the respondents' ages, genders, racial identities, levels of religious piety, and whether they came from the countryside or the city, lending Stouffer's findings added credence. Since that time, with a few notable exceptions (e.g., Selznick & Steinberg [1969]), the same correlation has been observed by countless other researchers, not only in America (McCloskey, 1967; Bobo & Bobo, 1989) but in Europe (Wagner & Zwick, 2006). The Wagner and Zwick study is particularly important because, unlike most surveys, it controls for the possibility that better-educated respondents are able to avoid being classified as bigots, not because they are necessarily more tolerant but because they are more adept at filling out questionnaires in conventionally acceptable ways.

To learn how classroom experience bears on tolerance, sociologists Debra Van Ausdale and Joe Feagin (2001) received permission to study a demographically diverse preschool staffed with state-certified instructors and with a curriculum devoted to instilling in pupils antibias attitudes toward different races. What they discovered was both illuminating and disturbing: The preschool was graduating children as young as three who were "reproducing" the same intolerance found in the larger society and deploying racial categories and "hurtful [racist] words" to wound their classmates. Furthermore, their teachers were unwittingly abetting them in this.

In one lesson plan, the children were asked "pick out" their own racial type from a set of photographs, as a preliminary to valuing their own race. Joey, a 3-year-old Asian, selected a picture of a black girl, proudly brought it to the teacher, and said, "Here's me!" The teacher shook her head, no, and told him to go back and try again. After witnessing the encounter, Van Ausdale tried to discern what had gone into Joey's thinking. Joey told her that the girl in the photograph had on a red sweater, just like he did. Evidently, Joey had used as a signifier of his racial group the sweater's color, not the color of his skin. By correcting him, the teacher was inadvertently aiding him to learn the criteria that underpin the American racial code (Van Ausdale & Feagin, 2001: 52–4).

Van Ausdale and Feagin report a second incident, this involving 4-year-old Taleshia, the daughter of a white American father and a black African mother. The children were each asked to choose a paint color to match their skins. Taleshia chose pink; the teacher strenuously objected. Not wanting to disappoint the teacher, Taleshia embarked on a series of small experimental steps, each of which got her closer to the "right" answer. She began by accurately identifying a T-shirt as black and then moved on to identify the teacher's hair as black.

Finally, she attached the color to herself, happily singing out her discovery: "I'm black, black, black. I'm *real* black" (Van Ausdale & Feagin, 2001: 72). Later, Taleshia had to fight another battle; this, over the accuracy of applying the term "daddy" to the white-skinned father who had come to pick her up after school. The teacher told her that she couldn't possibly have a white father; Taleshia disagreed, saying the teacher was wrong. As the debate continued, Taleshia grew increasingly irritated. Realizing the teacher's obduracy, in the end she resigned herself to the impossibility of her situation and sullenly replied, "Whatever."

Van Ausdale and Feagin go on to detail how, after the children had learned their "right" racial groupings, the teachers introduced them to finer distinctions, between Chinese whites and Japanese whites, for example, and between Hindu browns and Hispanic browns. Then they helped the children negotiate tearful disputes over each race's proprietary rights: for the right of a black boy to care for a white pet rabbit (which one little girl found unacceptable, saying "White goes with white, black with black"); for the right to pull a wagon (which is only for "white Americans," insisted another girl); for the right to swing on the preschool tire, and so on. Proprietary claims made in what the staff considered an unseemly manner were met with furrowed brows and frowns, as when a girl at nap time told a teacher that "I need to move this [her cot]. "Why?" asked the teacher. "Because I can't sleep next to a nigger. Niggers are stinky" (Van Ausdale & Feagin, 2001: 97–8). This encounter was deemed so unseemly by the staff that the little girl's parents and the preschool counselor were called in to intervene.

Already, then, by the time they were ready for first grade, the children in Van Ausdale's and Feagin's field study were able to articulate a (liberal American, in this case) racial cosmology. And contrary to what pop-psychology holds, they were not empty vessels into which adults could pour their own ideas willy-nilly. Rather, the children were able to recreate the American racial world (with the assistance of their teachers) by actively appropriating larger cultural texts to themselves and then reshaping them to suit their own interests.

In the course of my research, I too inquired into the educational backgrounds of ultra-rightists living in the greater Idaho area (encompassing Idaho, eastern Oregon and Washington, western Montana and Wyoming, and northern Utah and Nevada). What I learned seems to comport with Van Ausdale and Feagin's findings. After eliminating from the sample radical-right professors, legislators, and government administrators, the existence of whom might have biased my research, I was surprised to discover that the remainder had an equivalent, if not somewhat higher, level of educational attainment than their (admittedly very conservative) neighbors. Of this sample, 6.5 percent claimed to have earned graduate degrees, compared to 8 percent of white Americans at least 25 years of age, and nearly twice as many of them had been awarded undergraduate degrees than Americans generally. Most glaringly, only 10 percent of the radicals admitted to having dropped out of school, compared to almost one-third (31 percent) of white Americans (Aho, 1990: 140).

To be sure, the people I studied majored in what are acknowledged to be somewhat less than daunting academic fields: religion, education, business, and the social sciences. Furthermore, many of them attended nonsuperlative colleges such as Lenoire-Rhyne, Oral Roberts, Liberty Christian, Grove City, or lower-tier state schools. Nevertheless, I was able to uncover only a fraction of respondents who appear to have lied or exaggerated their educational attainments. One, I remember, eventually confessed to having earned his doctorate from a mail-order "university." Another more bizarre case concerns one of the three "co-authors" of the Pace Amendment, which I discuss in Chapter 6 under the section on immigration. When I interviewed him at the Aryan World Congress, he claimed to have graduated from Harvard University, that the second author had earned a BA in Japanese from Brigham Young University, and that the third had been awarded a law degree from Columbia University. I later learned that the three authors were, in reality, the same person or, perhaps more correctly, three personae inhabiting the same body.

After being unable to describe their dissertations, a handful of the sample meekly confessed to having been granted honorary doctorates. But more common were such cases as the then head of a splinter group of the Nazi Party known as the National Alliance, William Pierce. He had, in fact, earned a PhD in electrical physics at the University of Colorado. Using the pen name Andrew MacDonald, he authored *The Turner Diaries,* the "bible" of the *Brüders Schweigen.*

The possibility that public education may in fact aggravate, as opposed to mitigate, racism is indirectly confirmed by the case of Nazi Germany. The very nation that in the 1930s and 1940s boasted of having the world's most schooled population dedicated its prowess to constructing history's most heinous death machine. Before the Nazi SA (*Sturmabteilung,* storm troop—"brown shirts") was decapitated on "The Night of Long Knives" by the even more brutal SS (*Schutzstaffel,* defence corps—"black shirts"), its ranks were filled with liberal arts PhDs, poets, and artists, including Martin Heidegger, who is still considered his generation's greatest philosopher (Farias, 1989). As for the SS, who staffed the death camps, it is estimated that one-quarter of its elites had earned doctoral degrees (Kornhauser, 1959: 188).

Given the equivocal nature of the findings concerning the connection between tolerance and schooling, analysts have been forced to re-pose the question of the connection between formal education and the "infection," as historian Malcolm Hay once called it, of bigotry. Some say that the issue is not just the sheer number of years spent in school but how the reward systems in classrooms are structured. Elliot Aronson and Shelley Patnoe (1997) hypothesize that where an emphasis is placed on individual competition (the situation in most American schools), students can graduate with *higher* levels of hostility toward out-groups than when they entered school. When placed in cooperative "jigsaw" classrooms, on the other hand, where the success of each "piece" (pupil) depends on the help of their fellows, prejudice will decrease. (For a lengthy discussion, see Levin & Rabrenovic, 2004: 178–86.)

Other researchers argue that it is not so much the structure of the classroom that bears on (in)tolerance but what is "injected" into students during their stay there (Hay, 1981: 3).

In reaction to passage of federal civil rights legislation in 1964, which put an end to Jim Crow apartheid, private home and church-affiliated schools were established throughout the Deep South (Zeskind, 2009: 217–18); and not just there but in the Midwest and Rocky Mountain regions as well. The Aryan Nations Church, for example, set up its own academy and dedicated it to instilling in students the "4Rs": reading, 'riting, 'rithmetic, and race. Not surprisingly, many of its graduates grew up to be voluble racists and, in one case, a terrorist who is presently languishing in prison for murdering an Arkansas highway patrolman (see Appendix, Apr. 15, 1985). Evidently, he was on his way to visit friends at the Covenant, Sword and Arm of the Lord (CSA) compound, which boasted its own "Christian" academy. When CSA headquarters was later raided by the Bureau of Alcohol, Tobacco, and Firearms, one of the largest caches of illegal weapons in American history was uncovered (Zeskind, 2009: 60–68, 99–100).

April Gaede, cofounder of the National Vanguard, a splinter of the National Alliance, provides another case in point. She was raised in Fresno, California, by a father so devoted to Nazism that he branded his horses and cattle with swastikas (Southern Poverty Law Center [SPLC], no date). Predictably, Gaede sought out a fellow Aryan to marry and eventually birthed two blond, blue-eyed daughters. She then home-schooled the girls, "using my own curriculum" of material published prior to the civil rights era. When the girls reached puberty, she took on the role of stage managing their music careers as the so-called "neo-Nazi Olsen Twins." Dressed in Hitler-smiley-face yellow T-shirts, they organized a band called Prussian Blue that played the racist skinhead circuit. The band's title was said to honor Zyklon B, the residue found in Nazi gas chambers. This seems to be one generation after another of reliable hate.

But, for better or worse, the truth is rarely this simple. Although the twins continue to live with April owing to health problems, they claim to have renounced what she once taught them and now publicly embrace "love and light." They also confess to having smoked medical marijuana (SPLC, 2011). Another more chilling illustration of the difficulties involved in linking education with attitudes involves the recent shooting death of a neo-Nazi leader by his 10-year-old son in Riverside, California. Evidently the father's lessons didn't take, or perhaps they took too well. In any case, the boy claimed to have been psychologically abused.

Caveats aside, some of the most striking evidence in support of the proposition that political attitudes are traceable to the content of classroom lesson plans comes from observations on Christian Patriots themselves.

As their title suggests, Christian Patriots are a pious lot, yet they do not share the same theology. As a result, their venom tends to be directed against very different enemies. Patriots who report having been raised as Protestants are nearly six times more likely to espouse Christian Identity (CI) than

Mormon Patriots. (Recall that, among other things, CI claims that Jews are the masterminds of the supposed one-world plot.) Mormon Patriots agree there is a satanic conspiracy, but they are three times more likely than their Protestant counterparts to attribute it not to Jews but to such entities as the Hidden Hand, Shadow Government, the Global Elite, or the Insiders (Aho, 1990: 177).

One plausible explanation for this disparity is that when they were Sunday schooled as youngsters, Protestant Patriots absorbed Apostle John's diatribes against the "perfidious Jews" who, he says, worship at "the synagogue of Satan," and were "murderers from the beginning" (cf. John 8:44). Mormon Patriots read the gospels as well but, in addition, they have access to The Book of Mormon, which tells a very different story.

The Book of Mormon acknowledges the existence of what it describes as a "Gadianton conspiracy," headed by a so-called "Master Mahan." But instead of associating it with Jewry, it allusively ties it to the "abominable church" of the "gentiles," which is to say to orthodox Christianity. If this were not enough, when Mormon children are baptized they are taught that they are ritually "grafted into" or "adopted by" Israel; some Mormon commentators have gone so far as to argue that when this happens their blood-chemistry transubstantiates: They become literal blood brothers of the Jews, not just figurative relatives. Finally, when they receive what is known as their "patriarchal blessing," Mormon teens are apprised of their Jewish tribal origin: Ephraim, Judah, Issachar, or the like. According to sociologist Armand Mauss, these considerations explain why Mormons exhibit such extraordinarily high levels of "Semitic identification." Mauss shows that Mormons are, on average, more pro-Jewish than even members of the most liberal Protestant denominations (Mauss, 1968).

This is not to say that Mormon Patriots are any less politically vituperative than their Protestants compeers or, for that matter, less inclined to violence. Recall the tale of Cliven Bundy in the Prologue to this book, and his progenitor, one-time Mormon bishop Gordon Kahl. Kahl and his sons engaged in running gun fights with federal officials in 1983 that resulted in four deaths (see Appendix, Feb. and June 1983). Robert DePugh, who founded a paramilitary group in California known as the Minutemen and was imprisoned for firearms violations, was Mormon, as was the polygamist Adam Swapp, who declared his 2.5-acre property in Utah a sovereign nation and then murdered a government official for "trespassing" (see Appendix, Jan. 1988). Robert Mathews, co-founder of the *Brüders Schweigen,* was also raised in the Church of Latter-Day Saints.

In sum, then, while there is evidence for the claim that education or its lack plays a role in the formation of the far-right mindset, the data are far from conclusive. Most fundamentalist evangelicals and most Latter-Day Saints do not become Patriots. Furthermore, a number of Patriots report having had Catholic backgrounds and still others that they have no religious training at all. This suggests that it may not be just the structure of the classroom that bears on young hearts and minds, nor the content of the classroom lessons, but the *way* by which they are conveyed. Before entertaining this possibility, a short digression is in order.

Are They Crazy?

In 1982, Frank Spisak, Jr. hid a pistol in a hollowed-out copy of the Bible and, dressed as an old woman, embarked on a "search and destroy" mission to "exterminate as many niggers and Jews as possible." His several-month campaign resulted in three deaths and, ultimately, his own execution, during which he recited Bible passages for the witnesses (see Appendix, 1982).

On Christmas Eve, 1985, David Rice, a self-labeled Christian "soldier," bludgeoned to death a secular Jewish family of four in what he considered to be a "first step" in staving off a rumored invasion of United Nations troops across the Mexican border, an invasion that he believed the parents were about to order. During the trial, he said he regretted having harmed the kids but then added that "it might have been necessary to sacrifice these lives for the greater good of mankind" (Aho, 1994: 47).

Bruce Carroll Pierce, a member of the *Brüders Schweigen*, gunned down a popular Jewish talk show host in Denver as he was pulling into his carport, enraged at what he considered the host's unfair attacks on Aryan warriors such as himself (see Appendix, June 18, 1984).

The examples go on and on: Timothy McVeigh, who brought down the federal building in Oklahoma City in 1995; David "Joey" Pederson and Holly Grigsby, who, after murdering Pederson's father and stepmother, killed a black man and a teenager they mistook as a Jew, on their way to Sacramento to commence the "revolution"; Wade Page, who killed seven Sikh worshippers at an Oak Creek, Wisconsin, temple, August 6, 2012, and then took his own life; and Jason Ready, a member of the US Border Guard, a neo-Nazi group, who committed suicide after taking the lives of four undocumented Mexican immigrants in 2012. (For further examples, see Appendix.)

Obviously, these are all instances of aberrant behavior, but were the perpetrators also insane? If we could answer in the affirmative, then we might be able to avert future tragedies, perhaps by means of early diagnostic screening and preventive detention. The problem is, we can't. To quote James Fox and Jack Levin, "the sociopath is bad, not mad" (Fox & Levin, 2005: 58). (For a comprehensive bibliography of the crazy theory of right-wing extremism and its critics, see Blee, 2002: 213, n. 8).

After he was found guilty of first-degree murder, Spisak wrote to me that he had "conclusively refuted every suggestion that [he] might be mentally ill." He went on to say that for Nazis and racists such as himself, being hospitalized for insanity would be "a fate worse than death." This is because it would enable the public to ignore the real, "morally principled" motives behind his acts (Aho, 1990: 73).

Rice at first claimed to be innocent of murder on grounds of insanity but, after being presented with overwhelming evidence of his rationality, he agreed to plead guilty in exchange for a life sentence. The examining psychiatrist concluded that Rice did not "cook up" his fantasy about the impending UN invasion "out of the void" but was involved with a group of government haters who "validated these ideas as rational and important." The group leader, a female naturopath, had earlier spurned his favors; evidently, he killed the family in part because he wanted to impress her (Aho, 1994: 48).

Pierce, too, underwent a pretrial examination to determine his capability to stand trial, and the consulting psychiatrist found the same thing: "He is not psychotic and there is no evidence that he was ... under psychotic command during any of the actions having to do with the indictments." On the contrary, reported the psychiatrist, Pierce felt that in committing the murder he was obeying Yahweh's "electrifying and spine-tingling voice" (Aho, 1994: 47). He eventually died in a federal super-maximum-security prison of natural causes while serving a 252-year sentence.

Similar conclusions can be reached about McVeigh, Ready, Pederson, and Page, as well as about Andrew Breivik, who shot to death sixty-nine children at an interracial camp in Norway in the summer of 2011, appalled by the thought of what miscegenation might mean for the purity of the Nordic race. The court-appointed physicians agreed that Breivik was "borderline narcissistic" and that he had "antisocial" tendencies, but they were unable to diagnose him as psychotic. They nonetheless recommended that he be permanently incarcerated behind bars in a mental hospital. In words eerily reminiscent of Spisak's, he wrote that this was "the ultimate humiliation." "To send a political activist to a mental hospital is more sadistic and evil than to kill him." "It is a fate worse than death" (Reuters, 2012).

Given these and related observations, most analysts have come to renounce attempts to explain right-wing violence by means of psychosis. Instead, they have begun focusing on what are known as "normal neuroses," particularly the neurosis known as *authoritarianism*. A notable example of this is the work of German social psychologist Alice Miller.

Miller claims that the Germans were beguiled by Nazism not because they were stupid or crazy but because of the "poisonous pedagogy" that had been inflicted on them as children (Miller, 1984). Their so-called "concentration camp childhoods" were, in turn, she says, a product of neo-Calvinist theology (with its emphasis on human depravity) plus a culture of hyper-masculinity.

To support her contention, Miller summarizes the advice offered in nineteenth-century German childcare manuals, especially one authored by a Dr. Daniel Gottlieb Moritz Schreber (1806–1861), a book that was so popular at the time that it was reprinted no fewer than forty times. In it, Schreber writes that parents should spare no effort to "establish dominance"; that they "permit no disobedience"; and that they "suppress everything in the child." To facilitate this, he recommends a regimen of ice-water baths and torso restraints (the latter to encourage a rigid, rectal posture), the deployment of hand manacles (to avert masturbation and thumb sucking), leg fetters (to keep the child from assuming a fetal position in bed), and evening enemas (for a summary, see Griffin, 1992: 120). (Schreber is credited for introducing "medical indoor gymnastics" to Germans, facsimiles of the machines of which can now be seen in exercise facilities worldwide. Schreber hoped that such machines would firm up what he feared were the increasingly flaccid urban youth of the Fatherland.)

Besides Adolf Hitler (Miller, n.d.), Miller points to Heinrich Himmler, the fastidious SS mass murderer, as a prototypical product of Schreber's teachings. Already as a young boy Himmler was exhibiting traits that would later recommend him to Nazi Party officials to administer the death camp system: prudery (in response to an overly exuberant 3-year-old girl, he once wrote in his childhood diary, "One should teach a child a sense of shame" [Griffin, 1992: 117]); obsequiousness; a knack for meticulous record keeping; false bravado; and rage, not only at his own physical inadequacies but at the frailties of others. As an adult he was obsessed with *Schmutz und Schund* (filth and trash) movies, especially their depictions of sexual debauchery and abortion. (After "cleansing" this genre of mass entertainment of its "non-Aryan" [i.e., Jewish] content, the Nazis used *Schmutz und Schund* to mobilize the Folk to their own cause.) Jews, Himmler felt, were not just illicit couplers who routinely used abortion to destroy the incriminating evidence of promiscuity; he also believed they harbored an inborn propensity for secrecy and subversion.

Dr. Schreber's youngest son committed suicide. The eldest, at the time a respected judge, ended up in an insane asylum, horrified that God was turning him into a woman, a fact that Freud once diagnosed as an expression of the son's repressed homosexuality. Miller is not alone in hypothesizing that both tragedies are traceable to what their father had imposed on them as children. This, she says, explains the judge's gibberish about what he called the "compression miracle," a possible allusion to Schreber's torso restraints, and to the "freezing miracle" (the ice-water baths).

One implication of Miller's theory is that, insofar as children who are raised in abusive households grow up to be abusers themselves, then those brought up in emotionally nurturing settings are likely to become peaceful, compassionate adults. Although the evidence is scanty and anecdotal, this is exactly what sociologists Samuel and Pearl Oliner (1988) claim to have found. In their award-winning study of Europeans who, at great risk to themselves, rescued Jews from Nazi persecution, they show how many of them report having enjoyed happy, affirmative childhoods.

The problem with Miller's theory (and the Oliners' corollary), of course, is that while it may be able to explain things after the fact, given obvious research-ethics considerations, it is impossible to test. This is the reason why psychologists have tended to shy away from addressing the question of what *causes* authoritarian (or altruistic) personalities in favor of devising instruments that hold promise of identifying them in the population and, where appropriate, getting them into therapy.

The first result of this effort was the infamous fascist, or F-, scale (Adorno et al., 1950), a device that received a scathing reception from professionals, both for its "response set" (i.e., posing all the questionnaire items in the same way, so that if a respondent answers the first two or three with, say, an "agree," they will be habituated to do the same for the rest) and for its transparently left-wing bias. All the designers of the F-scale were Jews who had recently fled Nazi persecution, and several were outspoken Marxists.

In response to these criticisms, Bob Altemeyer (1988) has constructed a more sophisticated tool, which he labels the *right-wing authoritarian*, or *RWA*, *scale*. This thirty-item questionnaire estimates a respondent's "prefascist potential" by means of the individual's scores on three "attitudinal clusters": their submissiveness to legal and religious authority; aggression toward authoritatively identified deviants; and willingness to comply, without objection, to authoritatively decreed conventions, especially those relating to sexuality. Altemeyer finds that high scores on these clusters correlate with, among other things, support for torture during judicial interrogations, support for military trials of political dissenters, advocacy of execution, a willingness to inflict pain on peers who fail at tasks, racism, a tendency to conflate legality with morality, and religious piety.

In contrast to Miller and the Oliners, Altemeyer explains authoritarianism (and, by implication, altruism) by means of learning theory. One *learns* to become a proto-fascist or the opposite, he says, from parents, pundits, preachers, and peers. If the content of what they teach is "fascistic," then the longer a child spends time under their tutelage, the more likely is the child to exhibit RWA him- or herself. The reverse is also true. Altemeyer shows that regardless of their major in college, students produced RWA scores that dropped for each year of their matriculation. The scores of liberal arts majors in particular display a precipitous decline (Altemeyer, 1988: 93). It appears we have come full circle back to where we began.

Middle-Range Theories

Are They Socially Isolated?

RWA is an undeniably reliable predictor of attitudes, but Altemeyer is the first to admit that it is virtually powerless to forecast who will actually join an extremist group. After all, not everyone who exhibits high fascist potential becomes a far-right activist, and some who do register low RWA scores. To address the absence of a clear and direct link between attitudes and group affiliations, several analysts have seen the need for more middle-range theories. The rudiments of one of the most compelling of these, popularly known as *mass* or *mob theory*, was first introduced years ago by Gabriel Tarde (1843–1904).

Tarde's problematic was *la terreur* of the French Revolution (1789). How, he asked, could the Jacobins, the supposed proponents of liberty, equality, and fraternity, turn into (what he saw as) a mob and end up guillotining countless numbers of their own countrymen? His answer is this: Human beings are inherently "imitative" animals, and their gregarious instincts can only be satisfied through involvement in communities: through church-going, family routines, and shared work. If and when these channels are blocked, however, humans can become susceptible to the blandishments of *pseudo*-communities, to cults and/or causes that offer something greater than their ephemeral ego to believe in, the mundane contentment of food and shelter, and the simple pleasures of human contact.

Mob theorists postulate that modernization, with its concomitant industrialization, urbanization, central planning, and secularization, has the effect of untethering people from their local communities, producing in them a vertiginous sense of psychic mobility, and placing before them institutional specters of mind-numbing size and complexity. Fragmented, frightened, and alone, they become available to totalistic movements that promise "once and for all" to end their anxieties. Apart from the fundamentalist religious enthusiasms of the present era, the two most notable examples of this are Communism and Nazism.

Seymour Martin Lipset (1960: 175) says it this way: "Classical fascists" are "psychologically homeless ... personal failures," "socially isolated [and] uneducated." Conservative sociologist Robert Nisbet concurs: The greatest appeal of "the fantastic doctrines of the Nazis" to otherwise intelligent Germans, he writes, was their proffer of "refuge to the hungry sheep, hope to the hopeless, and faith to the disillusioned" (1953: 34–7). Nazism promised the advent of a New Man, one brought to completion through flag parades, midnight fires, one-armed salutes, ersatz Greco-Roman monuments, goose-stepping armies, martial music and, more than anything, the ever-fascinating, horrifying drama of blood sacrifice (Mosse, 1980).

Mob theory has the ring of plausibility but, as so often is the case with theories of history, it is exceedingly difficult, if not impossible, to test empirically. Instead, we are left with what seem to be—but may not, in fact, be—indicators of community collapse; with what might be—but are not necessarily—signs of individual atomization. To make matters worse, the few concrete data that do exist are not entirely consistent with its predictions.

In the 1960s, field observers conducted interviews with antifluoridation activists who believed that placing fluoride in public water systems was a plot to weaken the people and render them vulnerable to Communist subversion. Similar surveys were conducted around the same time with attendees at Christian anti-Communist Crusade rallies. In both cases, researchers found that the participants were not the hapless, homeless, helpless joiners that Lipset and Nisbet supposed them to be but were among the *most* integrated citizens of their local communities (Wolfinger et al., 1964). Analysis of German voting patterns during the pivotal election of 1932, during which the Nazi Party came to power, reaches a similar conclusion. The most avid supporters of Nazism did not come from the burgeoning cities of the time, where Lipset and Nisbet would say the most alienated and anomic souls resided, but from the decidedly settled, bucolically paced Protestant countryside (Hamilton, 1982: 40–1). Berlin and Hamburg did have extremists, but they tended to be left-wing radicals—Communists and anarchists—not right-wingers.

My own research on Christian Patriots living in greater Idaho in the late 1980s is consistent with this. First, they were older, by a considerable amount, than the average American. This indicated to me that they were a relatively mature bunch emotionally. Second, like most people of their age group, their early years had been spent in public schools, which are acknowledged to be a major integrative force in American culture. Third, although many of them reported having been geographically mobile, they were no more so than their neighbors, although residents of the inner–mountain west area are much more transient than Americans generally. Fourth, at least as measured by their marriage and divorce rates, their couplings seemed to be more stable than those of the average American (Aho, 1990: 151). The fifth factor concerns religion: While the Patriots were highly sectarian and even cult-like when I interviewed them, most had been raised as mainline Protestants or Mormons. This too, I felt, bespoke incorporation into their communities of origin.

The only finding consistent with mob theory concerns occupational isolation. Far more of the radicals reported working in structurally isolated jobs than Idahoans as a whole or than Americans generally: as farmers, ranchers, miners, and loggers. Many described themselves as freelance political organizers, independent "researchers," or itinerant preachers. In fact, there were twenty-five times more self-identified clergy in my sample than predicted, given their numbers in Idaho's overall job statistics.

The preaching, pronouncements, and policies of non–institutionally affiliated clerics and intelligentsia are customarily provocative, often uncivil, and occasionally violent (Kornhauser, 1959: 183–93). This is, first of all, because these individuals are perpetually insecure financially and in need of audiences to remunerate them for their services, which incentivizes them to be hyperbolic and inflammatory. Add to this the fact that competition in the American religious, broadcast, and publishing markets is particularly fierce. Second, because they work outside mainline denominations, recognized academic institutions, and established political parties, their oratory is not subject to the usual normative constraints. Not surprisingly, it is roving writers and itinerant evangelical ministers who gravitate to leadership positions in right-wing extremist groups.

However this may be, the bottom line is that Christian Patriots do not appear to be the lost souls portrayed by the popular press. Many have close friends, loving families, and trusted associates. The question, then, is, Are they perhaps the *wrong sorts* of friends, families, and coworkers?

Is It Who They Know?

The presupposition of most micro-level and middle-range theories is that, because the beliefs of right-wing extremists are bizarre, then the way(s) by which people acquire them must also be unique. Social network theorists dispute this, calling it the "fallacy of the uniformly profound" (Lofland & Skonvod, 1981). They argue to the contrary, that people are mobilized to become right-wing extremists in much the same way that others become vegetarians, antivivisectionists, pacifists or, for that matter, left-wing extremists—namely, through their relationships with people already in the movement. That is, they are recruited by means of their (largely accidental) involvement in a Christian Patriot "opportunity structure."

Imagine a *seeker* (S), who is undergoing a personal crisis owing to unemployment, a death in the family, or a faltering marriage, and for whom the kit of pat answers and solutions is unsatisfactory. Enter now the proffer of an *invitation* (I) from an acquaintance who is already in the Patriot movement. This "I" can take the form of a book or CD that explains the problem in question; it can be a formal summons to attend a Patriot meeting; or it can be an informal invitation to a social gathering of activists—say, a gun show, a punk-rock festival, or a party. The inviter, in turn, may be a neighbor, a coworker, a fellow prison inmate, an attendee at a Bible-study group, a love interest (such as a "good Christian man") or, most commonly, an esteemed family member. The point is that S's involvement with the activists is due largely to chance. Were S to live in a different town, work at a different job, attend services at a different congregation, or be born into a different kinship group, the likelihood of his or her even hearing about the Patriot group in question, much less joining it, would be nil.

Ordinarily, people do not join Patriot groups because of what the groups espouse. Rather, they are first *pulled* into them (P_1) and then set about converting themselves to conform to the group's beliefs—which is to say that bigotry is more a *consequence* of involvement with an extremist group than it is a cause (Blee, 2002: 27–30). Indeed, prior to joining, S may be entirely unaware of the group's distinctive teachings, dumbstruck by their weirdness (such as the idea that Jesus was an Aryan or that a Hidden Hand controls world affairs). Or, if aware of them, S may initially deny the group's credibility. Having once joined, however, everything changes.

At first, S may merely mouth the group's pet slogans, defamatory labels, and code words, announcing them with a degree of self-conscious detachment. But in the event this wins S what they crave—the backslaps, smiles, and handshakes of the group's members—S may be motivated in the future to shout out the slogans with more gusto and relish: What was initially an empty gesture can turn into a firm commitment. At this point, it is not uncommon for S's earlier friends, colleagues, and family members to express their disgust at what they hear. When they do, S may be inadvertently *pushed* (P_2) into the arms of "the only people who truly understand me": They may find themselves *engulfed* (E) in the Patriot world.

In the end, the group's gatekeepers determine whether and when S has become one of them. Full acceptance is frequently *marked* (M) by a rite of passage, at which point S may be granted a new title or awarded an identifying insignia. Typically, S will make sense out of his or her self-conversion by retrospectively reconfiguring his or her autobiography, seeing it variously as a development out of childishness into manhood, from naivety into enlightenment, from addiction into sobriety, or from sin into salvation (Blee, 2002: 35–46).

The rudiments of the SIP_1P_2EM model were first articulated by John Lofland and Rodney Stark (1965; Lofland, 1977) in their fascinating portrayal of how perfectly ordinary people were converted into "world savers," Moonies, members of the Unification Church. The model has since been corroborated by research on a variety of social movements (Snow, Zurcher Jr. & Ekland-Olson, 1980): from ex-hippie converts to the Jesus Movement (Richardson & Stewart, 1983), Muslim terrorists (Forest, 2006; Juergensmeyer, 2003), and women in the hate movement (Blee, 2002), to tea-party recruits (Williamson, Skocpol & Coggin, 2011; Parker & Barreto, 2013). It also comports to the way by which a right-wing anarchist militia was recently organized among soldiers at Ft. Stewart, Georgia, in the early 2010s. Known as The Family for its incestuously close ties, this group was responsible for the deaths of least two (possibly four) people (Labi, 2014. See Appendix, Dec. 5, 2011). This makes the SIP_1P_2EM model an especially powerful weapon in the sociological arsenal.

Two corollaries can be derived from network theory. The most important is that those who are truly isolated, atomized, and uprooted from their local communities, as mob theory supposes, are, in fact, "the last and the least likely" to become insurgents themselves, if for no other reason than that they have no way to learn about the movement (Oberschall, 1973: 135). The second concerns the theoretical possibility that individuals can *de*-convert "out of hate" into tolerance or even love of their one-time enemies. Specifically, if a fully engulfed Patriot becomes disillusioned with his or her relationships within the group—for example, with the "good Christian man" who first recruited the individual to the group, after learning, say, that he is an adulterer or a drunk— that Patriot may once again become a seeker. At this point, the seeker may bond with someone outside the movement and end up apostatizing, espousing an entirely new, possibly even liberalistic, world view (Aho, 1994: 122–38). Perhaps this is what happened to the "neo-Nazi Olsen Twins" mentioned previously.

Network theory is not without weaknesses. One of these is that if group pulls and pushes are overemphasized, the impression may be given that joiners and leavers are passive victims of forces over which they have no control (Wallis, 1982). Another is that while network theory may explain how people enter and leave hate groups, it leaves unanswered the question of how those groups originate in the first place. To deal with this, we need to consider a more macro-level approach to the subject.

Interlude 3

Dreams of a Right-Wing Homeland

By all appearances the frigid, windswept climes of North Dakota are the last place where one would think to set up a right-wing utopia. But this is precisely what a white-bearded, 61-year-old neo-Nazi, Craig Paul Cobb, has done (Donovan, 2013). After moving from Canada in 2010 following his indictment for inciting racial hatred, Cobb purchased twelve vacant lots in the tiny town of Leith (population twenty) for several hundred dollars each. Then, using the Wi-Fi link at a local library, he invited fellow activists to put down stakes in what he proposed to rename "Cobbsville." His goal: to create a white supremacist community adjacent to the high-paying jobs on the Bakken tar-oil field. "Imagine strolling over to your neighbors to discuss world politics with nearly all like-minded volk [*sic*]," he told reporters. "Imagine the international publicity and usefulness to our cause! For starters, we could declare a Mexican-illegal-invaders-Israeli … spies-no-go zone." So far, takers include Tom Metzger, an ex-Klan leader and founder of the White Aryan Resistance; the webmaster for the [National] Vanguard News Network, the country's largest neo-Nazi organization; and none other than April Gaede, mother of the Olsen twins, mentioned in the last chapter. Among the things that attracted them to Leith was a desire to flee the American "multicultural cesspool."

When Leith residents learned of Cobb's plans, they began buying up vacant lots themselves. The result was a minor land rush. One interracial couple, who expressed fear for their safety in the *Bismarck Tribune*, drew a stinging rebuke on the [Nazi] Stormfront online forum: "A negro is someone who needs to be in their own country separate from whites, a filthy race-mixing white woman like her has no place in a white nation." As it turns out, soon after news stories about his plans were aired, Cobb was fired from his job as a pilot car driver and flagman. Evidently, he had become a danger to his crew.

3 "White Man's" Victimhood and Heroic Redemption

The major macro-explanation for right-wing extremism introduces a subtle but important twist to the causal link said to exist between modernization and extremism. Whereas the approach discussed earlier—mass or mob theory— argues that the destabilizing effects of modernization unleash a quest for community substitutes, macro-level theory holds that right-wing radicalism grows from a revolt *against* modernization. Here, ultra-right activism is pictured not as an unconscious reaction to historical upheaval but as a relatively conscious rebellion against it.

This shift in emphasis has several advantages, one being its parsimony. It assumes that unless there is compelling evidence to the contrary—that they are idiots, wing-nuts, or isolates, which, as we have seen, is doubtful—far-rightists are relatively rational actors who are attempting to maximize their interests (as they see them), given what they know about their situations, even if what they know is minimal or false. A second advantage is that it takes into consideration the "insider" viewpoint described at the outset of the last chapter. Instead of ignoring or disparaging what activists say are their motives for joining the movement, in other words, it grants their words explanatory salience. To see how this is so, we must first distinguish between the two faces of modernization: modernism and modernity (Johnstone, 2004: 164–6).

Modernism refers to the material comforts and appurtenances of modernization: abundant food, electricity, sewage disposal, central heating, instantaneous communications, rapid transportation, and firearms. These, right-wing rebels gratefully embrace as tools to be used in the struggle. *Modernity*, on the other hand, refers to the nonmaterial ethos of modernization: its advocacy of egalitarianism, its openness to sexual and artistic experimentation, its support of epistemic ambiguity, its futurist orientation, and its secularism—the valorizing of scientific facts over religious dogma. (For the classic description of the ethos of modernity, see Berman, 1988.) These, ultra-rightists view with suspicion, or they explicitly denounce them altogether as contrary to "God's design," "the laws of nature and nature's God." The meaning of these phrases is not always clear, even to Patriots, but they appear to describe a status hierarchy in which adult, propertied, physically able, heterosexual, white Protestant males enjoy preeminence.

Patriots have a plethora of labels for those whom they consider the agents of modernity: "fenian monsters," "Edomites," "subhuman mongrels," "Force X," the "Bilderbergers" (so named for a Dutch hotel that hosts an annual meeting of supposed "one-world cabalists"). Regardless of the title, they evoke in Patriots a complex mood burnished with the following hues:

First is sentimental nostalgia for "everything we've grown up with, everything we've known," of feeling "discarded like trash on the side of the information superhighway" (Kimmel, 2013b; for a lengthy excerpt from this book, see Kimmel, 2013a). When the Supreme Court ruled that the antigay Defense of Marriage Act was unconstitutional, June 26, 2013, Rev. Mike Huckabee, a well-known Patriot minister, solemnly declared, "Today, Jesus wept." The next afternoon, talk-show host Glenn Beck asked in a breaking voice whether his audience fully grasped the enormity of the Court's ruling. "Can you recognize your own country? I can't … . Your country is slipping away" (Blaze Radio, June 27, 2013).

Second is angry resentment toward the "thieves," "takers," "dependents," and "moochers" who have "stolen our country." Radio pundit Rush Limbaugh describes them as "the new castrati" and says they have "dismantled" and "destroyed all our institutions." "Those of us who treasure America," agrees another right-wing commentator, are under attack by "a group of elitists hell-bent" on transforming the republic into "a fascist police state that regulates, coerces, bullies and spies … " This "is not just unacceptable, but … evil" (Larsen, 2013b). "Every freedom we have," concurs one of his cohorts, a self-described "conservative" talk-show host, "they will take. They will take it all": our communications, our treasure, our achievements, our hegemony, our law-abiding innocence, our conscience, our liberty. All of it is being "eroded, sold, corrupted, compromised, and co-opted." In the end, there will be nothing (Larson, 2014).

Third is what Michael Kimmel calls "aggrieved entitlement," the fierce determination to "get it back." "*I pay my taxes and I want my country back!*"

As Martin Heidegger (1995: 67) has shown, moods are not just chemically induced feelings located inside our bodies. They are also, more importantly, "outside" us "like an atmosphere" in which we find ourselves immersed. And in being immersed, we become "attune[d] through and through" to respond in preset ways: say, with bored indifference, nausea, hopeful anticipation, or panic-filled dread.

Heidegger goes on to say that the challenging thing about moods is that we are not always aware of having them. Indeed, he argues that the most telling mood of all, *angst*, which he defines as apprehension about "no-thing at all" (Heidegger, 1962: 24)—our diminishment, decay, and death—is significant *precisely because* it is unconscious and hence drives us to engage mindlessly in all distractions emblematic of modern life: from pornography and gossip to compulsive shopping and tourism.

The tempting thing about the mood of sentimental nostalgia/resentment/urgency is its precondition: forgetfulness. What Patriots forget is that the "sister" of nostalgia (to use Carl Jung's term) is brutality. And the more nostalgic one is, "the closer you are to violence" (Delillo, 1985: 258). Christian Patriots are blind to the despoliations, enslavements, rapes, and murders of the past that have provided them with the rights and privileges they enjoy today. When these are not blithely dismissed as ancient history—"Get over it!" (Buchanan, 2008)[1]—responsibility for them is projected onto the fenian monster, subhuman mongrel, or Edomite chosen to play the foil in their morality tale of national renewal, who can now be treated accordingly.

A striking example of willful blinkeredness is the National Association for the Advancement of White People (NAAWP), an organization cofounded in 1979 by David Duke, who at the time was a prominent Klansman. Paul Cobb, mentioned in the interlude to this chapter, has offered to donate one of his lots in "Cobbsville" to Duke. The other cofounder, presently housed in a super-maximum-security prison for soliciting the murder of a federal judge (see also Appendix, July 2, 1999), is Matt Hale, the self-styled "Pontifex Maximus" of the racist Church of the Creator. April Gaede is said to have named her youngest daughter, Dresden Hale, after Matt, and in honor of the German city of that name bombed by the Allies in World War II (Southern Poverty Law Center, no date).

Hale and Duke admit to having explicitly modeled the NAAWP after the National Association for the Advancement of Colored People (NAACP), which has a long history of successfully campaigning for the rights of African Americans and other minorities. By Hale's and Duke's reckoning, these victories add up to the "genocide of White American culture." The homepage of the NAAWP.org, reads: "Government is mandating the destruction of white people around the worlkd [*sic*] today … . God help all of us."

Keith Gilbert, who once headed his own neo-Nazi group, shares Hale's and Duke's sentiments. After gaining local notoriety for his swastika-embossed, camouflage Volkswagen and for training his German shepherd to lift his right paw at the command, "Seig Heil!," Gilbert filed a complaint with the United Nations against the United States government for "slander[ing] and caus[ing] by whatever means … the criminalization of all members of the [the 'white'] race … in order to destroy them as an identifiable group" (Gilbert, 1986).

Another, more recent, tech-wise case concerns the Montana-based National Policy Institute, which markets itself as a "white nationalist think tank" (NPIAmerica.org). Its purported goal: to stand tall against "antiwhite discrimination," which, it maintains, has imperiled "Western civilization." NPIA's spokesman, Richard Spencer, writes that he has no animosity toward other ethnicities but is solely concerned with "our [meaning *his*] children's future." "Don't they have rights too?" And if so, "Who stands for them?" Spencer's is a mournful cry to a dying world by one wholly vested in it.

To Duke, Hale, Gilbert, Spencer, and the like, the arc of history is not experienced as "bending toward justice" (to paraphrase Martin Luther King) but as a tale of "the dispossession of America's traditional majority" (NPIAmerica.org; Buchanan, 2008). As evidence, they and their cadres cite variations of the following legislative edicts, presidential executive orders, and landmark Supreme Court decisions.

- 1866   Fourteenth Amendment grants equal rights to ex-slaves
- 1920   Nineteenth Amendment grants suffrage to adult women
- 1947   Desegregation of the armed forces by executive order of President Truman
- 1954   Supreme Court declares as unconstitutional the segregation of public schools
- 1964   Civil Rights Act outlaws discrimination in public accommodations, public spaces, and employment on the basis of race, ethnicity, national origin, or religion
- 1965   Voting Rights Act outlaws discrimination against minorities at the voting place
- 1967   Supreme Court invalidates state miscegenation laws, legalizing interracial marriage
- 1968   Native American Civil Rights Act reiterates the Civil Rights Act of 1964
- 1971   Twenty-sixth Amendment grants suffrage to 18-year-olds
- 1973   Supreme Court legalizes abortion
- 1990   Americans with Disabilities Act expands the 1964 Civil Rights Act by outlawing discrimination on the basis of physical or mental disability
- 2011   End to the military's antihomosexual Don't Ask Don't Tell policy by executive order of President Obama
- 2013   Supreme Court declares antihomosexual Defense of Marriage Act unconstitutional

This is by no means an exhaustive itemization of all the affronts suffered by "white man" over the course of the last two centuries. Among other things, it omits the federal progressive income tax system (introduced in 1913), the Wagner Act (1935) that legalized collective bargaining for workers, Social Security, unemployment insurance, and Aid for (poor) Dependent Children, all of which were enacted under the New Deal. We might also mention Medicare, Medicaid (1965), and Obamacare (2010), which guarantee medical insurance for the elderly and destitute. There have also been such Supreme Court rulings as Miranda (1966), which protects (mostly minority) arrestees from self-incrimination, and *Gideon v. Wainright* (1963), which guarantees this same group competent legal counsel. A host of other recent federal court decisions have decriminalized sodomy and sanctioned contraceptive sales, protected flag burners from prosecution, granted "unAmericans" the right to teach in public schools, denied a place for creation science in public school biology classes, and disallowed compulsory prayer and Bible reading. The point, however, is clear: When standing in the shoes of "white man," modernity *does* seem like an unrelenting assault on "everything we've grown up with, everything we've known."

Not literally everything, of course: Without going into the various Supreme Court judgments that have favored corporate property rights over labor (addressed in Chapter 7) and its one-time endorsement of Jim Crow segregation, there is the "war on drugs" of presidents Richard Nixon and Ronald Reagan. This has resulted in the incarceration of (and loss of political rights by) hundreds of thousands, if not millions, of minority and poor people under the guise of "mandatory minimum sentencing" guidelines (Alexander, 2012). Just as the Prohibition Amendment of the 1920s was a strike by American white Anglo-Saxon Protestants against Catholics, Jews, the Irish, and Germans (Gusfield, 1980 [1963]) for their alleged appetites for wine, whiskey, and beer, today's war on drugs can be read as a veiled assault on African Americans, Mexican Americans, Asian Americans, and Native Americans for *their* supposed drugs of choice. Add to this various federal court gun rights decisions that have been (mis)understood by "white man" as authorizing the formation of private militias, and the implementation of stand-your-ground laws, which permit people to use deadly force to protect themselves from those whom they fear might do them bodily harm. The defeat of the Equal Rights Amendment in 1982 which, had it been ratified, would have guaranteed equal protection for women under the Constitution, was a signal victory for "white man," as have been the passage of state right-to-work laws, the introduction of physically intrusive antiabortion laws, antigay discrimination legislation, and local voter suppression measures.

In the fantasy world of the far-right, however, these rulings and laws have not been greeted with the plaudits that might be expected. Far from being hopeful about the future, many Patriots see a black curtain descending to the stage floor, announcing that *"All the signs of the End-times are here!"* It is at this point that they confront the existential question, the answer to which will define the remainder of their lives: Will I quiver like a mouse and surrender to the inevitable? Will I flee like a rabbit, provisions on my back, to my little hole in the mountains? "Absolutely not!" declares a self-titled "firearms trainer." "I will not stand quietly by while [my values] are threatened or sacrificed in even the tiniest and most insignificant way. Because when we sacrifice one particle of our freedoms, we open the door for evil men to take another, and another, and another … *I will never, ever, under any circumstance, back away … I will not be moved!"* *"It's time to stand, join me"* (Earl, 2013c, author's italics).

It is this kind of conviction that stirs the Patriot soul. In response to it, one writer gushed that the firearms trainer "is a brilliant writer … patriotic, spiritual, compassionate … and wise … . I wish he would run for president" (Bailey, 2013). Several days later, the trainer wrote back, saying that he "was touched," and it got him to thinking, "What if I were?" He then went on to enumerate the steps he would undertake as Commander in Chief.

To begin with, he would disenfranchise "any person or entity that can be identified as receiving government assistance in any form or fashion." Having expunged "takers" from the voter rolls, he would then enact mandatory sentencing laws to rid the nation of drug users and "illegal aliens." Following this, he would "exterminate" [*sic*] the rulings, laws, and orders listed above that protect minorities from discrimination. Finally, in no particular order, he would impose a flat 10 percent tax on earned income, issue a decree forbidding the Treasury Department from going into debt to subsidize "unconstitutional" policies, end the spurious separation between church and state, and return non–constitutionally designated powers to the individual states so they could run their internal affairs as they see fit (Earl, 2013b).

The Right-Wing Hero

Caller to Ground Zero, a syndicated radio talk show (June 14, 2013)
I was in the Navy. I'm down here [in Moore, Oklahoma, following a massive tornado]. When I see a homeless person, I give them ten bucks. If I don't have change, I give them a cigarette, even if it's not good for them. [But] I'm not a hero.

Clyde Lewis (the show's host)
You are a hero.

Caller
No, you're the hero. I agree with everything you say, everything. You tell it like it needs to be said. People need to listen to you.

Gino (the next caller)
I'm not a hero either; I'm a sucker, an imbecile, a failure." He goes on to describe how his parents fled Mussolini's Italy and emigrated to America. "They gave us everything, taught me right from wrong. I let them down. I'm a failure.

Clyde Lewis
Don't you say that. You're not a failure.

Gino
Yes, I am.

Clyde Lewis
No! [He breaks down, sobbing.] You're all [meaning, his audience] heroes. This is real. We're all struggling.

It is impossible to grasp the inner workings of the Patriot psyche without taking into consideration the appeal of heroism. Not that there is an absence of larcenous intent behind Patriot politics: Emergency foodstuffs, bumper stickers, t-shirts, off-shore tax havens, gold bars, tungsten, burglar-proof safes, home alarm systems, identity-theft protection, military-style weapons, conspiracy CDs, videotapes, and books and, revealingly, over-the-counter remedies for erectile dysfunction and testosterone deficiency have all grown into flourishing cottage industries since the 1980s, catering primarily to an aging male Patriot audience. Nor can we overlook the emotional appeal of Patriot activism: the adrenaline rush that accompanies attendance at tea-party rallies, the dressing up in camouflage or revolutionary-era garb, the hefting of the Confederate Stars and Bars or the jerry-rigged placard, "Obama is a black Muslin" [*sic*]. There are angry chants and country music and the warm flood of sentimentalism that accompanies Patriot speechifying. And then there are bleaker pleasures of contemplating retribution against those presumably at fault for America's ills. But to focus exclusively on profit making and emotion is to risk overlooking the fundamental reason for right-wing extremism in the first place, which is to be a hero.

In contrast to the "average man" who carefully weighs the costs of different choices before acting, the man of heroic temperament acts out of what Max Weber calls "pure intentions" (Weber, 1964: 15–16; Collins, 1982: 2–29). That is to say, he or she burns with a desire to do right *regardless* of the costs. What is important is what God commands, not what a cost-benefit analysis recommends. Michelle Goldberg quotes TEAvangelist motivational speaker, Pam Stenzel as "begging" the "People of God ... to commit yourself to truth, not [to] what works. To truth. I don't care if it works, because at the end of the day I'm not answering to you, I'm answering to God" (M. Goldberg, 2007: 136). (For the logic of pure intentions, as applied to jihadists, see Juergensmeyer, 2003: 187–215.)

Many Patriots concede that Social Security, the Environmental Protection Agency, occupational health and safety measures, federally subsidized farm insurance, affirmative action programs, legal abortion, civil rights for gays, and the like, do, in fact, enhance the general felicity of the population, as do progressive income taxes, rehabilitation instead of punishment, food stamps for indigents, Aid for Dependent Children, unemployment insurance, Medicaid, and Obamacare. But the problem is that these contravene what Patriots take to be "nature and nature's God." Thus they must be "exterminated," to quote the firearms instructor mentioned earlier. Better that America's economy falter and collapse than that her sacred covenant with the Lord be transgressed. *"Better dead than Red!"*

In 2014, the Idaho state legislature passed a measure to allow faculty, students, and staff at public colleges and universities to carry concealed weapons on campus. Several of the college presidents objected that this would increase the likelihood of injury, require increased spending to retrain and arm campus security, and cause liability insurance problems. In response, one senator indignantly huffed that "coddling" people was not his job. *"My job is to preserve freedoms!"* "We sometimes think our duty is to make everyone safe," he continued, but no: "It's to preserve liberty" (Staff, 2014, author's emphasis). Utilitarian arguments such as that offered by the National Rifle Association that more guns mean safer campuses (Lott, 2010) are beside the point. What is not is the sanctity of the Second Amendment.[2]

Patriot policies meant to dismantle public education, destroy labor unions, frustrate environmental protections, deny medical insurance to the poor, or legalize discrimination against gays follow a similar logic. Even when Patriots admit that such policies might cost millions, even billions, of dollars, they insist that they be implemented anyway—not because Patriots are stupid or crazy but because they are *rational*; rational, however, in a way that is difficult for the "average man" to comprehend. The word for it is *ends-oriented* rationality, the conviction that certain principles are worthy of compliance not because they might enhance domestic welfare but because they are good in themselves.

Patriots can barely conceal their contempt for "mushy middle-of-the-roaders," self-congratulating conservatives who seem too eager to sacrifice ultimate ends for the sake of peace. In their mind, compromise is little better than surrender and "bean-counting" and democratic procedures, "the great love of the failures and cowards of life" (Rushdoony, quoted in British Centre for Science Education, 2007; Clapp, 1987). Instead of negotiating with the devil, they urge one another to "grasp hold of the Lord's hand." Failure to do so is to risk God's wrath. Rev. Pete Peters claimed that "Voodoo Haiti" suffered a devastating earthquake for precisely this reason. Rev. C. Peter Wagner told his congregation that God visited a comparable judgment on Japan a year later because the emperor was having sexual intercourse with the Sun Goddess (Gross, 2011). Rev. Cindy Jacobs, a Wagner protégé, added that the tsunami that followed the earthquake was due to President Obama's refusal to enforce the antigay Defense of Marriage Act. Later that summer, she invoked the same theory to explain a mass die-off of drum fish in Arkansas (Jacobs, 2011).

To the Christian Patriot, ends are everything, and any means that might conceivably advance them are permissible. Among these are nonviolent demonstrations á la Operation Rescue, hunger strikes (Daily Beast, 2014), deceptive "stealth" campaigns to win seats on school boards and city councils (a tactic first proposed by Gary North in 1981 and subsequently endorsed by Ralph Reed), and attempts to seize control of state and county Republican Party apparatuses so as to campaign on explicitly Christian Dominionist platforms. Some Patriots have gone so far as to petition Congress to ban federal courts from hearing cases that bear on "God's concerns," such as school prayer, homosexuality, and abortion (Yurica, 2004). And when all else fails, there are always guns. The so-called "Army of God," inspired by Francis Schaeffer's *Christian Manifesto*, committed up to seven abortion-clinic murders in the 1990s and 2000s (see Appendix). But one thing Patriots find exceedingly difficult to question is the wisdom of their ends, even when what might be required to attain them is extraordinarily costly.

Max Weber considers the heroic politics of the far-right (and -left) "irresponsible" (Weber, 1958a). But the fact is that, contrary to what behavioral scientists might have us believe, human beings *don't* just want to feel good (or maximize their pleasure at minimal cost). Instead, we want to feel good about *ourselves* (Becker, 1975). Burdened with awareness of our existential frailty, we want to know that our short time on Earth has meaning and significance in the greater scheme of things. For one person, this might mean amassing a great fortune or having multiple offspring. For another, it might involve conquering the world's highest peak or breaking a land-speed record, and for still others, discovering a cure for cancer or AIDS. Christian Patriots dramatize their significance by laboring with like-minded souls to erect what they believe is a more God-pleasing society on a fallen Earth. Which is to say, the object of their veneration is not the "vulture capitalist" or Hollywood celebrity, much less "some Jewish queer looking sissy ... Pee Wee Herman" (Peters, 1994: 3), who is always calculating the benefits and costs of different courses of action. Instead, it is the golden-skinned Shamgar (Judges 3:31) or the armor-bedecked Samson (Judges 15:15), who slew evil-doers with ox-goads and jawbones of asses.

Glenn Beck (Blaze Radio, June 13, 2013) occasionally likens himself to a hero, and he urges his audience to be "giants" as well. He tells them to "enlist" in the "black-robed regiment" (an evident allusion to colonial-era Presbygationist ministers) and to "raise a standard for all men." He cautions that "they [i.e., their neighbors] will laugh at us, ridicule us, call us freaks ... But that's okay ... The whole story of America is about the misfit." Abraham Lincoln, George Whitfield, Steve Jobs, Ben Franklin: They were "outsiders" too, Beck assures his listeners. Of course, the "cool people will isolate you ... mock you, and call you a 'loser.'" But that's only because deep down "they are scared of us." So, be like George Washington, Mahatma Gandhi, and Martin Luther King Jr. Or better, be like Beck himself. "I've had doubts. I was offered fame, fortune," but I gave it all up, knowing I could "be better than I am." I promise you, "If you lose your life for His sake, you will be saved." "The time is now!"

Beck (Blaze Radio, September 26, 2013) once compared himself to Tokyo Rose, the infamous radio announcer who aired Japanese propaganda messages to American troops fighting in the Pacific. Although she was imprisoned for treason after the war, Beck maintains that actually she was a hero. "If this [pointing to her] microphone could speak, it would say, 'Listen to the voices of the past; you are the bastion of freedom.'" "Don't follow the crowd ... Do the right thing."

Christian Patriots see themselves as "God's battle axe and weapons of war" (Jer. 51:20), as a "remnant" who fear no church, no government, nor "any other tool used by the Adversary" (Crawford, 1984: xv). Thus, whatever the final outcome of their fight against Them—ethnic minorities, gays, "femi-nazis," and liberals—its ferocity justifies these Patriots in their faith. It proves to them that their God is an "awesome God," not a wussy, indulgent *abba*-daddy deity, but a stern, jealous, and angry King.

Notes

1 Buchanan is an ex-speech-writer for President Nixon and was a relatively successful GOP primary presidential candidate. In his keynote address to the 1992 GOP convention, he invoked the phrase "culture war," which subsequently became a major rallying cry for Dominionists.

2 "It was bound to happen," said the president of Idaho State University. Within two weeks of the new semester, a chemistry professor had shot himself in the foot with a concealed weapon while teaching class (O'Donnell, 2014). Why he was armed with a loaded, un-holstered pistol in his pocket with the safety off and how he managed to pull the trigger are still unclear.

Interlude 4

"Cut It or Shut It!"

Critics called it "economic terrorism" and "legislative chicken." The editorial staff of *The Washington Post* dismissed it as "a reckless, wastefully irresponsible dereliction of leadership": In October 2013, a rump caucus of far-right House members threatened to shut down the federal government and/or refuse to pay its debts unless Congress defunded the Affordable Care Act (Obamacare). Although the law had earlier passed both houses of Congress and had been signed by the president, declared constitutional by the Supreme Court, and subsequently ratified de facto by Obama's landslide reelection, right-wing extremists viewed it as "socialized medicine," a "criminal act," and a "monstrosity." The more cynical among them realized that if the public ever became "addicted to the sugar" of Obamacare, their political fortunes would be compromised.

After voting to take the government hostage in order to get their way, supporters of the "cut it or shut it" strategy reportedly emerged from the caucus room giddy at the prospect of battle. "Let's roll!" one of them exhorted, referring to the last words uttered by passengers on a terrorist-hijacked airplane. "It's like 9/11!" GOP detractors called the caucus's move "a fool's errand." Nonplussed, the caucus returned the insult, labeling its critics "appeasers" or "RINOs" (Republicans in name only) and as "squishy." They compared them to Neville Chamberlain, the British Prime Minister who futilely sought peace with Adolf Hitler. What the times called for, they insisted, was a grand, heroic gesture. True patriots needed to stand tall for the Bible and for constitutional principles regardless of what this might entail for their own careers, the fate of the GOP, or the economic well-being of the country or the world. They reminded themselves of Barry Goldwater's infamous campaign slogan: "Extremism in the defense of liberty is no vice."

4 The Communicative Preconditions of Far-Right Fantasy

Far-right fantasy is a knowledge form that emerges from a particular kind of communication structure, technically known as a *closed system*. The distinguishing feature of a closed system is that its claims are validated tautologically by reference to its own presuppositions. This is in contrast to an open system, wherein assertions are available to criticism or rebuttal from information sources outside it.

Closed and open communication systems are emblematic, respectively, of authoritarian (leftist or right-wing) and democratic social orders (Popper, 1995 [1945]), and they find expression in variant forms of erudition: respectively, in mythology and laboratory science. Most claims-making enterprises fit somewhere between these extremes. Among them are the "pseudo-sciences," as Karl Popper (1965) calls them, of astrology, Freudianism, Adlerian psychology, and vulgar Marxism. Others examples are intelligent design (creationism), conservative sociological theory (also known as *structural functionalism*), rational choice theory, and racialist cosmology.

Phrenologists, spiritual channelers, palm readers, tarot card interpreters, and medical pleomorphists (who believe that disease causes germs, not the opposite) contend that because their theories are supported by empirical data, they deserve to be grouped with bona fide sciences. But, as Popper tells us, "the world is full of verifications … ." "It is easy to obtain confirmations … if we look for them" (Popper, 1965: 35–7). What demarcates scientific inquiry from pseudo-science is not that one is necessarily more highly "verified" but that *scientific* conjectures are, to paraphrase Popper (1965), inter-subjectively challengeable. That is, they generate "risky predictions" that, when they fail, can result in the theory in question being falsified. Pseudo-scientific confirmations, in contrast, have "the quality of defensive acts," which shut the investigator's "receptive apparatus" and protect them from "having to attend to disturbing considerations that do not fortify [their] ideas" (Hofstadter, 1963: 38).

A pertinent case of pseudo-science is provided by the thousand-plus book conspiratology concerning the assassination of President John F. Kennedy (1963). All of it is copiously documented, tightly argued, and insightful, yet there is no agreement among its authors about who the assailants were. Some say they were CIA officials who felt Kennedy had betrayed them during the

Bay of Pigs and was now about to withdraw troops from Vietnam. Others insist that they were New Orleans mafia hit-men who had once worked for Kennedy's bootlegging father, Joe, and still others, that they were Texas Ku Klux Klan allies of Vice President Lyndon B. Johnson. And the speculation goes on: His killers were conservative Dallas oil magnates who detested the Yankee Kennedy for his British inflections; Federal Reserve bankers fearful that Kennedy was going to pull the plug on their control over the nation's money supply; FBI agents carrying out orders from J. Edgar Hoover; Soviet KGB spies; pro-Castro revolutionaries; anti-Castro exiles; and so on. A handful of conspiracy theorists point to friends of Kennedy's wife, Jackie, who they say was scandalized by her philandering husband. Each account is accompanied by verifying anecdotes, think-tank testimonials, and study group opinions. What these accounts do not provide, *cannot* provide, is an assertion of what they would accept as *disconfirmation* of their narratives. But if they can never be disconfirmed, then strictly speaking they are certain and, in being certain, are instances of pseudo-science.

Far-right conspiratology is particularly notorious in this respect. Richard Hofstadter once counted 313 citations alone in Senator Joseph McCarthy's 96-page pamphlet, *McCarthyism*, and the canonical John Birch Society text, candy-maker Robert Welch's *The Politician*, which fingers President Eisenhower as "a dedicated, conscious agent of the Communist conspiracy," contains more than 100 pages of footnotes and bibliographic references (Hofstadter, 1963: 37). What McCarthy and Welch fail to offer is a statement of what they would accept as disproof of their claims. This is because, without a Communist conspiracy to rail against, their politics would be pointless. But because this is unthinkable, the conspiracy *must* be true.

To illustrate the difference between science and pseudo-science, Popper (1965) describes a classical test of Einstein's claim that light is composed of tiny particles called *photons*. If this is true, physicists supposed, light emitted from a distant star should be measurably deflected by the gravitational pull of the Sun, which effect can be measured during a total solar eclipse. (When the test was eventually conducted, its findings supported Einstein's theory.) Compare this to the reasoning characteristic of, say, a creation scientist. The basic proposition of creation science is that a transcendent "Intelligence" has designed life. (Creationists are reluctant to use the term "god,'" because it does not sound scientific enough.) As confirmation, they offer the fact of the eyeball in all its beautiful complexity, the intricacies of a bird wing, and the minute cilia in a worm gut. Initially, this all seems promising. The problem is that it generates no predictions, let alone *risky* predictions. Because of this, it does not constitute real science.

Another more prosaic example directly relevant to the subject of this book is the proposition widely held on the far-right that Barack Obama was not born in the United States and thus is (was) ineligible to be president. Popper would insist that this not a scientific assertion, because there is no way to refute it, which, to repeat, is another way of saying that it is nontestable. "Birthers" have shown themselves unwilling to accept as valid any document or witness that might conceivably contradict their belief, including publication of Obama's birth certificate, which is rejected as fraudulent, or the testimony of the Hawaiian Department of Vital Statistics, the honesty of which they question. In effect, denial of President Obama's American birth is an article of faith, along the lines of the myth of a god-man said to be born to a virgin, an amazing story of immeasurable psychological significance but not a historiographic (i.e., testable) assertion.

Popper (1995 [1945]) argues that open systems of communication encourage skepticism and doubt. These, he says, are the distinctive qualities of a "critical attitude," a disposition mirrored in such institutions as free speech and, in regard to empirical inquiry, the practice of having anonymous referees, instead of friends and ideological comrades, assess the quality of journal submissions. Closed systems, in contrast, engender a "dogmatic attitude." Dogmatism discourages criticism and rewards work that verifies predecreed, authoritative truths.

When faced with what appears to be negative evidence, say, about a diabolical one-world plot, a notion with which we will become intimately familiar in the next chapter, dogmatists resort to "magical thinking." One species of this is what Popper (1965) calls the "soothsayer's trick." This is a forecast about the future posed in such vague terms that virtually any event can be said to confirm it. Soothsayer's tricks are closer to religious prophecies, says Popper, than to bona fide predictions. A classic example, which will also be introduced in the next chapter, is the solemn, much ballyhooed "prediction," made every decade or so, that ours are the End Times. Because a precise date for the Last Days is rarely provided, this is a forecast that is always a good— and typically, profitable—bet.

Dogmatists also fall back on the "conventional twist" to defend their pet theories. That is, they invoke *ad hoc* assumptions to explain away evident anomalies. Thus, Dr. Martin Luther King Jr. is held up as a so-called "exception" that proves the rule that colored people in general are stupid. Another example is the "explanation"—again, recited approximately every decade—for why the world did not come to an end after all—namely, because believers prayed so fervently to God that He withheld administering His final judgment.

Related to the conventional twist is *mythologizing*, which refers to the tactic of using the same theory to explain both one thing and its opposite. Gruesome media reports of school shootings are, as we shall see, routinely taken by conpiratorialists to prove the existence of a federal government plot. Yet the failure of that same press to report on other events is *also* taken as proof of a plot and, furthermore, that the mainstream media are in on it. A case in point is the press's silence about a story that spread like wildfire in right-wing circles in the 1990s, that Presidents George H. W. Bush and Bill Clinton were dealing in illegal drugs—Clinton for the purpose of seducing young girls—the drugs being shipped to the presidents through an airport in Mena, Arkansas, by CIA operatives working out of Latin America (Momenteller, 1998). That major media outlets neglected to comment on it was understood to mean that they too were involved in the plot.

Still another move used by dogmatists is argumentum ad hominem, the rhetorical dismissal of counterevidence by showing that its bearers are "fakirs" (Rush Limbaugh's description of environmentalist Rachel Carson) or "frauds" (his assessment of Carson's "science, bought and paid for by liberals" [Rush Limbaugh show, April 29, 2013]). As "Nazis," "fascists," or "Fabian socialists," they are unworthy of being heard.

In the end, dogmatists simply cover their eyes, stamp their feet, and scream, "Shut up!" They want neither to see nor hear anything inconsistent with what they already know to be true.

Popper (1995 [1945]) points out that the difference between closed and open systems of communication has nothing to do with their respective levels of technical sophistication. As we saw earlier, right-wingers are happy to use modern communications technology to fight against what makes that technology possible in the first place: the ethos of modernity. They purchase quality paperbacks from Amazon.com and read e-books on their Kindles; they consult slick-papered magazines and self-publish their exposés of world events on their PCs; they sell cassette tapes to less savvy older folks, and digitally engineered CDs and podcasts to youngsters; they are comfortable in the cable TV studio as well as behind the short-wave radio transmitter; they handle mobile camera phones with ease and are more than able to hold their own with the snarkiest liberal bloggers. By far the most widely listened to radio talk shows in America are right-wing syndicates but, invariably, their format gives the game away: Invited guests and call-ins are prescreened to assure that any feedback they offer re-affirms the host's biases (sometimes by allowing a particularly obnoxious call-in a back-handed opportunity to reveal his or her ignorance, thereby magnifying, by comparison, the host's intelligence and graciousness). It is not at all uncommon to hear listeners gush to the host, "I love you man; thank you for all you do." "Finally, there's someone who speaks the truth!" "You're doing the Lord's work." "Mega-dittoes." Rush Limbaugh says that "no one questions what I say; that would be pointless." Exactly. Whatever he proclaims is indisputable because he has access to "talent on loan from God." At least in regard to right-wing extremist communications, then, Marshall McLuhan appears to have been mistaken: The medium is *not* always the message. True, modern communications can advance openness, but they can also stifle it.

Closed systems are hermetically sealed off from contamination, but this does not mean that what is conveyed through them is senseless, unimportant, or even necessarily untrue. As Popper (1965) shows, both mythology and pseudo-science have repeatedly served as sources of scientific breakthroughs. Take continental drift theory. Until a few decades ago this was ridiculed by geologists as a concoction of charlatans; today, it is accepted by mainline scientists as a fact. The once-maligned theory of medical monomorphism has a similar history. This is the notion that tiny organisms, which, until the invention of the microscope, were invisible, cause diseases. In the nineteenth century, the Austrian pathologist who hypothesized that childbed fever (septicemia) had a bacterial cause (and then forced his interns to scrub their hands before examining pregnant patients to avoid spreading it) was considered crazy for his "germ obsession" and nearly lost his job. Today, his recommendations are standard hospital protocol.

That claims generated within closed systems are irrefutable is considered a virtue by their advocates but, from a scientific standpoint, this is a vice, because what is irrefutable is certain, and certainty obviates the need for further investigation. An irrefutable theory is already known to be true; therefore, all that remains is to memorize its passages and regurgitate them back, like a church catechism. In open systems, on the other hand, there are no certainties. "All theories without exception" are considered tentative and hypothetical, "even when we feel unable to doubt them any longer" (Popper, 1965: 51).

Theories generated in closed communication systems "act upon weak minds like revelations," says Popper (1965: 39). So it is with far-right fantasy. Those granted access to it become "inside dopesters," members of an exclusive club. They have revealed to them two definitive secrets of which even academic "dococrats" with their federal grants and so-called research are unaware, secrets that the government and liberal progressives have been trying to hide from us all this time. The first secret is: *There's a plot!* This is why "they" are mapping the brain; why they are implanting radio-frequency identification (RFID) chips under the skin of elderly Medicare recipients, with plans to do the same to children; why they are installing fiberoptics in the pavement of the nation's freeways, capable of receiving messages from black boxes installed in cars; why home utilities now come equipped with smart meters; why the government eavesdrops on cell phone calls and emails in search of "flag words"; why drones are being unleashed on our borders. It is not to satisfy idle curiosity or promote the general welfare but, in the manner of Michel Foucault's Panopticon, to spy on us and keep us under control (Clyde Lewis, Ground Zero, April 29, 2013; May 5, 2013). Since every discomfiting event, factual and imagined, confirms the existence of the Plot, it can never be disproved. Therefore, to be let in on it is to be ushered into the sanctum sanctorum of cognitive surety. One is provided with what scientific inquiry, fuzzy borders, endless debates, and piecemeal reforms never can supply: something firm, something imperishable on which to stand. In an age when "[a]ll that is solid melts into the air" (Berman, 1988, quoting Karl Marx), this is priceless.

The second indubitable secret is: *There's a cure!* The firearms trainer introduced at the end of the last chapter explains it this way (Earl, 2013d). When "elements of the government … lust after ultimate dictator [*sic*] control … in a world that is changing faster, and in ways more extreme than I ever could have imagined," I "anchor my soul" in "the things I know": the "organic" Constitution (the original articles plus the Bill of Rights) and the Bible, the first read in an "originalist" way (i.e., according to the presumed intent of the Founding Fathers), the second understood literally. Using these as guides, says the trainer, we can re-Christianize America and foil the Plot. Exactly how this is to be done is the subject matter of Chapter 6.

Far-Right Certainties in Uncertain Times

We can speculate forever about what it is that Christian Patriots find so beguiling about the Plot and its Cure (for example, see Hall-Jamieson & Cappella, 2008). As a starting point, it is worth noting that their attraction appears to have grown concomitant with the rise of the national security state since World War II and a growing sense of *insecurity* on the part of the public. This is not to say that the security state has caused far-right fantasy. In fact, the causal connection may well run in the opposite direction: The anxiety and panic generated by far-right fantasy feeds calls for more government surveillance, more drug testing, more loyalty oaths, more mandatory sentencing, and more militarization of local police forces.

However this may be, the enormous increase in defense spending during the Cold War, the rise of a vast but covert nuclear weapons industry, and the authorization of furtive military operations worldwide have helped foster suspicion and paranoia about happenings in high places. Add to these the War Powers Acts of 1941 and 1942, which were never rescinded, and a variety of Homeland Security measures introduced under auspices of the Patriot Act after 9/11. Together, these have legalized, if not exactly legitimized, the expansion of government authority to conduct clandestine supervision of the public by means of the CIA, the National Security Agency (NSA), Naval and Army Intelligence, the FBI, and the Bureau of Alcohol, Tobacco, and Firearms (BATF) (Bamford, 2008).

At this writing, the Department of Homeland Security is erecting a massive data center in Bluffdale, Utah, with the capacity to review 500 billion terabytes (TBs) of information on American citizens annually (as contrasted to the Hubble Telescope, which amassed only 45 TBs during its first 20 years of operation); this with virtually no congressional or judicial oversight and gathered from satellites, surveillance cameras, wiretaps, and telecommunication intercepts. Unauthorized revelations in the spring of 2013 that secret Foreign Intelligence Surveillance Act (FISA) courts had, for years, been granting permission to the NSA to gather metadata on the locations, number, length, and time of day of landline and cell-phone calls between private citizens, together with information on their credit card purchases, emails, file downloads, electronic photos, and Internet searches, confirmed the worst fears of many of those on the far-right (and -left). When he heard the news, Glenn Beck sobbed as he told his radio audience that "this is the death knell of the country!" "We are putting our children on the altar, the altar of Moloch" (Blaze Radio, June 12, 2013). (It is worth pointing out that private corporations such as Yahoo and Google routinely gather even more intimate data on the personal lives of their customers and have been doing so far longer than has the government.)

Even when undertaken for what are seen initially as legitimate reasons, the actualities of warfare almost always render hollow the romantic clichés of patriotic duty and heroic sacrifice. This effect is amplified when deception is used to mobilize public support for combat. Americans have always exhibited a healthy skepticism about military action, so much so that it may almost be considered an American folkway. Witness the doubts expressed about the sinking of the USS *Maine* in Havana Harbor, Cuba, in 1898 or the questioning of news stories concerning the *Lusitania* in 1915. In 1941, American isolationists, some of them parents of today's Patriots, aired doubts about whether the attack on Pearl Harbor was, in reality, the "surprise" officials claimed it to be. The nation's unhappy military engagements since that time have only added to public misgivings. Most notable was the transparently fabricated naval engagement in the Gulf of Tonkin in 1969 that precipitated the invasion of Vietnam and, a generation later, misleading reports about "weapons of mass destruction" that goaded the public into supporting Operation Iraqi Freedom. This is to say nothing of the Watergate scandal, Iran-Contra, the Clinton impeachment, and tales of possibly criminal, if hyperbolized, Internal Revenue Service investigations of political action groups during the Obama administration. With each breach of trust, imagined or real, the presumed sinister nature of government is exposed and doubts about its fidelity increase.

The clearest evidence of growing public skepticism about the government concerns news reports about domestic tragedies. As we will see in the next chapter, some on the far-right have gone so far as to question videotape evidence of the destruction of the World Trade Center on 9/11 or, if they do acknowledge it as valid, take the buildings' collapse as proof of an "inside job," presumably set up by the government to justify a preplanned conquest of Middle Eastern oil fields. Other Patriots wonder who was "really" behind the bombing of the Murrah Federal Building in Oklahoma City. Was it Timothy McVeigh, as we have been led to believe? Or was it BATF officials who, after planting explosive devices in the walls, are rumored to have exited the building moments prior to the blast? Still others harbor suspicions about recent guns massacres. Were the assailants lone wolves acting out of psychotically induced resentments, or were they government brainwashed dupes? There are even some on the far-right who believe that the Moon landing in 1969 was videotaped inside an airplane hangar in the desert outside Las Vegas.

A still unexplained irony is that many who express doubts about these and related official claims exhibit gape-mouthed credulity when it comes to stories of alien abductions and "moth men," about "chem trails" and communications with deceased souls via "spirit boxes." This is reminiscent of what was seen during the McCarthy era. Around the time that the House UnAmerican Activities Committee opened investigations into Communist subversion (1947–8), the first reports of flying saucers near Mt. Rainier in Washington State were broadcast, and tales were told about a UFO crash in Roswell, New Mexico. Anecdotes soon were leaked to the press about autopsies conducted on tiny-limbed, green-skinned extraterrestrial corpses. It is difficult to avoid concluding that the investigations into internal subversion and the revelations about UFOs and extraterrestrial beings were facets of the same postwar moral panic. Likewise, disclosures of the machinations of the Insiders, the Hidden Hand, and Shadow Government today: Patriots who claim to have finally identified the puppet-masters of the global cons-*piracy* also revel in tales about quasi-human "reptilians" and "grays," about "shape-shifters," crop circles, and spacecraft piloted by alien Ebens who inhabit the Zeta Reticuli star system.

McCarthyism involved more than the outrages of a single, some claim drunken, demagogue. Rather, it was a nationwide witch hunt, the frenzy of which seeped into churches, schools, universities, and businesses from Washington, DC, to Washington State and everywhere in between. So, too, in our era, far-right fantasy fills the airwaves and permeates the internet. In both cases, we witness a public made anxious by a federal government using new technologies to gather and store information and, in both instances, they make sense out of a chaotic, fast-moving world by falling back on age-old children's fables about evil dragons, shining knights, and fairytale endings.

In the 1950s, McCarthyites hardly knew who or what to believe and ended up accepting as true what today are acknowledged as the least plausible things. The same is true of contemporary Patriots: They have been so deluged by "*de*formation" that what was once a settled difference between fiction and fact, simulacra and reality, has collapsed. They question who, if anyone, they can trust and end up putting their faith in the least reliable. Their epistemic paralysis whets an appetite for unassailable truths, what can be held onto for certain, what is nonfalsifiable and sure. Evidently, this is a hunger that only a portentous Plot and a scripturally inspired Cure seem able to satisfy.

Interlude 5

The Rhetoric of "No-Spin" News

Roger Ailes is chairman of Fox cable news (est. 1996), and he is derided (or applauded, as the case may be) for devising a closed system of communication that has helped create and sustain the modern Christian Patriot movement (Sherman, 2014). Ailes admits to being a conservative, and he also evinces an authoritarian streak. Apocryphal legend—Ailes calls it his "rosebud story"— traces this back to his childhood and the experience of being brutalized by his father. (Roger stands on the top bunk bed. Father opens his arms, smiles, and tells him to jump. Roger complies. Father steps back. Roger crumples to the floor. Lesson, asks father? "Don't ever trust anybody.") Leni Riefenstahl is one of Ailes's great infatuations, not because of her Nazism but for her reputed skill as a propagandist. She uses camera angles to foster impressions of selected characters, portraying Jews and Slavs from a distance, amidst unruly mobs. Meanwhile, she lingers adoringly over close-ups of square-jawed Nazi storm-troopers and Olympic Games competitors. She uses the eroticism of pageantry and partially clad females to convey messages and has them recite slogans to buttress their truth. Fox TV news draws on all these devices. Besides turning minor events into theatrical spectacles, it panders to the (mainly elderly white male) audience through the sex appeal of its primarily blond female hosts, who are sometimes caught on camera with their legs provocatively crossed. To give the impression of fairness and balance, Fox invites physically less attractive token dissenters to opine and then has them verbally bullied into silence. Lastly, its (Ailes's) agenda is reinforced through Fox staff's incessant repetition of slogans: "war on Christmas," "black voter intimidation," "Fast and Furious," "Muslim no-go zone," "Benghazi cover-up," "Obama–illegal immigrant–ISIS–Ebola." To its audience, Fox proudly proclaims, "We report, you decide." But in the end, what the audience finds is comforting confirmation of its prejudices.

5 Far-Right Fantasy 1

The "Satanification" of America

As Richard Hofstadter (1963) has shown, the "paranoid style of politics," with its "heated exaggeration," suspiciousness, and grandiose victimhood, is longstanding American tradition. In fact, its first expression occurs in the very first years of the republic in the form of a pamphlet titled, *Proofs of a Conspiracy against All the Religions and Governments of Europe, Carried on in the Secret Meetings of Freemasons, Illuminati, and Reading Societies* (1797). Here, liberals of the day are portrayed as libertines, godless advocates of Reason who would destroy the church and imperil female virtue.

Authored by British conservative John Robison, *Proofs* was cited by New England academics and Presbygationist clergy in what turned out to be their losing struggle against the followers of Thomas Jefferson and a gaggle of renegade Baptist/Methodist tent preachers. One document of their fervor was passage of the Alien and Sedition Acts in 1798 that allowed for the imprisonment and/or deportation of those considered "dangers to the peace and safety of the United States." During his campaign for the presidency, Jefferson vilified the Acts as nondemocratic but, once in office, he used them to harass his enemies. Since that time, *Proofs* has served repeatedly as a template for right-wing conspiracy mongering, up to the present day.

Hofstadter acknowledges that all politics and, for that matter, all commerce, to say nothing of all American religious enterprises, are about setting strategic goals and then devising tactical plans to carry them out—which is to say, *conspiring*. The difference between this and conspiratology is that the latter *cosmologizes* this mundane fact by positing the existence of a fiendish, virtually omnipotent cabal that "breathes together" to achieve world domination: a coterie of demonic *Übermenschen* who are rumored to meet at night in cemeteries, caves, gothic castles, synagogues, war rooms, or exclusive men's clubs. It is a fantasy composed in equal measure of a Manichean division of the world between good and evil; a belief that there are no accidents, coincidences, or confusion but that every historical misfortune is the result of the cabal's secret plan; an exclamatory urgency that the Apocalypse is nigh; and "secular Adventism," an insistence that, if Patriots remain vigilant, it is not too late to save the republic from catastrophe. "Big wheels turn slowly," a guest on a conspiracy radio show reminded the audience, "but if you take your eyes off them, you'll be crushed" (Ground Zero, March 21, 2013).

That fundamentalist Christians are drawn to conspiratology is not surprising. Joan Acocella (2013: 84) observes that "paranoia and religion have a lot in common". Both argue that beneath the humdrum routines of everyday life lies a mysterious Presence and that a skilled hermeneutist is needed to decipher signs of the times, each clue pointing to the next, which brings one closer, but never quite all the way, to Truth. What this means is that, like Bible stories, conspiratology should not be understood as offering a testable (i.e., falsifiable) account of the world but as a metaphysical doctrine in a never-ending search for confirmatory proofs. Each item in its literary corpus reveals more about the inner demons of its authors than it does about reality "out there." It is, says Hofstadter (1964: 100), the unconscious projection of "concerns, not only largely private but essentially pathological, into the public scene."

Conspiratology evinces what I like to call the "narcissism of lived time." By this I mean the presumption that my (or our) fleeting moment on the endless timeline of history is not just unique but has immeasurable, eschatological significance. Thus, the passing of my little moment on Earth represents more than just the end of my existence but stands for the termination of *all* things once and forever. The narcissism of lived time accomplishes two things simultaneously. First, it inflates my tiny ego into a psychic giant of unmatched proportions. Second, it projects the inevitable and imminent decline and death of this ego onto an *alter*-ego of equal majesty: a fantastical Other who can be blamed for ego's (hence, the world's) demise. Psychoanalyst Stephen Grosz views the narcissism of lived time in ironic terms, as a psychological defense against "the catastrophe of indifference": "the feeling that no one is concerned about us [me], that no one cares." According to Grosz (2013: 82–3), "it is less painful to feel betrayed" by, say, a liberal progressive president or the IRS "than to feel forgotten." They may hate me, plot against me, and spy on me, but at least I matter; at least someone cares.

The Spokesmen of Modern Conspiratology

For all their differences, and there are many, all contemporary American right-wing conspiracy buffs are narcissists of lived time. The three I focus on here are Glenn Beck (Blaze Radio), Alex Jones (Infowars.com), and Clyde Lewis (Ground Zero Radio).

Beck tends to find his solace in God, Jones in guns, and Lewis in gore or, as he calls it, "blood cement," the "unity by atrocity" propounded in the Book of Revelation. When one of the callers to Lewis's talk show urged listeners to "follow the money" while tracing the lineaments of the conspiracy, Lewis demurred. "It's not about the money. You are thinking like a normal person would." Rather, "It's about power." And the way to "prove your power is by destroying, burning, scorching things, including people." A better guiding principle, Lewis said, is to "follow the Demon." Like a "hydra, the Demon is headless, and its tentacles are everywhere, marauding, raping, killing." "The Demon," he added, is the "vampire that we deny exists." It is the federal government (Ground Zero, March 21, 2013).

On his afternoon talk show, Beck can seem preachy and unctuous. Occasionally, he weeps out of an inflated sense of his own persecution as he contemplates the grim future that awaits the country. As for Jones, he underwent his minute of fame during a brief appearance on CNN when he broke into angry tears after the host, Piers Morgan, refused to acknowledge "the obvious"—that a school massacre just days earlier had been staged by government officials as an excuse to confiscate guns. In a highly polished, widely disseminated 90-minute video, Jones reveals that Bohemian Grove, California, is the site where "the secret rulers of the world" meet each July to plan the next step in their nefarious designs. There, he says, they seal themselves to the cause and to each other by making burnt offerings to the ancient fire god, Moloch (Jones, 2009).

Lewis appears better read than either Beck or Jones, particularly in comparative religions and mythology. He can laugh at himself—more than one listener has accused him of "mocking my Christ"—and sometimes he tries to preempt criticism by describing himself as a neutral "investigator." Nevertheless, he too can become defensive (and sob) when listeners challenge his authority; this as he spins deeper and deeper into esoterica in a futile search for solid ground.[1]

There is also a host of lesser lights. Among them are the (deceased) anti-Semites Elizabeth Dilling (*The [Jewish] Plot against Christianity*) and Henry Ford (*The International Jew*), both of whom continue to be cited as authorities on the subject and both of whom were influenced by the *Protocols of the Learned Elders of Zion*, a fabrication of the nineteenth-century Tsarist secret police. When he awarded Ford with the Iron Cross in the 1930s, Adolf Hitler is reported to have said, "We look to Heinrich Ford as the leader of the fascist movement in America" (Cohn, 1967: 162). To buttress her claims on the subject, Dilling plagiarizes selections from the Jewish Talmud, using as her inspiration Father Justin Bonaventura Pranaitis's notorious *The Talmud Unmasked*. In her introduction to *The Plot*, she boasts of having dined in the executive lunchroom at the Ford car factory in Detroit.

Gary Allen, author of the John Birch Society bestseller *None Dare Call It Conspiracy*, and Ralph Epperson (*The Unseen Hand*) deny that Jews are the puppet-masters of the one-world plot. (Their constant harping on the machinations of the Jewish Rothschilds, Warburgs, Loebs, Schiffs, Ochs, Baruchs, and Morgenthaus, however, seem to belie their protestations.) Instead, they attribute the conspiracy to what they call "Insiders," to "Shadow Government," or the "Hidden Hand." These are literary devices that enable the authors to stoke readers' anxieties while discouraging them from focusing their hostility on a concrete ethnic group. In this way they shield themselves from being held responsible for any violence their words might incite. Furthermore, and more to the point, in the manner alluded to in the last chapter, the use of these titles inures their conspiratologies from being falsified. After all, how can one disprove the existence of a hand that is "hidden," of a government that resides in the "shadows," or of a cryptic "insider?"

Caller to Ground Zero (Jan. 2, 2014)
You asked if we are going to be willing to fight. Damn right, I'm willing, but who's the enemy? You [Lewis] are not being definitive enough.

Lewis
I don't know … It can't be seen. It's a shadow government … the global oligarchy. [After naming a handful of possible oligarchic candidates, including the Rothschilds, Zbignew Brezinski, and Henry Kissinger, he admits] we won't know for sure until the catastrophe … .

Allen and Epperson are often found shelved in the Patriot library with radical Mormon constitutionalists, Cleon Skousen (*The Naked Capitalist*) and (recent Latter-Day Saints Church president) Ezra Taft Benson (*A Nation Asleep*). There is also Jerome Corsi (*Obama Nation*) and Gerald Celente, who was once accused of "pessimism porn" for his gleeful ruminations about the imminent collapse of civil society. Finally, there is the more scholarly and circumspect Anthony Sutton, whose *America's Secret Establishment* reveals that it is the Yale University Skull and Bones Club where one-world cabalists meet, not Bohemian Grove or the Bilderberg Hotel.

Lying deeper in the recesses of the right-wing imaginary are countless writers, some of whom might well be rebuked by Beck, Jones, Lewis, Allen, Epperson, Benson, and Skousen. Among these is Rev. Pete Peters (*None Ever Call It Conspiracy* and *The Real Hate Group* (an "exposé" of the Jewish Anti-Defamation League of B'nai B'rith). (For more on Peters, his church, and annual family Bible retreat, see Zeskind, 2009: 172–83.) Also included are Col. (ret.) Gordon "Jack" Mohr (*Know Your Enemy*), which exposes "Satan's Kids," Jews, as committers of "terrible pollutions at their secret gatherings"; ex-Methodist minister Rev. Wesley Swift, *The Mystery of [Jewish] Iniquity*; Rev. Jarah Crawford, *Last Battle Cry*; and the one-time head of "prison outreach" for the Church of Jesus Christ Christian, Louis Beam (*Essays of a Klansman*). Beam's self-published collection contains a scoring system for earning the one point required to be officially recognized as an Aryan warrior. He estimates that the value of a dead sociologist is about 1/500 of a point. Finally, there is Rev. Sheldon Emry, *Billion$ for Bankers*, the content of which is reviewed in the next chapter.

None of these individuals has manufactured their world views out of thin air but have inherited them from a well-established literary tradition, and all frequently cite one another to validate their claims in the circular, self-referential manner mentioned in the previous chapter. They also take pains to cite fiction, two favorites being George Orwell's *1984* and Ayn Rand's *Atlas Shrugged*. On his radio show, Beck once plaintively cried, "I want my John Galt," referring to the hero of Rand's novel. There are also movies like *The*

Matrix, *Minority Report*, and *Star Wars*. The latter refights the final battle between good and evil with the antagonists garbed in spacesuits and firing laser weapons.

Cosmic Conspiracy through Time

For convenience, we can begin our brief survey of American conspiratology with Adam Weishaupt, "the monster," as Gary Allen calls him, a Bavarian Freemason who did in fact organize a secret group called the Illuminati in 1775 (Illuminati = bringers of light = Lucifer = the Devil). To maintain perspective, however, it is crucial to bear in mind that the elements of the conspiracy archetype were already present in European literature centuries prior to Weishaupt. According to historian Norman Cohn, the first mention of a sinister cosmic plot is found in Gaius Sallust's history of the Roman republic (written *c.* 65 BCE) (Cohn, 1975). But an even clearer anticipation is the apocryphal Book of Enoch (attributed to Noah's grandfather), which is routinely cited by modern conspiratologists to buttress their claims. Enoch, in turn, displays traces of Zoroastrian influence, perhaps attributable to the time when the Israelites were exiled to Babylonia (*c.* 600–500 BCE).

In Enoch, Azazel, the name of the goat originally sacrificed to Yahweh during Yom Kippur (Lev. 16:20–1), is reconfigured into a cloven-hoofed, hairy goat-*man*, whom we know today as Satan (1 Enoch 6–8). As chief of the "fallen angels" alluded to in Genesis, Azazel mates with "the daughters of men" and, through them, produces a race of swarthy giants, the familiar "sons of darkness." It is they and their descendants who are said to be responsible for the misfortunes humanity has since suffered, and it is against them that the "sons of light" are prophesied to fight and defeat in the Last Days.

Whether we go back to the final moments of the Roman republic, then, or earlier to Jewish mythology, we are dealing with a stock of symbols and images that inhabit the most primitive regions of the Judeo-Christian psyche.

Saint Augustine (345–430CE) was the first Christian of any importance to incorporate the theme of satanic conspiracy into his exposé of the "carnal shamelessness," "vile fornications," and "sacrifices to the devil" allegedly engaged in by the Manichean cult, of which he confesses to having been a member prior to his conversion (Augustine, 1960, books 2–5). Variations of Augustine's libel subsequently were transferred onto a succession of Church enemies: Jews, Montanists, Paulicians, Bogomiles, Cathars, Waldensians, Albigensians, and the Knights Templar (Cohn, 1975: 75–98). The female cult known as the Free Spirits (or Beguines) also fell under the projective strobe of the Church. Evidently, they frightened Church fathers with their "nonpious" independence and antinomian indifference to conventional morality and marriage. (This indictment eventually figured in the persecution of European witches.) The libel finally settled on the Illuminati, the early Franco-American advocates of democracy, who were accused of consorting with the anticlerical French revolutionary Jacobins.

As mentioned in the first chapter, the indictment against the Illuminati quickly died off. It then enjoyed a brief rebirth three decades later in the hands of the Anti-Masonic Party. From there it evolved into slander against the Mormon Church, urban legend at the time supposing that the word "Mormon" was a neologism composed of the last names of two men allegedly murdered by the Freemasons: Morgan and Monroe.

It is no small irony that, although Mormonism endured persecution for its Masonic connections, because it appeared when anti-Masonic hysteria was cresting, it absorbed anti-Masonry into its own mythology. The Book of Mormon reiterates the opposition between good and evil that plays a central role in the conspiracy narrative. Here, however, the respective principles are represented by the "white and delightsome" Nephites and the "dark and loathsome" Laminites, alleged forebears of the American Indian. Second, again consistent with the conspiracy trope, within the Nephite nation the two warring principles reappear, this time in the guise of the "freemen," who are described as "friends of the republic," versus the conniving "kingmen." Following the anti-Masonic storyline of the day, the kingmen are accused of being a "murderous combination" whose goal is to destroy liberty and, with it, "agency" (free will). Furthermore, they are said to wear "lambskin aprons" (as did Masons), communicate through "secret signs" (as did Masons), and swear self-condemnatory "oaths" not to divulge their plans to noninitiates. Lastly and most revealingly, the kingmen are reported to having been led by a "Master Mahan." This is an obvious allusion to the despised Master Mason, who was accused by anti-Masons of directing the Masonic plot.

A complete answer to why Mormonism became an object of hostility for anti-Masons takes us beyond our immediate concerns. Suffice it to say that like Freemasonry, Mormonism was, and still is, a notably secretive enterprise: After they are blessed by Church authorities, Mormon temples become off-limits to "gentile" nonbelievers. Furthermore, like Masons, Mormon churchgoers take oaths not to reveal what transpires in the course of their sacramental ordinances, elements of which appear to have been borrowed from Masonic rites. (The founder of the LDS Church, Joseph Smith, was at one time a practicing Mason.) Above all, there is the issue of the so-called "Mormon seraglio," the once ecclesiastically endorsed practice of polygamy. This was taken by prurient Protestants of the time as an indicator of the Church's involvement in sexual depravity (cf. Bennet, 1842).

However this may be, it is a measure of the Mormon Church's assimilation into mainstream American culture that many of its contemporary confessors agree with the descendants of those who once persecuted them, that federal government "kingmen" are engaged in a one-world conspiracy. Something similar happened in German-Irish Catholicism, which, after Mormonism, became the next object of popular American odium.

Protestant vilification of "Romanism" first emerged during the Reformation and reached a high point during the Thirty Years' War (1630–1660), after which it was carried to America by English Calvinists. In the late 1840s, antipapist bigotry was coupled to the traditional British abhorrence of "simian Irish Celts," giving rise to the Know-Nothing Party. Once again, the alarm was sounded: *It's a plot!* Already reviled as a nondemocratic institution, the Church was accused of harboring its own secret cabal. Some claimed it was the earlier-banned Knights Templar; others said it was the black-robed Society of Jesus (Jesuits). In any case, the charge was that Catholics were seeking to resurrect the Holy Roman Alliance, this time not merely in Europe but across the Americas. Add to this salacious, if largely fictional, revelations about sexual improprieties taking place between priests and nuns in underground chambers and the charge that the products of their illicit unions were being baptized, strangled, and thrown into lime-stained pits (Monk, 1999 [1836]).

With this last development, American conspiratology neared the richly textured narrative familiar to most readers, broadcast nightly on right-wing radio. The primary difference is that today the toads and cats once said to oversee the oath takings and orgies have been replaced by beings more suitable to a scientific age. They are Anunnaki astronauts from the planet Nibiru, half-human cyborgs (mechanical humanoids), or soulless robots. And hapless Americans are no longer said to be in thrall to succubi or incubi who fly to their destinations by brooms to penetrate their victims' orifices. Instead, they are abducted by saucer-riding aliens or enslaved electronically by technologies ginned from pop-science. Lastly, Mormons and Catholics—and except for self-proclaimed neo-Nazis, Jews—have lost much of their earlier standing as leading figures in the conspiracy, having been replaced, at least momentarily, by the "towel-headed" legions of Mohammed and their liberal-progressive allies. But as ever, the American Evil One par excellence is en-fleshed in the government hireling.

A Foul and Loathsome Plot

No horror or unpleasantness is immune to conspiracy theory: From the Civil War to both world wars, and from these to the Cold War; from the Great Depression of the 1930s to the Great Recession of 2007–8; from the U.N. to the U.S.S.R. (which is said to have been "Made in the U.S.A."); from "The Great Immigration Conspiracy" to "alien-generated diseases"; from "medical allopathic slavery" (read *modern medicine*) to movies that picture minority people as articulate, sensitive professionals. There are two caveats to this truism: First, much of what ordinary Americans consider to be good either "never happened," say conspiratologists. (Thus, Osama Bin Laden's death by Navy Seals on May 2, 2011, was "all a big show," a "lie" for which there "is no hard evidence." "There was no photo of his body. Why not?" asks Clyde Lewis. His callers supplied the answer: According to "my intel," said one, "O.B.L. is alive and well in Monaco" [Ground Zero, April 26, 2013].) Or, second, if the good did happen, it must have been bad. Thus, Martin Luther King Jr.'s "dream" is, in reality, "our ('white man's') nightmare"; public education is the reason for declining student performance; female suffrage is the driving force behind pornography, artificial birth control, and "a holocaust of child murders"; public vaccination programs are the cause of growing number of autism spectrum disorder diagnoses; and labor unions are "organized thugs," the reason that American business is no longer globally competitive.

In the gloom-filled world of conspiratology, every presidential assassination is traceable to the machinations of Wall Street bankers or their ilk. Global warming is said to be "the new Communism," a "hoax" second in outrageousness only to "The Hoax of the Twentieth Century," the Jewish Holocaust. The increased ferocity of hurricanes is attributable to a secret government program known as HAARP (the high-frequency active auroral research program). The destruction of the Murrah Federal Building was a "state-sponsored" atrocity, and 9/11 an "inside job." Talk of overseas military involvement is a "setup," and reports of declining unemployment rates are "rigged." Sex education is "a filthy Communist plot," Beatles music is "Communist hypnotism," advocacy of gay rights is a "hidden agenda," food stamps are a "scheme," and smart meters are a way to spy on citizens and "program their brains." Even republicanism (lowercase) can be accounted for by means of conspiracy theory: the idea that government authority should rest on the will of the people instead of on divine election. Ralph Epperson maintains that republicanism was part of the Illuminatist plot to rid Europe of its royal families, all of whom, he asserts, "have the blood of Christ in their veins." It was the first step along the path to today's tyranny: a precursor to scientific geology, paleontology, and Darwinism, all of which have culminated in the "worship of mankind," the cult of secular humanism (Epperson on Ground Zero, March 4, 2013). Clyde Lewis agrees: It is all the unfolding of a "sick, sick, sick diabolic plan ... A dark cloud hangs over us." Today, "the god of the state is Lucifer" (Ground Zero, Feb. 7, 2013).

There are no built-in limits to the applicability of conspiratology. And undoubtedly, by the time the following case studies see print, attention will have moved on to other crises and demons. The ensuing discussion should therefore be read not as a definitive account of conspiratology but as an introduction to its logic, the assumption being that the same reasoning can be generalized to any future (or past) event. I purposively present the cases in an obsessively detailed way, similar to the manner in which I heard them broadcast. My intention is to evoke in readers the same dread, depression, and rage that plague the prototypical Christian Patriot.

Shootouts

Although they are relatively few in number compared to the total number of deaths by firearms, mass shootings at American schools, shopping centers, and theaters almost always animate negative impressions about guns. They also inspire calls on the far-right to defend them. An example of this followed the massacre of twenty children and six teachers at Sandy Hook elementary school in Newtown, Connecticut, November 30, 2012, by one Adam Lanza, an obviously disturbed teenager, hefting a semiautomatic assault rifle. (Lanza took his own life when police arrived on the scene.)

In the ensuing days, conspiratologists from across the country offered their own accounts of what had occurred. If indeed it happened at all, which several doubted, it must have been staged by the government with the use of paid "actors." Why, we might ask, would the government collude in such an abomination? According to Clyde Lewis, a clue can be found in the fact that on the very day of the shooting, President Obama allegedly signed a United Nations protocol that called for the confiscation of private firearms (Ground Zero, April 12, 2013). When implemented, Lewis warned, this would make citizens more "vulnerable to attack" than they already are and would justify declarations of martial law, encouraging people to place responsibility for their safety in the hands of police (Ground Zero, March 26, 2013).

As to why Lanza allowed himself to be played as a government dupe, Lewis also has an answer: His rampage was the result of CIA and/or NSA mind control. Although he fails to detail how this was done, he suggests that it might have had something to do with "en-training personal brain waves electronically." This could have produced "visual and auditory hallucinations" that "cause people to commit gun violence" (Ground Zero, April 11, 2013). "The implantation of suggestions to murder" might have been accomplished either through minute drones flying over Lanza's head, through his cell phone, or through his personal computer located in the home of his mother (whom he also murdered).

Lewis uses the same theory to account for a gun massacre at a Tucson, Arizona, grocery store that critically wounded a U.S. Congresswoman (January 8, 2011), a mass killing by an Asian American student at Virginia Tech University (April 6, 2007), and a deadly shooting at an Aurora, Colorado, theater (July 20, 2012). He has also invoked it to explain the bombing of the Murrah Federal Building (April 19, 1995), the destruction of the Twin Towers in New York City on 9/11, and the explosions set off by two Muslim terrorists that killed three spectators near the finish line of the Boston Marathon (April 15, 2013). Lewis's suppositions appeared to receive confirmation when a person named Aaron Alexis murdered twelve government employees at the Washington, DC, Naval Yard (Sept. 16, 2013), after blogging that "an ultra low frequency attack is … what has driven me to do this." On his shotgun, Alexis had etched his intention to "end the torment" with "my ELF [electromagnetic low frequency] weapon" (Marimow & Hermann, 2013).[2]

That "the calcium ion equilibrium in brain tissue" of American citizens is being altered by means of giant ELF wave magnifiers operating at "the fourth harmonic of the earth-ionosphere Schumann Resonance" is an idea that first appeared in far-right circles in the 1980s (Baker, 1985). It has since become fully absorbed into its worldview. In addition to shootings and bombings, ELF weaponry is now being used to explain such medical conditions as tinnitus (ringing in the ears), insomnia, anxiety, and lethargy (cf. George Norry, Coast to Coast AM Radio, March 2, 2014). When ELF weaponry was first disclosed, activists at the time asked, "Why do we know so little about this?" Answer: "Our ignorance is solid proof of Jewish thought-control over America ... . Because these pro-Marxist, anti-American, degenerate Sodophiliacs control all aspects of the U.S. television industry, there should be no surprise" that it "has been totally covered-up and suppressed" (Baker, 1985).

Bombings

Glenn Beck reports on the presence of "a bad, bad, bad man" at the scene of three separate terror attacks: the Boston Marathon bombing, the Murrah Federal Building explosion in Oklahoma City, and 9/11. In each case, says Beck, the man in question was detained by local police as a person of interest, released, and then spirited back to Saudi Arabia before he could be prosecuted. In the Boston case, he was "blood-covered," taken to a hospital, allegedly visited by President Obama's wife, and then disappeared. Some conspiratorialists claim that this same Saudi national was also seen with Presidents Clinton and Bush at the Mena, Arkansas, airport in the 1990s, awaiting arrival of drug-laden CIA planes (discussed in the last chapter.) The "bad, bad, bad man" has since sued Beck for defamation of character (McCoy, 2014).

Beck goes on to claim that the man in question has connections to the Muslim Brotherhood, an Egyptian political party which, after the overthrow of President Hosni Mubarak during the Arab Spring of 2011–12, seized control of the government. Among other things, again at least according to Beck, the Brotherhood is "kidnapping Christian girls, raping them," and then forcing them into marriage so that their "souls will be saved by Allah" (Blaze Radio, May 8, 2013). Beck maintains that President Obama not only supports the Brotherhood verbally but has been "running guns" to them, presumably the very weapons used to kill American diplomats in Benghazi, Libya, on September 11, 2012. "This is the biggest scandal in American history!" he says, but because it involves "everybody in the State Department" and the Pentagon, no one is willing to acknowledge it.

Beck never explicates the reason for American arms sales to the Muslim Brotherhood, but he suggests that it is either because President Obama is himself a closet Muslim (a good likelihood, given his "birth" in Kenya and "madrassa-schooling" in Indonesia), and/or because the White House, State Department, and Defense Department all have been infiltrated by Brotherhood cadres. This explains the existence in McLean, Virginia (a suburb of Washington, DC) of a "compound" owned by a Saudi diplomatic attaché where, according to Beck, Christian girls are forcibly taken and abused. "Saudi Arabia is absolute poison," he proclaims. They are "pumping poison into our country."

Oddly, the day that Beck exposed the "bad, bad, bad man," an actual kidnapping, imprisonment, and rape of three young women was uncovered by police in Cleveland, Ohio, "just down the street from Toledo" (quoting Beck) where there is a large Muslim population. While he never spells out the links between this event and the Saudi attaché, he offers them as proof of an insidious plot involving the president. "I'm sorry," he says, voice quivering. "But [Sen. Joseph] McCarthy was right!" He then adds, "We have [only] a short time" to save America from tyranny. "Please help us" with a donation (Blaze Radio, May 8, 2013).

Just here, we glimpse the oratorical style characteristic of conspiratology, as well as the mercenary impulse that frequently lies behind it. First, the audience is presented with a handful of plausible, if not quite accurately reported, unrelated events, each of which is disturbing. Then, by means of a gigantic inferential leap, they are woven into a menacing narrative about treachery in high places. When the tension is palpable, a sales pitch is made for life insurance, emergency food stuffs, fireproof safes, property in the tax-free refuge of Belize, or survival gear, or a franker plea is made for money.

Clyde Lewis, for one, does not buy Beck's tale of the Saudi bogeyman. Nevertheless, he does see a hidden hand at work (Ground Zero, April 15, 2013). Instead of a Muslim conspiracy, he attributes the Boston bombing to "an act of organized crime," to "cover the tracks" of the bankers who "collapsed the economy" in 2007. In other words, it was all "a dog and pony show" intended to "distract" Americans from seeing what is truly happening. He cites as evidence passage of a stocks law by Congress that same day and the presence near the finish line of several banks on Boylston Street, down which the marathon was run. At the time of the bombings, says Lewis, these "banksters" were being investigated for securities fraud, and all of them had posted crew-cut, khaki-dressed security guards at their buildings' entrances. (Lewis also offers this as the reason for the collapse of "Building Seven" in New York City on 9/11. Building Seven, he says, is where records of ongoing investigations into stock market manipulation were being stored, all of which, naturally, were lost in the rubble.)

The Boston bombing and 9/11, then, were "false flag operations," "typical new world order operations," as was, Lewis adds, the shooting at Sandy Hook Elementary in Connecticut. This is why federal authorities were seen at all three sites the mornings of the incidents, conducting fake training exercises. Numbers, he says, cinch the argument: Just as there are 26 miles to a marathon, there were twenty-six victims at Sandy Hook (actually, the number was twenty-eight). "Is this a coincidence?" (Ground Zero, April 15, 2013). No. In the metaphysics of conspiratology, there can be no coincidences. Everything, good or bad—essentially, everything is bad—must be attributable to acts of will. Adam Lanza, the Boston bombers, and the al-Qaeda hijackers all were "patsies," puppets whose strings were pulled by a Demon in "a test run for martial law." And after they served their foul purposes, "they were taken out in a crime mob hit."

Even the victims of the tragedies are illusory, says Lewis (Ground Zero, April 22, 2013). If the amputees witnessed on TV after the Boston Marathon bombing, being wheeled down Boylston Street, with their legs "supposedly" gone, had actually been wounded, they would have "bled out and died" before reaching a hospital. "These were all actors," most likely unemployed Iraq war veterans, paid by the government to remove their prostheses and pour "canisters of artificial blood" onto the sidewalk when the bombs exploded. This gave the "impression that the bombs had injured them." But what, we might ask, about the tangled scaffolding that had to be removed before first-responders could reach them to perform their (supposedly prescripted) roles? "How convenient," Lewis sneers. It is not just coincidental, he says, that just days prior to the bombing, Obama had lost his gun control campaign to a stubborn Congress. "He was angry" and frustrated, so he tried a "different, more direct tack" to confiscate private firearms. (Likewise, 9/11: "Holograms were used, not real planes," says Lewis [Ground Zero, April 26, 2013]. Jewish "Mossad agents" were seen in downtown Manhattan after the Twin Towers collapsed "celebrating their success," looking forward to the war on Israel's enemies that would soon be declared. In a slang voice, a caller agrees: "What we got here is full Heglian [*sic*] dialect [*sic*].")

The bloodshed witnessed at the Boston bombing and 9/11, then, was just a prop. The *real* victim is Lewis himself. Proof: "It's not the action," the bombings, that are important, he says. "It's the [government] *reaction* (Ground Zero, April 19, 2013). The phrase he uses to characterize this tactic is "tension anxiety," a phrase, he maintains, that was coined by socialist community organizer and supposed Obama mentor Saul Alinsky. First, stage an atrocity and then promise to alleviate the ensuing terror by urging citizens to renounce their constitutional liberties. Thus, in response to the killings at Virginia Tech, Tucson, and Aurora, Colorado; to the sham disasters at Sandy Hook, 9/11, and Oklahoma City; to the Washington, DC, Naval Yard massacre; the conflagration at Waco, Texas (April 19, 1993); and the gigantic fertilizer explosion in West, Texas that killed fourteen people (April 17, 2013), the public demands that government *do something*: Build more prisons! Deploy more drones! Conduct more intrusive electronic searches and seizures! Post more soldiers in the streets! Understood in this way, the death and prosecution of the Boston bombers "isn't a victory for the people." It is, instead, a victory for the state. The citizenry "were celebrating the Stasi," the so-called American equivalent of the notorious East German secret police (Ground Zero, April 26, 2013). "It's a victory for the new world order! It's a design! It's a farce!" "We have people celebrating in the streets because they [i.e., the citizenry] were imprisoned!" (Ground Zero, April 19, 2013) "The criminal [i.e., the government] has become the savior!" (Ground Zero, July 22, 2013) As a result, "We [meaning himself] are all suspects now" (Ground Zero, April 26, 2013). "We're in the cross-hairs now." And those who refuse to "go along" with the government narrative "are being fired and replaced with more compliant *foreign correspondents* [Lewis smirks] who speak with an *accent*, like Christiane Amanpour." "We are the new scapegoats, the *real* victims" (Ground Zero, April 22, 2013). The audience is urged to avert its eyes from the injured and killed and cast its gaze instead on the primary casualty, the sobbing Clyde Lewis.[3]

Common Core: "A Trojan Horse"

If there is a government program more benign, at least in sound, than the Common Core State Standards (CCSS) Initiative, I am unaware of it, for at least outwardly Common Core appears to be little more than a federally funded, state-led effort to establish a single set of educational guidelines from kindergarten through twelfth grade in English and mathematics to ensure that graduates are prepared to enter college or take jobs in a postindustrial workplace. This, however, is not how the radical right sees things. To the far-right, Common Core "is about the Constitution; it's about states' rights; it's about slavery. They're enslaving your children. [And] since [given what we saw in the previous sections] you have no gun to protect yourself, "*you* are a slave too" (Blaze Radio, April 12, 2013).

Under Common Core, says Glenn Beck, "you won't have the right to teach your own religion," which will now be labeled as "intellectual abuse." "They're coming for your kids" because now they belong to "the collective." In his typically mixed-metaphoric hyperbole, he describes Common Core "as a monstrosity!" "They are building a machine!" "Now, it's for all the marbles!" "The missiles are in the air!" (Blaze Radio, April 8–9, 2013). "It's the biggest story in American history! If it is not stopped, American history is over!" (Blaze Radio, March 29, 2013) (It's not too late, please send in your donation today.)

According to representatives from Eagle Forum, a far-right lobby, Common Core is not a locally initiated effort at all but the creation of an "international cartel," of which Bill and Melinda Gates, George Soros, and Bill Clinton are frequently mentioned as members, along with Bill Ayers, the Chicago "terrorist" with whom President Obama is accused of "palling around." All of them "want commonality across the entire world," where "everything will be the same." "We will have the same standards as Sweden" or, heaven forbid, "as *Zimbabwe!*" (Neal Larson Show, April 18, 2013).

The indictment against Common Core is partitioned into three arguments:

First, contrary to what its proponents claim, it has nothing to do with the three *R*s at all but everything to do with the "three *E*s": environmental sustainability, equity (i.e., social justice, "so big in all this" and a very bad thing indeed), and economics (meaning profits for the school equipment suppliers Microsoft and Pearson Education). The SATs, ACTs, and GREs, the three standard achievement tests, will be "retooled" to assess "student compliance" with the three *E*s by means of open-ended questions. This is "the same technique used by 'hidden persuaders,'" salespeople, to manipulate consumer choices. In addition to administering "socialist tests," teachers will also try to decipher whether their charges are exhibiting the appropriate attitudes toward the 3Es. The classic literature "we enjoyed," says Beck, as youngsters—Beck is a junior college dropout and autodidact whose understanding of classic literature is highly suspect—are to be replaced with government pamphlets. As for the math section of the tests, process and teamwork will be emphasized over correct answers and individual achievement. In this way, students will be "encouraged to 'construct' their own reality," including their mathematical reality, communally. Thus, presumably, if they agree that $1 + 1 = 3$, then so be it; this is their reality. The idea of fixed truths and absolute values goes out the window, which plays right into the relativist agenda of secular humanism. "It's all part of the new world order" to make us good socialists, says Beck, adding that Common Core also will encourage "moving wealth from rural areas to poor urban centers." To say it simply, it is a "progressive-ist, statist, Fabian socialist, Communist" plot.

Second, according to Beck (Blaze Radio, March 28, 2013), Common Core will entail a massive "data-mining operation on our children for the good of the collective." This will encompass everything from the child's self-reports of their parent's income, religious affiliation, and voting preferences, to their bus-stop sites. "Bio-metrics" will be gathered on the child's hair and eye color, birthmarks, and blood type. There will be iris scans, fingerprints, DNA swabs, and magnetic imaging of their brains. To enable 24/7 monitoring, schools will distribute wristband monitors with miniature cameras. Chairs capable of measuring the child's weight and posture will be distributed. Beck recoils in horror: "It's *1984!*" "The progressives are lining up for the kill!" "It's an end-run around your state, your communities, your school boards, your parental rights!" "*This* is the line in the sand!" "Your children's freedom, their life is at stake!" It's the final battle between good and evil prophesied in Revelation 13. (Again, it's not too late. I urge you to send in your donation. Today.)

The third indictment is that Common Core will introduce "tracking" (a routine practice in American schools since the 1950s but, for the ill-schooled Beck, something shockingly novel and "insidious"). On the basis of their assessed competencies, aptitudes, and attitudes, in other words, children will be assigned either to precollege curricula or to less academically demanding vocational technical tracks. The upshot of this is that "your [child's] lot is cast by the age of seven." This will render them "cogs in the system forever" (Blaze Radio, March 28, 2013).

Advocates of Common Core claim that it was never intended to be either a federally administered program or mandatory, but Beck is unconvinced. Cash-strapped local districts will be "bribed" with federal monies to comply with Common Core recommendations, he warns, with "billions" of dollars. He makes no mention of why American local school districts today are strapped for cash or of the role the far-right has played in this development.

Dramatic Weather

In the months following his second inauguration in 2013, President Obama suffered what right-wing pundits nationwide gloated was a "trifecta of scandals": publication of doctored emails "proving" that the Benghazi attack (mentioned earlier) was "covered up"; revelations that the Department of Justice was secretly monitoring the electronic transmissions of journalists; and exposés of how the IRS had "targeted" right-wing groups who were supposedly engaged in educational and charitable activities. Talk turned to the possibility of impeachment for high crimes and misdemeanors.

This is not the place to examine the veracity of these claims or the plausibility of the hopes. It is enough to say that just as fervency reached an apex on May 20, 2013, a catastrophic tornado leveled a suburb of Oklahoma City, killing twenty-four residents, including nine children. Within hours, bloggers were reporting that the "Oklahoma Tornado Proven False Flag Conspiracy" (Jeffness, 2013).

The storyline goes like this: After police ordered the townspeople to leave their homes, ostensibly for safety reasons, government officials moved in. Equipped with explosives, bulldozers, and wrecking balls, they quickly turned the suburb into a rubble of sticks and bricks. As this was going on, other agents, using a "giant projector," produced a "hollogram" (*sic*) of a tornado image in the sky, analogous to the hologram images of passenger jets flying into the Twin Towers twelve years earlier. "One of my friends," the blogger continues, "heard a self-proclaimed Zionist talking to a shape-shifting [*sic*] white guy. They said that all the earthquake [*sic*] in Oklohoma [*sic*]" were the result of "Jews ... building massive slave labor camps under Oklohoma [*sic*]" (the reader supposes, to imprison "white guys" like himself).

It is not clear what Jewish underground slave labor camps have to do with tornadoes but, ignoring this, the question is once again raised: Why? Why would government officials do this? The next day, Alex Jones provided the answer: The tornado allowed President Obama to "take a pause" from the trifecta of scandals and "reconnect with the American people" by giving "authoritative speeches about aiding disaster recovery." The speeches were intended to show government skeptics, with which Oklahoma is amply supplied, that contrary to their doubts, federal relief would be their "savior." But, Jones editorializes, "you cannot count on government to protect you. You can only protect yourself ... by self-sufficiency and sensible planning."

In response to a listener's call, Jones admitted that he was not certain that the Obama administration had used holograms to generate the illusion of a tornado, yet "of course" the government has deployed "weather weapons" (read *gigantic ELF wave transmitters*) in the past: once during the Katrina hurricane that swept through New Orleans on August 29, 2005, and again during the Sandy superstorm that devastated the New Jersey shoreline on October 25, 2012, just days prior to the presidential vote, virtually guaranteeing Obama's reelection. And the government "can," if it wants, "create and steer groups of tornadoes" to serve its purposes today. He tells the audience that if it saw small planes or helicopters hovering over Oklahoma City the day of the tornado, "You better bet your bottom dollar they did this." But again, he adds, "We don't know" (Willis, 2013).

Little wonder that in a reputable poll taken in 2013, 20 percent of the respondents agreed that President Obama is the Anti-Christ (Public Policy Polling, 2013). "Yes," Glenn Beck opined, he certainly does look "exactly like pictures we've seen of Satan." Clyde Lewis, however, takes issue with Beck.

"Obama is not the puppet-master" of the conspiracy (Ground Zero, March 21, 2013). That honor goes solely to "the Demon." Obama is merely the Demon's "shadow," "the Dark Lord of the Sith." In the *Star Wars* trilogy, the Dark Lord of the Sith is the symbol of all that is "evil and vile," the personage whom the heroic Luke Skywalker awakens to realize is his own "Darth Vader" (Dutch = dark father) (Ground Zero, May 24, 2013). But whatever his name—Devil, Demon, Dark Lord, or malevolent Father—"Under his [Obama's] rule democracy dissolves."

Conclusion

Considerations of limited space and the reader's indulgence require me to forgo discussing other conspiracies. Among them is the plan to "mega-cull the population" (Clyde Lewis) by means of compulsory euthanasia (allegedly written into Obamacare in the form of "death panels"), "abortion on demand," and the government promotion of homosexuality, which "discourages reproduction." Lewis relates that "portable FEMA [Federal Emergency Management Act] cremation units" have already been deployed in poor neighborhoods. Modeled after the death cars used by the Nazis to murder Jews, each is capable of eliminating 100,000 bodies a day. To accommodate those not killed on sight, FEMA has erected gigantic concentration camps. Lewis admits that "you can't see the barbed-wire or the pillboxes," but rest assured, "they are there." The goal of the death cars and camps is to free up scarce resources for use by government elites who, at this very moment, are constructing underground bunkers for themselves, perhaps the same bunkers alluded to by the "Oklohoma" blogger cited previously.

"It's no longer a secret," a caller to Ground Zero agrees. "It's an open book" (Ground Zero, March 26, 2013). Secret Level 4 (low-security) government labs, surreptitiously staffed with technicians from the hostile nations of Pakistan, Malaysia, China, and India, are working on pathogens to infect Americans with hemorrhagic fever, dengue, and Ebola, flasks of which have mysteriously "disappeared." "We don't need to worry about them infiltrating across the border. They're already here!"

Nor do we have time to do more than mention how the Department of Homeland Security is buying up ammunition and ammo-making supplies to prevent Americans from defending themselves when FEMA agents knock on their front doors; or the rumors about how President Obama has encouraged countless "alien Gonzaleses," with their "anchor babies," to illegally cross America's borders; or attempts by gay activists to "politicize" and thus destroy the Boy Scouts of America; or how "atheists seek to take God off our currency"; or how President Obama's mother-in-law uses the White House kitchen to sacrifice chickens as part of her Haitian voodoo rites; or how Obamacare "literally kills" people (Michelle Bachmann). Even the dread that you, dear reader, feel as you contemplate these possibilities is part of the plot. "Those in authority want you to be anxious ... selfish ... in pain. They want you to numb yourself so they can continue … controlling you" (Ground Zero, March 15, 2013). There is no acknowledgment by Lewis of the role *his* conspiracy mongering plays in engendering your psychological state.

And so it goes. On and on, without end. The point is that "anyone who tells you that our government is not tyrannical is themselves a tyrant" (Ground Zero, May 6, 2013, in reference to a commencement speech given by President Obama days earlier at Ohio State University). If we remain blind to what is right before our eyes, that America is either a crumbling "banana republic" or a Soviet-style totalitarian society, then we are no better than "sheeple," imbecilic *campesinos*, or dull-eyed proletarian slaves. In any case, we don't deserve to be citizens of a free land.

This is what I mean by *fantasy*.

Notes

1 In 2014 Lewis dedicated an entire show to the mystical political significance of the number seven, a presumed sign of the End Times. Among other facts, he pointed to the disappearance of a Boeing 777 airliner (Malaysian flight 370) weeks earlier over the Indian Ocean, saying that seven is also the sacred number of Neptune, Greek god of the seas; that the name "Ukraine," where a second Boeing 777 was shot down on July 17, 2014, has seven letters; that the assassination of Archduke Ferdinand occurred on June 28, 1914 and that the First World War triggered by that assassination began on July 28, 1914 (all of which, divided by 4 or 2 = 7). In short, Lewis said, "Everything's coming up 7s." When a caller gently reminded him that in tables of random numbers, seven is listed only 10 percent of the time and that "You're not counting the 8s or the 3s," Lewis exploded. "You haven't read the papers!" "I've done research," the caller sheepishly replied. "You haven't done jack! You haven't done jack squat!" Lewis boomed (Ground Zero, re-aired Sept. 2, 2014).

2 The ELF theory was given added credibility when a young black lawyer, Myron May, opened fire at the Florida State University library, wounding three students, on November 20, 2014. After May was killed in a police shootout, a search of May's computer revealed that he, too, feared he had been targeted by government ELF weaponry.

3 Why do so many terrorist attacks seem to take place in spring? Lewis asks. His answer: It is because spring is the time for "pagan Slavic blood rites" and sacrificial fires (Ground Zero, April 19, 2013). This, in turn, is because spring resides "under the reign of the fire god, Ignis" (Ground Zero, March 8, 2013). Thus, when flowers bloom and trees leaf out, the "fire-meme" begins to "creep into the Zeitgeist." At his second inauguration party held in the waning days of winter 2013, President Obama was extolled by vocalist Alicia Keyes for being "on fire"; during halftime at the Super Bowl that same year, Beyoncé danced to smoke and flames; young women throughout the country complained at the time of having "brains on fire"; and Obama nominated John Brennen (German = burner) to head the CIA and direct its "fiery" drone program. All this was done in honor of the "dark father, Saturn," "the Black Pope," "the exalted One."

Interlude 6

Nullification

When right-wing extremists realize that they are not "sovereign citizens" after all, that they will be unable to impeach "tyrants" such as President Obama, that they are powerless to convene constitutional conventions to rid the nation of the IRS, and that ridicule will follow talk of secession or shutting down the government, their fantasies fix on nullification: invalidating "unconstitutional" federal laws, among them, gun laws, which, they say "infringe on the People's right to keep and bear arms." To this end, in 2013 both houses of the Missouri state legislature overwhelmingly passed a "Second Amendment Preservation Act." On paper, it preemptively voided federal laws that would restrict the manufacture, ownership, or use of guns, magazines, or ammunition; it called for the arrest on misdemeanor charges of federal or state officials who attempted to enforce such laws; opened these officials to citizen lawsuits for false arrest; criminalized the outing of any Missouri gun owner by the media; lowered to 19 the age required for obtaining an open/carry gun permit; and licensed teachers to serve as armed "school protection officers." After reminding voters that he was a gun-lover himself, Democrat governor Jay Nixon vetoed the Act, arguing it was "unsafe," "imprudent," and "unconstitutional," because it violated the supremacy clause of the U.S. Constitution, which grants precedence to federal statutes over state laws that violate them. The Missouri House of Representatives defiantly voted to overturn Nixon's veto by a two-thirds majority. When the veto measure was sent to the state senate, it failed to pass by a single vote. With this, a constitutional crisis the likes of which had not been seen since the Civil War was averted. Undeterred, one legislator vowed, "This fight ain't over, it ain't over, it ain't over, … We'll be back … Guns save lives!" The gun enchantment of Missouri's state legislators has since spread to Idaho, Ohio, Kentucky, Louisiana, Oklahoma, Georgia, and Arizona.

6 Far-Right Fantasy 2

The Christian Reconstruction of America

Ignoring the handful of pagan Odinists and SS-garbed neo-Nazis, America's contemporary ultra-rightists are almost exclusively white, middle-aged Baptists, Pentecostals, Presbyterians, and Mormons, animated by a doctrine known as *Dominionism*. It is so named after the admonition in Genesis 2:26–8 and 9:2, the most frequently cited passages in its corpus of literature—which directs mankind to "dominate" "all that moveth upon the earth." Dominionist leaders claim that "there is not one word of Scripture to declare that this mandate was ever revoked" (Rushdoony, 1973: 14; North, n.d.b) and take this to mean that they are commanded by God to "reconstruct" America on the basis of biblical/constitutional teachings. I say *re*construct, because this will entail restoring the country to what presumably prevailed at its founding (Barron, 1992). "It is dominion we are after, not just a voice ... not just influence ... not just equal time ... [but] dominion ... " (quoted in M. Goldberg, 2007: 41; Rushdoony, 1973: 375; Tabachnick, 2011). This chapter traces the roots of Christian Dominionism, describes its stylistic variations, and discusses the main elements in its political economic program. I leave off debating its merits until the next chapter. To underscore the historical particularity of the Dominionist agenda, however, I occasionally contrast it with traditional Roman Catholic teachings on the same subjects.

A Brief Survey of Dominionism(s)

Dominionism is an "umbrella term" for a variety of far-right orientations (Ingersoll, 2011), and the disputes between them can be nasty (Clarkson, 1997). The most well-known is Christian Reconstruction (CR), originally promulgated by Dutch Reformed (i.e., fundamentalist Presbyterian) preacher Rousas John Rushdoony (1916–2001), in a turgid, three-volume, nearly 2,000-page text (1973). A second, more virulent type of Dominionism is represented by Christian Identity (CI), the ideology mentioned in the introduction to this book and the inspiration for the terrorist group known as the *Brüders Schweigen*. The reader may recall that CI maintains that white Europeans and North Americans are blood descendants of one or more of the lost tribes of Israel. Until his death in 2011, Rev. Pete Peter's Scriptures for America

Ministry in LaPorte, Colorado, exemplified the most sophisticated version of this viewpoint. Another CI preacher is Rev. Sheldon Emry, one-time pastor of the Lord's Covenant Church, presently headquartered just north of Coeur d'Alene, Idaho. Emry died in 1985, but his easy-to-read, cartoon-illustrated pamphlets on banking and money continue to influence Dominionist thinking. A third form of Dominionism is exhibited by Kingdom Now, whose clapboard church buildings can be seen sprinkled along rural roads throughout Colorado, Oklahoma, and Texas. It is a charismatic variation of Dominionism, the roots of which are traceable to the Pentecostal movement. Its latest manifestation is the New Apostolic Reformation, discussed later.

Since 1980, Dominionism has been disseminated through countless organizational networks. As a result, its tone has become less strident and more palatable to mainstream conservative evangelicals. A pivotal player in this development has been the Institute for Christian Economics, located in Tyler, Texas, and run by Rushdoony's ex-son-in-law, Gary North (b. 1942, PhD in history, University of California–Riverside). North has dedicated himself to wedding Rushdoony's Calvinism to the Austrian school of free market economics, whose foremost carriers are Friedrich von Hayek and Ludwig von Mises.

A second figure is Rev. Pat Robertson who, after his failed presidential bid in 1988, founded the Christian Coalition and, later, Regent University, the stated goal of which is to inculcate Dominionism in the younger generation. At the time of his appointment, the first dean of Regent University, Herb Titus, was a devoted follower of Rushdoony. It is speculated that Ralph Reed, then executive director of the Christian Coalition, recognizing that CR—which he considered "an authoritarian threat to a free society"—was bad for public relations, urged Robertson to replace Titus with a more politick administrator (M. Goldberg, 2007: 164). Robertson eventually complied but insisted on hosting Dominionist ideologues, including (while he still lived) Rushdoony, on his popular cable TV show, the "700 Club." Titus supervised the thesis of one-time Virginia governor Bob McDonnell's 1989 master's thesis, in which he recommends using government policies to discourage "cohabiters, homosexuals, and fornicators" (Gardner, 2009).

An even more crucial vehicle for the assimilation of Dominionism into conservative evangelicalism is Francis Schaeffer (1912–84). Schaeffer's widely read *Christian Manifesto* (1981), his supposed "answer" to Karl Marx, was the inspiration for the antiabortion "pro-life" movement (Diamond, 1995: 246–8). Schaeffer was consuming Rushdoony's moral theology as early as the 1960s but subsequently broke with him because of Rushdoony's sometimes over-the-top militancy. This parallels the biography of Schaeffer's son, Frank, who disavowed his father for much the same reason.

Francis Schaeffer agrees with Rushdoony that humankind is on the threshold of a final battle between a "man-centered," "piecemeal," "pluralistic," "secular/ relativist" worldview (traceable to the liberal Enlightenment) versus a "God-centered," "totalistic," "Christian" viewpoint (his own). And while he concurs with Rushdoony that fighting this battle may require civil disobedience to the point of violence (Schaeffer, 1981: 131), Schaeffer is a proponent of premillenialism, which Rushdoony, a postmillenialist, considers anathema.

Long before Schaeffer arrived on the scene, most evangelicals shared the conceit that America is—to paraphrase seventeenth-century Puritan minister Jonathan Winthrop—a "City on a Hill," the New Jerusalem, a shining example of probity and prosperity to the world (Cherry, 1998). This is a phrase that Ronald Reagan invoked in his acceptance speech for the GOP presidential nomination in 1984; it won him the enthusiastic support of evangelicals nationwide. But as *pre*millenialists, most evangelicals believe that Christ's Second Coming will occur *prior* to the 1,000-year utopia of peace and justice prophesied in the Book of Revelation. This being the case, their traditional concern has been to Christianize their private lives in anticipation of the so-called Rapture, when they are to be bodily lifted into the heavens, so to evade the Time of Tribulations: to be chaste, and to avoid cursing, gambling, and drink. If they had any politics at all, it rarely strayed far from efforts to police their neighbors' bodies by organizing committees of decency or by campaigning against Sunday alcohol sales, strip clubs, and the "devil's anthem" (rock 'n roll).

Rushdoony ridiculed the premillenialist lifestyle, claiming that its go-to-church-and-leave-the-rest-to-God religiosity is "escapist and self-indulgent." At worst, he believed, it was a betrayal of Christ's true message. Instead of privatizing their faith, Rushdoony said that Christians must "occupy" secular institutions and then "reconstruct" them after biblical principles. Only after this would Christ come again.

While the significance of this dispute may be lost on most readers, that Schaeffer was an unapologetic premillenialist positioned him to offer Dominionism to evangelicals in a language they could understand. This effort was further facilitated through the 80+ book opus of one of his first followers, Tim LaHaye (b. 1926). With Jerry Jenkins, LaHaye authored the Christian fantasy series, *Left Behind*, sales of which are estimated to have totaled 70 million copies since 1995. To reach an even larger audience, contracts for movie rights are presently being negotiated.

The sixteen volumes of *Left Behind* provide a valuable insight into what it is in Dominionist homiletics that gives Dominionist politics such potency (the difference between fiction and fact often being elided by its readers.) First, there is the customary division of the "left behind" population into "Tribulation Saints" (those "born again" too late to have been Raptured earlier) versus the secular "Global Community" which, readers are told, is led by a racially ambiguous secretary general of the United Nations, working in cahoots with the Illuminati to establish world peace and equality. Second, is the cliché about the Tribulation-era Catholic Church being led by a "Pontifex Maximus of Enigma One-World Faith," a fetid amalgam of "non-Christian" (read *nonfundamentalist*) beliefs. Finally, there is the predictably lurid, gut-spattering portrayal of the pains the saints visit upon the global humanists in the Last Days.

After Schaeffer and LaHaye, a third premillenialist whose teachings have been absorbed into Dominionism is Hal Lindsey (b. 1929, DTh, California School of Theology), author of the *New York Times* bestseller, *The Late, Great Planet Earth* (1970). Lindsey is worth mentioning because of the profound impact he had on, among other Christian Patriots, the Weaver family, who were involved in a deadly shootout in northern Idaho in August 1992 (see Appendix). What made Lindsey's work so compelling for Randy Weaver and his wife is Lindsey's gift for reinterpreting contemporary events in biblical terms. For example, he claims that the European Union is the revived Roman Empire; that Russia is the Gog of Revelation; that Gog's "Harlot" is the World Council of Churches; and so on. Before the Weavers fled to Idaho to escape "the war against the white sons of Isaac" (the Isaacsons, the Saxons, the Germans), which they believed ZOG had already declared, they regularly met in their basement with Pentecostal neighbors to decipher signs of the times, using Lindsey as their guide (Aho, 1994: 61–2). Lindsey is credited with being the first commentator to identify President Obama as the Antichrist.

Still another purveyor of the premillenialist/Dominionist distillation is Jay Grimstead. Like LaHaye, Grimstead is a Schaeffer disciple, describing him as "a personal friend." He cofounded the Coalition on Revival with Gary North and Rushdoony in 1984 (M. Goldberg, 2007: 39–40). The Coalition subsequently issued a series of pronouncements that prescribe the positions Christians are to assume on virtually every aspect of daily life, from health care, sexuality, and art, to counseling, work, and taxes (Grimstead, n.d.).

Other prominent popularizers of the fusion of premillenialism with Dominionism are listed here:

- Rev. D. James Kennedy (b. 1933, PhD, New York University), pastor of (fundamentalist Presbyterian) Coral Ridge Ministries, Florida. Coral Ridge has its own cable TV studio, a K–12 Christian academy, and a theological seminary, all devoted to the promotion of Dominionism. Rev. Kennedy once argued that "the Mayflower Compact was the first draft of the United States Constitution" (M. Goldberg, 2007: 43).
- David Barton (b. 1954, BA religious education, Oral Roberts University), founder of Wallbuilders. This name derives from Ezra's attempt in the Old Testament to erect an "impenetrable fence" of ritual obligations to separate the Chosen People (in Barton's case, fundamentalist evangelicals) from the Babylonians (i.e., liberal humanists). Barton gained notoriety for the historically questionable assertion—which, since 2010, is required to be acknowledged in all Texas secondary-school social science textbooks— that America's founders were Protestant evangelists on a "divinely appointed mission" to promote "the liberty and purity of the Gospel of our Lord Jesus Christ" (McKinley, 2010). Glenn Beck has called Barton his

"favorite" historian; before his death, Rev. Pete Peters warmly embraced Barton at his annual Rocky Mountain Family Bible Retreat.

- Rev. Michael Farris, a Baptist minister and another LaHaye protégé. A graduate in constitutional law from Gonzaga University, Farris founded the Home School Legal Defense Association in 1983 and, in 2000, Patrick Henry College (perhaps named for the fictional campus where Ayn Rand's hero, John Galt, is said to have been educated). Its stated objective is to offer "apprenticeship methodology" to future "warriors for God" so that they can take control of American institutions and remold them on Christian lines. Patrick Henry graduates are reported to have provided 7 percent of White House interns in 2004 (M. Goldberg, 2007: 1–4).

What this boils down to is that although Dominionism and premillenialism are distinguishable, they are far from separable, and the line between them has blurred in the last three decades. Together they constitute a core element of Christian home-school and vacation-Bible-school curricula. (For a trailer of a video that features children at a Dominionist summer camp, see Ewing & Grady, 2006.) They also occupy a seminal place in conservative evangelical Sunday-school lesson plans. They are preached from evangelical campus ministry pulpits at public universities as well as at evangelical institutions of higher learning and law. They are transmitted nationwide by "patriot pastors" through videotaped "sermonars" and by means of publications sold at discount through Christian book clubs. There are Dominionist shortwave and FM radio broadcasts, Dominionist biology and geology textbooks and theme parks, children's video games, and cinema. There is even a musical based on *Left Behind*. Last but not least, Dominionism is a frequent, and sometimes the only, topic discussed at various "reclaiming America for Christ" conferences.

For all this, it is a grave mistake to equate any type of Dominionism with mainline denominational Christianity, with the politics of most born-again Christians, much less with the views of a majority of Americans. LaHaye, Grimstead, Barton, and Farris routinely rebuke these alternatives for being overly "accommodative," "other-worldly," "defeatist," and "peace-loving" (Grimstead, n.d.). Spokespeople for CR and CI are even less forgiving. As we saw in the first chapter, less than 20 percent of the American public can rightly be labeled *Dominionists*.

At this writing, the most notable expression of Dominionism is the New Apostolic Reformation (NAR), a movement with roots in Kingdom Now and its social base in Texas, Oklahoma, and Missouri. The immediate inspiration for the NAR is the writing and preaching of a soft-spoken, boldly assertive Pentecostal minister, C. Peter Wagner (b. 1930). Rev. Wagner holds a PhD degree in social ethics from the University of Southern California and, before becoming a full-time author of more than 70 books, served as a professor of church growth at Fuller Theological Institute.

Wagner (2011) waxes enthusiastic about what the NAR represents, namely, "the most radical change in the way of doing Christianity since the Reformation."

It is a "New Dispensation," he says, wherein the offices of prophet and apostle have been "restored." He traces NAR back to the apocalyptic anxieties suffered by his congregants as the second millennium drew to a close and today speaks of it as an "army of God" whose strategic mission is to "infiltrate" what he calls "the Seven Mountains" of modern society (a likely allusion to the seven hills of the original biblical "Beast," Rome): the family, religion, arts and entertainment, the news media, education, business, and government. After infiltrating them, the NAR is charged to undertake "spiritual warfare" to defeat the "principalities" (i.e., demonic forces) that presently control them and to "revive" them on the basis of biblical rulings (Wilder, 2011).

Apart from co-founding the NAR, what makes Wagner more than a figure of minor interest is that he first achieved acclaim by helping design the "mega-church," evidence of which can be seen in virtually every American city of any size. Based on the idea of using marketing research to win "consumers" for Christ, Wagner's model includes a TV-talk-show preaching format as opposed to the traditional pulpit, arena-style theater seating instead of uncomfortable pews, breakout rooms to serve the demands of niche markets—single moms, recovering addicts, retirees, and the like—and strobe lights and professional musical entertainment (for a scathing critique, see Guinness, 1993). Rev. Rick Warren, noted for his "purpose-driven" music CDs, coffee mugs, screensavers, books, and calendars, received his DMin, degree from Fuller Theological Institute. From virtually nothing, he used Wagner's program of church growth to build Saddleback Church in Orange County, California, into the eighth largest congregation in America. Warren himself is a political moderate.

Wagner's advocacy of modern marketing would likely have scandalized the earlier, more sober generation of Dominionists, such as Rushdoony. However, the NAR shares with them the same sanctimoniousness. For example, Oprah Winfrey, at one time the most popular daytime TV celebrity in the country and an early endorser of Barack Obama for president, is spoken of as a pleasant, comely looking "*harlot*"; the Statue of Liberty is judged a "French Masonic idol" (by Rev. John Benefiel or "Johnny" to Wagner); the Democratic Party is repudiated by Rev. Alice Patterson to be a "demon-possessed," "skinny-legged Jezebel"; and Catholicism is slandered as a "godless theology of hate" (Rev. John Hagee), whose saints "honor the spirits of darkness" (Rev. Cindy Jacobs). The reader may recall that Jacobs attributed the deadly Japanese tsunami of 2011 to President Obama's refusal to enforce the antigay Defense of Marriage Act. Hagee, Jacobs, and Patterson are all Wagner disciples (Wilder, 2011).

Reflecting its accommodation to the laid-back, prosperous suburban lifestyle of its followers, the NAR shows a kinder, if patronizing, face toward Jews and racial minorities than do Rushdoony, North, or Peters, even as its stance toward birth control, homosexuality, and abortion have hardened. Patterson, for instance, has organized what she calls a "Rainbow Right" to recruit black and Hispanic ministers who share her moral and political convictions; Rev. Lou Engel, it seems flippantly, has adopted the title, International House of Prayer (instead of "Pancakes") for the name of his devotional center. But details aside, all that readers need to know at this point is that the NAR has stood firmly behind the political ambitions of Pentecostal Sarah Palin, Michele Bachmann (on whom, she says, Francis Schaeffer had "a profound influence") and, most notably, Texas ex-governor Rick Perry. Perry's prayer meeting, The Response, held in Houston, Texas, in August 2011, is estimated to have drawn 30,000 attendees. It was organized by clergy associated with the NAR. Rev. Wagner and his wife, a recognized exorcist, were among them.

Strategic Ends

To facilitate the re-Christianizing of America, Dominionists have assembled what are variously named "Worldview Documents," "Legal Institutes," and "Remnant Resolves." While there is by no means consensus among them concerning what a renewed country will look like, its basic contours are clear. The guiding jurisprudential rule is this: Unless expressly abrogated by a New Testament pronouncement, each and every Old Testament prescription shall remain legally binding under the new dispensation, if not in detail, "at least in principle" (to paraphrase Schaeffer). For example, insofar as "no food is unclean in itself" (Acts 14:14), then the Kosher meal, which figures prominently in Judaism, will not be actionable in a reconstructed country. "Do not," Paul warns, "wreck God's work over a question of food" (Romans 14:20). On the other hand, insofar as neither Jesus nor the Apostles explicitly decree to the contrary, then biblical law requires that in a remade America the following shall be taken to the local plaza and stoned to death: disobedient youth, witches, blasphemers, astrologers, soothsayers, false witnesses, adulterers, women who lie about their virginity, and homosexuals (British Centre for Science Education, 2007).

Rev. Peters writes that "End-time abominators" (sodomites) must be executed (Peters, 1992), a policy that Rev. Engle recommended to the Uganda national legislature before American public outcry forced him to relent. Following the moderating influence of Schaeffer, most Dominionists demur at talk of killing gay citizens and "fornicators," favoring (as Engle says he now does) jail time and fines or, according to Michele Bachmann, reparative treatment of the "disease" that causes their "perversion" (but see Mazza, 2014).

Jesus and the Apostles have little to say about political economics; thus Dominionists feel free to incorporate their understanding of ancient Jewish practice into their design for America's future, an understanding inflected by their decidedly nonancient libertarian convictions. Readers should bear in mind that while I make some effort to nuance differences of opinion, the following sketches present the most radical Dominionist positions.

Liberty, Commerce, Labor, and Capital

Notwithstanding their awareness that "the root of all evil is love of money" (1 Tim. 6: 10), Dominionists call for the restoration of commercial "freedom" in

America, a codeword for the unfettered pursuit of profit (North, n.d.a). If each person is given the liberty to pursue his or her commercial interests in open competition, say Dominionists, then by means of Adam Smith's "invisible hand," the nation's aggregate prosperity is assured. All other paths lead to "serfdom" (von Hayek, 1994). As we will see below, "aggregate" prosperity refers to the total sum of a societies' wealth, not to the equity or lack thereof of its distribution.

Gary North, who once worked as a researcher for Christian libertarian Ron Paul, shares with him the extraordinarily naïve conviction that conscientious businesspeople do not resort to fraud or force, an idea presumably (but not in fact) asserted by Smith. In the unlikely event they do, their eventual elimination from the market is guaranteed and will thus be self-correcting.

Dominionists take the laws of laissez-faire economics for granted as universally valid and eternally binding. To appreciate how they are not, it is helpful to contrast them with a very different way of looking at things, taught by the scholastic thinkers of the Roman Catholic Church.

In traditional Catholic philosophy, commerce is morally suspect at best; at worst, it is an expression of avarice, a sin second in order of seriousness of the seven deadly vices. (In the root of "commerce" is found Mercurius, the ancient Roman god of travel, business, and theft.) Echoes of this taint are still evident in the linguistic relatives of commerce, "mercenary" (venal) and "mercurial" (fickle or insubstantial). Even mercy, the forbearance without which justice can descend into cruelty, is morally problematic in scholastic literature because, strictly speaking, it is unearned and thus undeserved.

In the medieval Catholic world, "Seldom or never can a man who is a merchant be pleasing to the Lord" (Gratian, quoted in Aho, 2005: 43).[1] Renaissance poet Dante Alighieri (1265–1321) pictures him as Geryon, "that loathsome counterfeit of fraud," who has a kindly face but comes equipped with the body of a scorpion and the rapacious claws of a four-footed beast. Geryon perilously perches on a cliff wall above the frothing fires of hell ("Inferno," canto 17, 28–30). In his *Didascalion*, Hugh of St. Victor (1096–1141) describes sales work as a "peculiar kind of rhetoric," because it requires the cleverness to anticipate customers' objections and the artfulness to mollify their concerns, sometimes deceitfully.

The medieval Church never objected to profits earned from the fashioning of things out of raw material. What it frowned upon was the buying of a commodity at one price—say, land, textiles, or housing—for the purpose of selling it later at a higher price, capitalizing on the difference. And of the varieties of capitalism, the most questionable was financial banking, the marketing of money. This is because it offers for sale what is presumably God's alone to dispose of: time. To accommodate to the emerging realities of financial capitalism, of course, the Church found it necessary to relax its attitude and, by the nineteenth century, its views had come to mirror what was being preached from the pulpits of the Calvinist-influenced sects, the progenitors of today's Dominionists. There nevertheless remains a radical difference between the two orientations: Catholic casuistry begins with a general prohibition against unregulated financial commerce and then finds exceptions; neo-Calvinist Dominionism does the opposite, starting off fully embracing high finance and only then introducing regulations to temper its worst abuses.

To say it differently, Dominionism prioritizes capital over labor; scholastic tradition does the reverse (Noonan Jr., 1957: 375–91). The "dignity of labor," say the scholastics, is affirmed by the fact that Jesus himself was a carpenter and that he expulsed money changers from the temple (Mark 11:15–19; Matt. 21:12–13). Church teachers acknowledge that labor cannot exist without capital and that both are "legitimate," but they relativize its value. Capital is reduced to a means or an "instrument" to be used by labor to advance *its* worth (Gregory, 1988: 149). "Money must serve," says Pope Francis, "not rule" (in his papal exhortation of November 2013, quoted by Cassidy, 2013). The so-called "inalienable right" to private capital so central to Dominionism is, in Catholic economics, superseded by the right "common to all to use the goods of the whole creation." "The right to private property is subordinate to the right to common use, to the fact that goods are meant for everyone" (Pope John Paul II, *Laborem Exercens,* iii.14, quoted in Gregory, 1988: 149). (For an exhaustive bibliography of writing on this subject, see Gregory, pp. 127–8, n. 31.)

In the utopia of Christian Dominionism, all capital is to be owned and disposed of by private entrepreneurs, not by the government. In Catholic scholasticism, by contrast, the question of ownership is largely beside the point: Sometimes public property is preferable—say, in water supplies, electricity, and transportation routes—whereas other times private ownership is preferred, as in agricultural land, furniture making, or car manufacture. Occasionally, a mixture of both is recommended. Rather, the proper question is what are the *consequences* of different forms of property. Does private ownership in a particular case confer respect for human life, or does it aggravate misery? If the latter is true, then reform is called for. This kind of spirit is alien to the "absolute and untouchable" conviction in private property that is emblematic of Dominionism.

Taxes

To promote economic liberty, Dominionists propose to rid America of what they see as her confiscatory, "Pharaoh-like" federal income tax system (North, n.d.c). In their histories of the income tax system, Dominionists claim that after Progressives abandoned efforts to socialize production to achieve social justice, they discovered the same end could be accomplished more directly, by "stealing" from the rich through taxation and then redistributing their wealth to the poor in the form of social services (von Hayek, 1976: 66). To do this, however, they had to resort to supposedly unconstitutional means. Martin "Red" Beckman (so named after his brilliant shock of hair) and William Benson argue that the Sixteenth Amendment, which legalizes the federal income tax system, was fraudulently ratified and is thus null and void (Beckman & Benson, 1985).

(Benson was convicted for tax evasion after he refused to file a 1040 tax form. His appeals were subsequently rejected by various federal courts on grounds that they were "patently frivolous," "a waste of Internal Revenue Service resources," and "deceitful.")

In place of progressive income taxes, Dominionists advocate revenue measures that "God favors." For some, this will be a "flat" tax that assesses the same proportion—say, Herman Cain's widely advertised 9 percent proposal—of each citizen's income. For others, like Gary North (n.d.d), it will be a national sales tax. This would have the advantage of levying higher tax burdens on the rich when they purchase sailboats, vacation homes, and Lear jets. For still others, the most god-pleasing tax is a tithe (about which I say more later).

Slaying the Beast

To address the inevitable federal budget deficit that will result when income taxes are eliminated, Dominionists recommend axing from the budget sheet biblically unsanctioned government programs, bureaus, and agencies. While these may be laudable in intent, they are the prime instruments used in the "foul and loathsome plot" to "satanify America," as described in the last chapter. Given the presumed inherent goodwill of Christian businesspeople, laws set up to regulate commerce and protect consumers from fraud are considered superfluous and costly. Furthermore, they are counterproductive in that they interfere with the "spontaneous ordering" or "catallaxy" (von Hayek's term for unfettered exchange), which is the precondition of economic well-being (von Hayek, 1976: 98, 139).

Without being exhaustive, the organs of the Beast to be "starved" include public housing, Aid for Dependent Children (or its latest iteration, Temporary Assistance for Needy Families), the Supplemental Nutritional Assistance Program (food stamps), WIC (food for poorwomen, infants, and children), unemployment benefits, OSHA (the Occupational Safety and Health Administration, which Senator James Inhofe describes as a "Gestapo bureaucracy"), mine safety regulations, the National Labor Relations Board (which protects collective bargaining rights for labor unions), the Consumer Financial Protection Agency, the Food and Drug Administration, and the Centers for Disease Control.

Besides being considered overly intrusive, public health monitoring and vaccination programs are believed to be plots to stifle parental rights, harm young children, and render children susceptible to anti-Christian subversion. Public health programs, public broadcasting, the National Endowment for the Arts and Humanities, Social Security (to Rick Perry, 'a monstrous lie,' a 'Ponzi scheme'), Medicare for retires, Medicaid for the poor, Obamacare ('a criminal act,' says Perry) for the medically uninsured, all must be placed on the chopping block. Again, the reason is that there is no precedent for them in the law books of the Old Testament or the prophecies of the New. Therefore none are scripturally sanctioned.

Public schooling is a special target of hostility for Dominionists. This is because it promotes Darwinism, sex education, and the toleration of human difference, which fundamentalist author Dr. James Dobson of Focus on the Family claims is a "buzzword" for homosexual advocacy. (For further analysis, see the Common Core curriculum "conspiracy" in Chapter 5.)

"Gangster government" (Sarah Palin's phrase) or "the synagogue of Satan," with its reams of red tape, thin-necked "thugs," "nanny-state" meddlers, and "pointy-headed intellectuals" is not merely distrusted by Dominionists; it is reviled. The only possible exceptions are its military and police functions and prisons; and many Dominionists favor outsourcing these to profit-making corporations. Erik Prince, founder and CEO of one such company, a notorious mercenary outfit known as Blackwater (Prince, 2014), was asked on the Glenn Beck show to estimate how many "private contractors" it would take to defeat ISIS, a brutal Muslim terrorist organization made up of 30,000 cadres. "Thirty-thousand?" asked the host. "Twenty-thousand? Ten-thousand?" "Less," Prince replied. With heavy artillery and some American airpower, the job could be done with 5,000 (Blaze Radio, October 29, 2014).

Compassionate Conservatism

Dominionism rejects the idea of public welfare. It nevertheless enjoins Christians to act charitably toward the poor, the crippled, and the blind (Deut. 15:10–11; von Hayek, 1976: 87–91). "For I was hungry and you gave me food, I was thirsty and you gave me drink … As often as you did it for one of my least brothers, you did it for me" (Matt. 25:35–40). Alms giving is said to "sanctify" believers (the Methodist term) by proving that they have accepted Christ as their savior or, in the case of neo-Calvinists, it confirms that they are among the Elect. True, beggars will likely never be able to redeem their debts to the charitable, but alms givers are assured that they will "be repaid for [their generosity] at the resurrection" (Luke 14:13–14; see also John 3:17–18; Matt. 6:1–4, 10:8).

To avoid becoming another byway to "creeping socialism," however, charity must be dispensed privately. For many Dominionists, this will entail something along the lines of "compassionate conservatism." This is a campaign slogan borrowed by President George W. Bush from Marvin Olasky, a one-time leftist, Francis Schaeffer protégé, and self-declared Dominionist (Grann, 1999). (For the text of Bush's speech in which he announces compassionate conservatism, see Olasky, 2000: 215–26).[2]

According to Olasky, charity in a reconstructed America will be distributed through "tithe agencies." These are private organizations, mostly churches, subsidized by grants awarded them from a government "compassion capital fund." Taxpayers will be allowed to tithe up to 10 percent of their income to such agencies. Furthermore, instead of receiving tax credits for their donations, they will be able to subtract the entire amount from their gross incomes, which is a sizable benefit. They will also have the option of designating the nongovernmental organization or religious group to which they want their tithe awarded (Olasky, 2000: 94–9).

To implement compassionate conservatism, President Bush issued two executive orders. The first established a "faith-based" subsidies and grants agency that directed millions of dollars to religious groups to underwrite prison outreach, foster care, afterschool activities, emergency room and board, charter schools, job training, and addiction, chastity, and antiabortion counseling. The second order launched Access to Recovery, which provided money vouchers to indigents exchangeable for services delivered by "preferred [primarily Christian] providers." Neither of these programs required that service deliverers be professionally licensed; however, the Bush administration did encourage them, where appropriate, to invoke "conscience" laws. These laws permitted them to fire workers unable to demonstrate fidelity to the sponsor in question, to refuse offering particular kinds of services (such as contraceptive information), and/or to withhold aid from those deemed morally unworthy of help.

Olasky understands that full implementation of compassionate conservatism will require revisiting Colonial-era practices that allowed states to use public money to underwrite the charitable and educational activities of established churches. It will also necessitate altering our present understanding of the First Amendment regarding the separation of church and state (Olasky, 2000: 94–9). As a starting point, Olasky recommends that the constitutional provision regarding "freedom *for* religion," not be taken to mean freedom *from* religion" (Olasky, 2000: 20, 106–7). Second, the Constitution should not be understood as *providing* for the general welfare but only as *"promoting"* it (Olasky, 2000: 16).

To deflect the objection by some Dominionists that compassionate conservatism is soft and wimpy, and in a manner congenial with his newly acquired neo-Calvinism, Olasky recommends that tithe agencies employ "tough love." That is, they should make their aid contingent upon "those who have dug their own hole" suffering the negative consequences of their bad choices and then repenting their sins (Olasky, 1996: 110). In this respect, while it may be inspired by a warm heart, compassionate conservatism has "iron in its spine." "This is a demanding love—at times, a severe mercy"—but without it, says Olasky, social problem remediation is impossible. During the waiting period prior to receiving aid, Olasky proposes that candidates undergo mandatory drug testing to determine their suitability for benefits.

Right here, we see the major difference between the Dominionist line of attack on indigence versus liberal alternatives. Olasky, along with many Dominionists, renounces social Darwinism, at least in its vulgar, Sumnerian form, but he also rejects liberal welfare economics, which offers unconditional aid to the needy, regardless of their self-destructive habits. If the first is sometimes vindictive, the second is open-minded to the point "that its brains drop out." Compassionate conservatism plods a middle way: It ministers to the poor but does so only after they have undertaken efforts to *rid themselves* of the vices that presumably got them into their desperate situation in the first place.

Charity, Not Justice

Dominionist charity is *not* distributive justice, the idea that human beings have an inviolable right to health, education, food, and shelter. Distributive justice is an aspiration of the Social Gospel, against which Christian fundamentalists have fulminated since they first declared "war on modernism" after World War I (Dorrien, 2009). It has also been Roman Catholic doctrine at least since Pope Leo XIII's encyclical *Rerum Novarum* (1891), if not centuries before that. Pope Leo's call for economic fairness was reaffirmed by Pope Pius XI in 1931, by Pope John Paul II 50 years later, and then again in 1986 by the American bishops in *Economic Justice for All* (Gregory, 1988; for an extensive bibliography on this subject, see 127–28, n. 31).

Catholic doctrine is based on the assumption that as a "creature" made after God's image and likeness, every human being without exception is owed a reasonable amount of shelter, food, clothing, and health care. While it acknowledges the importance of charity, it teaches that charity is motivated by love, an intention based on the perceived "oneness of mankind." Justice, in contrast, "is directed to the other" (*Justitia est ad alterum*), to the person whom one does *not* know, the stranger. This is to say, justice presupposes a separation between giver and recipient. "To be just means to recognize the other *as other*" (Pieper, 1966 [1954]: 54).

To Friedrich von Hayek and the Dominionists, the idea of distributive justice is not only "entirely empty and meaningless," a "superstition," and a "hollow incantation"; it is "no more truthful than ... belief in witchcraft or the philosopher's stone." Granted, says von Hayek, it is "certainly tragic" that some fall in the course of economic strife, as others rise. But even if our sensitivities are wounded by witnessing the cruel outcomes of competition, that does not make them unjust. To claim otherwise "is clearly absurd and itself unjust" (von Hayek, 1976: 65–6, 69–70). In a way that the neo-Calvinist Olasky could never agree with—because Calvinists believe that good fortune is a sign of God's favor and man's virtue—von Hayek (a Jew) argues that riches and poverty have nothing whatsoever to do with God. Instead, they are the result of blind fortune or "fate," about which little, if anything, can be done. For "the race is not to the swift, nor yet the battle to the strong, neither yet bread to the wise, nor yet riches to men of understanding, nor yet favor to men of skill; but time and chance happeneth to them all" (Eccl. 9: 11).

Olasky repudiates Catholicism because of its "preference for the poor," its support of the custom of begging, its emphasis on prayerful leisure (the supposed end of economic life, but which Dominionists view as idleness) and, above all, its presumed advocacy of collectivism (Olasky, 2000: 205–8). In Olasky's mind, there is no such thing as a *common*wealth. There is only *aggregate* wealth, a totality of individual riches. Insofar as this is true, if justice has any meaning at all, it is reducible to the commutative equity that obtains between satisfied buyers and sellers. In other words, it is for sale at a price on the free market. So, as it is for a flat-screen TV, a car, or an MP3 player, if one cannot afford health, education, food, clothing, or shelter, then, strictly speaking, they don't deserve them. However, to repeat, *as individuals* the merciful may provide them to those unable to pay. The bottom line is, "If anyone is not willing to work, let him not eat" (2 Thes. 3:10; Olasky, 2000: 14). How this injunction is to be applied in an increasingly automated economy that requires less and less human labor remains unanswered.

The Balanced Budget and the Federal Reserve

A major tool to be used in eliminating nonbiblical government programs is contemplated enactment of a balanced budget amendment to the Constitution. The theory behind this is as attractive as it is simple-minded: Like a family, government must "live within its means." This is a proposition that owes a good deal of its popular appeal to the homilies of Benjamin Franklin, whom Max Weber cites as the embodiment of the Calvinist (capitalist) "spirit" (Weber, 1958b). According to Franklin, honesty, orderliness, industriousness, and temperance all presuppose that individuals are scrupulously caring for their household finances, making sure that their expenses never exceed their income; Franklin models his system of personal moral improvement after the commercial accounting practices of his day. We can therefore sympathize with their unease when Dominionists first learn of the seemingly counterintuitive Keynesian notion of deficit spending, that the federal government can meliorate unemployment and stabilize the national household by taking out loans to fuel demand for goods and services.

For Dominionists, the relevant biblical injunction is to "let no debt remain outstanding" (Rom. 13:8) lest one become a slave to their creditor (Prov. 22:7). Some take this to mean that they should cut up their credit cards, avoid taking out car loans, and refuse home mortgages; the idea of taking out loans for college is disdained. When applied specifically to government fiscal policy, Dominionists believe that America may rightly lend to other nations, but she must never borrow. In this way, "[America] shall reign over many nations, but they shall not reign over [her]" (Deut. 15:6). The specter of Asian nations underwriting American debt is for many Dominionists a barely tolerable affront.

The bank from which the federal government draws credit is the Federal Reserve Corporation (FRC, established in 1916). To Dominionists, the FRC must be disbanded immediately. This was the centerpiece of Ron Paul's series of futile presidential bids, a cause that has since been taken up by his son, Rand. Besides being considered contrary to the requirement in Leviticus 19:36 that an economy be based on "honest scales and honest weights" (Fraud, n.d.), the FRC was allegedly set up illegally by the "stranger that is within thee," warned about in Deuteronomy 28:44–45. Exactly who this stranger is remains a matter of never-ending contention in Dominionist circles. As we saw earlier, conspiratologists such as Ralph Epperson, Gary Allen, Cleon Skousen, and Glenn Beck prefer to label them with such purposively vague titles as "Insiders" or the "Hidden Hand." Proponents of CI, on the other hand, finger them as Jews. Rev. Sheldon Emry (1984) even provides readers with cartoon caricatures of "Jews" to prove the point.

However the question of the stranger's identity is answered, the problem Dominionists have with the FRC is that it "prints money" and then lends it to the government (and, thereby, to taxpayers). This makes the FRC the de facto "head" of society, and the rest of America its wagging tail. So that the tail might be free, the head must be destroyed. To this end, Dominionists advocate once again making the dollar "sound"—that is, tying it to the gold standard (North, n.d.d). President Nixon eliminated the gold standard in 1971, effectively creating "fiat" money, the value of which is fixed according to its supply and the demand for it on the international money market. Because the demand for greenbacks has gone down and its supply (due to uncontrolled printing) has increased, confidence in the dollar's value as the world's reserve currency has, at least according to Dominionists, declined. This makes it increasingly doubtful—again, to Dominionists—that the federal government will be able to redeem its debts by printing more of it. Fears of imminent federal government bankruptcy have led some to prophesy that explosive inflation looms in America's near future. This will result in "a huge decline in the standard of living" (Larsen, 2013a).

To avoid this, some Dominionists have gone so far as to call for ridding the country of paper currency altogether and going back to gold, silver, and copper coins. But even the harshest critics of the FRC confess that, given the ponderous weight of metal, this would be unworkable in all but a primitive barter economy (Emry, 1981). Most Dominionists therefore advocate putting "The Beast" on the severe diet mentioned earlier and simply eliminating "unnecessary" (i.e., nonbiblically endorsed) government programs.

Debt Slavery

The Old Testament disallows the enslavement of Israelites. It also condemns slavery conducted through "abduction." It nevertheless allows both foreigners and guest peoples to sell themselves into bondage; this, either to pay off debts, to make restitution for torts, or to buy protection. Both Exodus and Leviticus spell out protocols for the humane treatment of bond servants (Ex. 21:1–11, 16; Lev. 25:45–6).

Neither Jesus nor the Apostles say anything in opposition to debt slavery but implicitly endorse it, even when given the opportunity *not* to do so (Luke 12:45–8; Eph. 6:5–9; Tim. 6:1–2; Col. 3:22–5). It therefore follows, according to Dominionists, that while it is not part of "God' s original [Edenic] plan," and is a "regrettable evil," slavery "will end only when sin does"—which is to say, never.

Although Jay Grimstead disagrees, a handful of Dominionists claim that the voluntary enslavement of non-Christian debtors is permissible (for example, Wilson, 2011). Stephen McDowell even quotes Rousas Rushdoony as proof. Rushdoony writes that "the law here is humane and also unsentimental. *It recognizes that some people are by nature slaves and will always be so*" (Rushdoony, 1973: 286; author's emphasis). McDowell adds that slaves must, of course, "be dealt with in a godly manner," but he also insists that "the slave recognizes his position and [per St. Paul's injunction] accepts it with grace" (McDowell, 2003).

McDowell serves on the board of WallBuilders, and he cites David Barton to bolster his revisionist history of the early American "Atlantic triangular market," his euphemism for the slave trade. Barton argues (correctly, as it turns out) that while several of America's founders frowned on slavery, a number of them practiced it. Their objection was not that servitude is wrong in it itself—to repeat, the Bible condones it. Rather, it is that in the American case it was conducted through force and that slaves were occasionally "mistreated" (Barton, 2011).

But this, says Barton, was the exception. On the whole, the slave experience was characterized by "lenience," "unity and companionship." Furthermore, far from being an unmitigated disaster, enslavement was actually beneficial in that it allowed Africans to escape "the cruelty and barbarism typical of unbelieving cultures," and provided them the opportunity "to hear the liberating message of the gospel." Indeed, Barton continues, African slaves enjoyed a vast increase of freedom" over what they had earlier endured, to say nothing of longer life expectancies (for amplification, see Buchanan, 2008). Thus, the Emancipation Proclamation (an executive order issued by President Lincoln during the "War of Northern Aggression"), "was both inhumane and irresponsible" (British Centre for Science Education, 2007). This is a position with which not only Michele Bachmann (Lizza, 2011: 63) but a host of other Dominionists (cf. Celock, 2012) agree. One of them, Loy Mauch, asks, "If slavery were [*sic*] so God-awful, why didn't Jesus or Paul condemn it, why was it in the Constitution and why wasn't there a war before 1861?" (quoted by Brantley, 2012).

Barton's apologia notwithstanding, most Dominionists find the possibility of slavery reemerging in America profoundly discomfiting. And to avert it they have proposed several policies.

One is reinstatement of the Old Testament Sabbatical and Jubilee years (Emry, 1984; Deut. 15:1–3, 7–9, 12–17; Lev. 25:8–17). The Jubilee is so named after the ram's horn, *yobel*, trumpeted to announce its onset. To be held every 49 years (or 7 cycles of 7 Sabbatical years) at the debtor's request, it would forgive their debts, return their alienated property, and free them from slavery. (Prices on loans would be adjusted to take into consideration the number of years until the next Jubilee.) However, Gary North, among others, worries that while noble, such magnanimity would go against the admonition that Christians not spend beyond their means.

A second proposal is to outlaw usury or interest taking on loans. Again, following the Old Testament, this would apply only to credit extended to Christians, while allowing it for guest peoples and foreigners, a subject to which I return below (Deut. 23:20; Lev. 25:35–8). But this, too, faces objections in that it runs counter to John Calvin's (read, *North's*) rulings (North, n.d.d).

Calvin claims that because every Christian "brother" is in effect an "other" (i.e., a Cain), then charging them interest is perfectly licit, as long as it does not infract commonsense notions of love and equity. Calvin adds that insofar as the latter is unlikely, it is preferable that usury be abolished (Nelson, 1949; Noonan, 1957: 365–7).

A handful of Dominionists have endorsed a third idea: that college students be allowed to sell claims on their future earnings (i.e., their labor) in exchange for tuition grants and room and board subsidies awarded to them by patrons. Although this would appear to solve the problem of student loan debt, critics believe it would reintroduce the "spirit" of indentured servitude under a different name (Levine, 2012). The alternative, however, that public college education be made a free civil right, is inconceivable to Dominionists.

There exists a facsimile to debt slavery that Dominionists fully embrace: the federal H-2A guest worker program. Here, foreign laborers voluntarily bond themselves to recruiters who provision them with green cards to legalize their temporary residence in America. They are then transported to this country and assigned to work in food-processing plants, on corporate farms, or at call centers. Since most guest workers are unable to pay recruitment fees up front, they agree to have a portion of their monthly wages taken out make to a dent in their bond, until their debts are redeemed. John Bowe (2010) describes how impoverished Thai guest workers, besides being forbidden to leave their places of work, are forced, sometimes by beatings, to sleep in company-owned dormitories and/or to purchase food at company stores, the costs of which are added to their debts, in a vicious, ever-deepening cycle. If and when guest workers pay back their loans, they can be sent home, with, as it is said, "no pathway to citizenship."

Their crocodile tears spilled over the issue of debt slavery is belied not only by the Dominionists' support of the foreign guest workers program but more directly by their hostility to collective bargaining and fair wages for American laborers. In Dominionist economics, the price of every commodity, including labor, is to be a function of the demand for it and its supply. Period. To take any other factor into consideration would be a "nightmare" leading to "the end of law" (von Hayek, 1976: 86–7). To underscore the significance of the Dominionist objection, consider once again traditional Catholic teachings on the subject.

In scholasticism, a fair or just wage is assessed not only by the demand for a particular occupation but by its estimated value to society and by the time, money, and effort invested in acquiring its skills (Roover, 1958). In operational terms, this means a wage that enables a worker to live "reasonably" and sustain his or her household "in frugal comfort." This is not a privilege to be conferred (or not) by society, but a natural right growing from the inherent dignity of the person (Ryan, 1971 [1906].)[3] Therefore, to violate it would be a *laeso enormis* (an enormous wrong).

Immigration

Dominionists claim that America is a "Christian nation." Therefore, immigration to it by non-Christians is to be discouraged and, except for legally registered temporary guest workers, those already here should be repatriated. Nonbelievers who continue to reside in America shall have neither political rights nor the right to free speech, although, as a "courtesy" and at the discretion of local authorities, these may be temporarily granted (Fischer, 2011a). (Rev. Bryan Fischer has a BA in philosophy from Stanford University.) Dominionists concede that the First Amendment protects religious expression but, following the pronouncements of Rushdoony (1973: 294), they also believe that this applies "only within the bounds of Christianity."

These rulings apply to immigrants of all non-Christian persuasions but particularly to Muslims. Muslims, says Fischer, are "toxic cancers" and practitioners of "oriental despotism" (Fischer, 2011b). Islam has long been a target of exclusionary American immigration policy. Originally, this was because of its association with the Barbary pirates and, later, for its polygamist practices (rumors of which were also used to exclude European Mormons from entering the country). Today, it is for Islam's alleged attempt to "impose" Shari'a (Muslim law) on the republic, a whimsical terror that several Dominionist-dominated state legislatures have undertaken to remedy.

That far-right resistance to foreign immigration is based on more than just considerations of faith is indicated by Dominionist hostility to Hispanic immigrants, virtually all of whom are Christian. The so-called Pace Amendment (Johnson, 1985) expresses it in legalese: The only people with "the right and privilege" to permanently live in the United States are citizens; and "no person" can be a citizen unless they have "no ascertainable trace" of Negro, Asian, Middle Eastern, Arab, Hindu, Thai, Vietnamese, or Indonesian blood. (In his fatuous legal brief sent to every member of Congress, the author, William Johnson, asks that both the Fourteenth and Fifteenth amendments to the Constitution be repealed and that America return to the definition of citizenship asserted by the Supreme Court in its 1857 Dred Scott decision. Here, the Court determined that whether they are slaves or free, black people have no civil rights. Hence, Scott had no standing in court and could not sue for his freedom.) The only exceptions, says Johnson, are to be white Hispanics who are "in appearance indistinguishable" from northern Europeans or Brits. The fates of "nonwhite Caucasoids" such as Iranians, Armenians, and Turks, Johnson continues, are to be "artfully" determined, using a combination of blood type, ancestry, and looks. Those who fail to meet "Caucasoid" standards must be deported, preferably in an orderly, nonburdensome manner, reimbursing those who suffer property losses as a result (Johnson, 1985: 109–20). Money presently "wasted" on public welfare programs and schools can be budgeted for moving allowances and for the leasing of mass transportation facilities. Against the objection that this would be overly draconian, Johnson replies that in fact it would be "compassionate," for deportees would now be able to return to cultures more compatible with their values.

Johnson believes that Native American Indians and Hawaiians should be allowed to remain in the country but only on reservations set apart for that purpose. However, American Jews "who desire the continued existence of Israel" should be "encouraged" (exactly how is not stated) to emigrate (Greenberg, 2008; Johnson, 1985: 99, 117).

In contrast to Johnson, most Dominionists have resigned themselves to the presence of "non-Caucasoids" on American soil. Some, in fact, have proposed that they be resettled in a manner reminiscent of apartheid South Africa. David Duke, for instance, has offered a detailed plan for relocation and has given each ethnic and racial enclave its own cartoon title (Ridgeway, 1996: 150–1). Indians, he says, can be assigned to "Navahona" in Arizona and New Mexico, Cubans can be relocated to "New Cuba" (Florida), Jews to "West Israel" on Long Island, Frenchmen to "Francia" in northern Maine, Hispanics to "Alta California," blacks to "New Africa" (Mississippi and Alabama), and assorted others to "Minoria" in New York City. Duke naturally dedicates the balance of American territory to white Christians.

At this writing, anti-immigrant sentiment finds its harshest expression in animus toward undocumented Hispanics. The question for Dominionists is not *whether* they should be repatriated but how. Internal debate revolves around two proposals. The first, offered by Mitt Romney in the course of his 2012 presidential campaign, is self-deportation. This is to be facilitated by denying them access to public services, including schools and medical care. A caller to Glenn Beck's Blaze Radio says it this way: "If you give a mouse a cookie, they'll keep coming around." In the event that self-removal cannot be accomplished within a reasonable period, says Doc Thompson, a stand-in host on Beck's talk show, then "round 'em up!" and forcibly remove them (Blaze Radio, July 12, 2013). "We don't care where you go, but you can't stay here."

"Little border-hopping hoodlums" (Idaho talk show host Neal Larson's label), undocumented Latinos brought to the U.S. as toddlers, have no memory of their place of birth; many do not speak Spanish. To these, Thompson graciously recommends a compromise. If they voluntarily return to their "homeland" and reapply for admission, then after 2 years, he promises, "they'll have my respect." He gives no guarantee, however, that their requests will be honored. In the manner typical of Dominionist ideologues, Thompson fails to address the immense police and logistics challenges involved with exiling millions of residents, many of whom are likely to undertake evasive moves to stay in the country. Instead, we are left with grinning, "aren't I cute" expressions of cynicism and spite.

American citizens who aid "criminal invaders" with rides, jobs, or housing, says Thompson, should have their vehicles and shelters confiscated and auctioned off. Money from sales can be reinvested to construct stronger fencing along the Mexican border. For their part, businesses that hire these people should face stiff fines and imprisonment but, since they already are subject to onerous government regulations, Dominionists believe that in their case a certain amount of lenience is called for.

Conclusion

The phantasm that haunts Dominionist nightmares is this: "Corruptors" have succeeded in destroying God's house in America" (Crawford, 1984: 587). To some, this means "our federal coffin is sealed," and we have no alternative but to "bow [our] heads and tearfully whisper goodbye to the USA" (Daugherty, 2013). But others caution, not so fast. They vow to "corner any sewer rat that has invaded the halls of government, expose, trap, and banish them with their debauchery back to the dark places from whence they come" (Andersen, 2014). Still others fantasize about revenge. "Warfare is inescapable," gloats Rushdoony (1973: 781). Rev. Pete Peters concurs: *"The Christian God ... will only be appeased by blood. If America is to be redeemed, there needs to be a blood bath"* (Peters, 1994: 20; author's italics), as does the fictional hero of *The Turner Diaries*, who says "there is no way we can destroy the System without hurting many thousands of innocent people—no way. It is a cancer too deeply rooted in our flesh" (MacDonald, 1980: 42).

We can give thanks that, like pornographers, most Dominionists are content to get their satisfaction vicariously, by reading about it from the comfort of their living room couches. (Rushdoony, Peters, and MacDonald [i.e., William Pierce] all died peacefully in bed.) Nonetheless, as the Appendix shows, there have been enough acts of Patriot terror in the last few decades to worry about even a small number taking the call to arms literally.

This is not to say that Dominionists are beasts or nuts. Nor do they resemble the Klansmen of the 1920s, whom H. L. Mencken derided as "gaping primates of the upland valleys," to whom formal education is deemed an excessive burden for all but "snobs." Rather, they see themselves as articulate messengers of "good news," God-fearing supplicants tasked with remaking America with the tools ready at hand. Burning with resentment over recent court decisions about abortion, Ten Commandments monuments, prayer in schools, and the extension of rights to those whom they consider perverts, they are frightened about a future that seems out of control.

As we saw earlier, compared to the larger population, Dominionists constitute only a tiny minority of the public but, as Max Weber writes, it is not troop numbers alone that win victories, but discipline (Weber, 1958a). And if Dominionists have demonstrated anything, it is their willingness to march in lockstep when given orders. This explains why their influence far exceeds what their small numbers would predict.

This does not mean that Dominionist fantasies are anywhere near to being realized. In fact, their more likely fate will be that of the anti-Illuminatists, anti-Masons, anti-Mormons, anti-Catholic Know-Nothings, Judeophobes, and anti-Communists of earlier ages: Like a shingles virus, they will recede back into the spinal cord of the body politic to fester until the next stress-induced flare-up. If the past is any basis for prediction, we can also anticipate who will be in the vanguard of the future movement: the offspring of today's Dominionists, already in training to be cultural warriors. Of course, the reemergence of religiously inspired political fanaticism will array itself under a different banner than "Christian Dominionism." Perhaps it will call itself "Joshua Generation," the label Michael Farris gives to the graduates of his Patrick Henry College. However they are christened, they will repeat the refrain uttered by their parents and *their* parents before them: "The End is near! Arm yourself for battle!" Whatever the case, this much is certain: Right-wing extremism is not likely to disappear any time soon from the American scene. This is because it is not really about the quotidian cares of everyday life. It is, instead, driven by vague feelings of disenchantment with the current state of affairs relative to the standards of Christian perfection. Like utopians everywhere, in other words, Dominionists hunger for the kingdom of God on earth (Barron, 1992). This is an appetite that no mere mundane politics, liberal or conservative, can ever truly sate. If we want to grasp their mood and its political expression, we need to supplement our knowledge of "Rorschach techniques or the construction of the F-scale with a rereading of the Book of Revelations [*sic*]" (Hofstadter, 1964: 103).

Notes

1 Johannes Gratian is credited with the first compilation of Roman Catholic canon law, ca. 1150.
2 There is a good deal of debate over whether compassionate conservatism has ever been fully embraced by the far-right. The first two directors of the initiatives set up by President George Bush to implement it quit in disgust after the notion was received by ultra-rightists with "snoring indifference" (Kuo, 2005). One of the two went so far as to criticize the concept as an empty campaign slogan devised by what he calls "Mayberry Machiavellis" to win the support of evangelical voters. He goes on to say that the Bush administration "never wanted 'the poor people stuff'," that "pure 'com-cons' were never terribly popular" on the far-right, and that, in any case, it was not right-wingers who took the idea to heart but their archenemy, Barack Obama (Posner, 2013) .
3 Ryan was a prominent Catholic moral theologian whose recommendations concerning the minimum wage were incorporated into New Deal legislation.

Interlude 7

"Justus" Served

In June 1996, after 81 days of negotiations, the twenty-four "sovereign citizens" of Justus Township, Montana, surrendered to federal marshals (Zeskind, 2009: 355–66; Pitcavage, 1996). They called themselves "Freemen" and claimed they had been "enslaved" by a "foreign government" (the United States of America) that mandated they pay taxes, secure driver's licenses, purchase building permits, and obtain car insurance. After incorporating themselves on a foreclosed 960-acre farm, the Freemen established short-wave radio connections with the outside world, designed their own flag, and prepared to defend their "God-given rights" from "jack-booted thugs." Instead of resorting to guns, however, they sought refuge in paper. They flooded local courts with frivolous appeals and meritless motions, printed their own money, issued bogus checks and money orders payable by a "Norwest Bank" (their living-room coffee table), and set up a "common law" court. They issued subpoenas and tried, found guilty, and sentenced to death state senators, judges, and a county sheriff for acting "unconstitutionally." They issued fraudulent bank drafts to loyal followers (including future murderer Scott Roeder, Appendix, May 31, 2009), urging them to "overpay" creditors and then demand remittance in American cash, plus interest. They warned those creditors that failure to heed their demands would result in liens being filed on their property.

Since the poor, sparsely populated county where the Freemen were ensconced was powerless to do anything about the situation, the feds were called in. Justus Township was surrounded by armed guards and electronic surveillance. Reporters from across the globe gathered in anticipation of a shootout. Wary of repeating Ruby Ridge (Appendix, Aug. 21–31, 1992), however, the government held back, enlisted the expertise of behavioral scientists and hostage negotiators, and eventually arrested the Freemen without firing a shot. They were later found guilty variously of bank, mail, and tax fraud, for threatening public officials, for trafficking in stolen property, and for firearms violations. Many were sentenced to federal prison, where their leader later died.

7   Far-Right Fantasy 3

A Critique

Christian Dominionism can be criticized on any number of grounds. Among them are its impiety, its hypocrisy, and its "falsity." Because impiety frequently leads to hypocrisy, and hypocrisy to falsity, none of these appraisals can be adequately grasped without taking into consideration the others. Nonetheless, they are distinguishable enough to bear separate scrutiny. Before starting, however, a disclaimer is in order, namely, that the censures of impiety, hypocrisy, and falsity are not immune to criticism themselves. The demand of piety, for instance, imposes on neo-Calvinist Dominionism an ethical standard derived from Roman Catholic social teachings, the validity of which it denies. The criticism of hypocrisy is also problematic, not because it is untrue but because anyone who stands on principle is bound to deviate from it at some point and thus betray him- or herself. The third criticism, that Christian Dominionism is false, evaluates it against its own its professed goals. Thus, it is both more germane and less frivolous than moral posturing but, because it derives from an orientation known as *critical theory*, which is rooted in Marxism and Freudianism, both of which Dominionists disavow, it too will raise hackles. However this may be, it is the third critique that will occupy the balance of our attention in this chapter. But first, a few words on impiety and hypocrisy.

Impiety and Hypocrisy

Impiety

Aside from criminal punishment, Christian Dominionism acknowledges but a single form of justice, that which pertains between equally satisfied buyers and sellers, the technical term for which is *commutative equity*. If it grants validity to distributive (in)justice at all, which is rare—recall Friedrich von Hayek's dismissal of the concept as a "superstitious incantation" on a par with witchcraft or the philosopher's stone—Dominionism considers it little more than propaganda for socialism. This conjures visions of shabby public housing, empty-shelved grocery stores, collective farms, and gaunt-faced peasants. To paraphrase Clyde Lewis, distributive justice is merely an excuse to advance the agenda of the "surveillance state" and its policies of "identification, isolation, and extermination." Rush Limbaugh says it more frankly: Distributive justice is "a crime against humanity" (Rush Limbaugh radio, August 16, 2013).

Given their ignorance about or denial of distributive justice—and with it the postulate that people are morally obliged to pay back to society in proportion to what they have received—it is not surprising that Christian Patriots find it even more difficult to acknowledge debts to society that they can *never* repay. The word for this is *impiety*. Ironically, of all American political actors, Christian Patriots are among the least pious.

Piety has lost much of its luster recently with the rise of narcissistic individualism and the deterioration of American community life. To retrieve its full meaning, therefore, we must go back to the ancient tradition of Greco-Roman civic virtue. And here, piety has a very special meaning. It refers not to religious devotion or churchgoing as such but to a habit of recognizing one's obligations to the republic, particularly to the institutional representative and agent of that republic, the state (Pieper, 1966 [1954]: 107–9). Christian Patriots do recognize the obligations they have to mentors, neighbors, and parents, but these are *private* actors whose interests do not always comport with those of the national community. True, Patriots never tire of proclaiming their "love" for America. They daub their eyes when the flag passes, hold hands over their hearts, and report having throat lumps when the national anthem plays, but then they add, "*I hate the government!*" What they are reluctant to acknowledge is that without a government, a nation is little more than an empty abstraction, a fanciful myth, or an unrealized aspiration. Beyond their mouthed idolatry of the Founders and the Constitution, and their annual ritual observance of those who have "sacrificed their lives, fortunes, and sacred honor" to protect it, Christian Patriots refuse to grant that, at least in a functioning democracy, *they* are the government they revile.

To speak of one's obligations to government is not to argue that it be glorified or "divinized," to use Jonah Goldberg's unfortunate term, that it be worshipped like a mystical body. Enough of that was seen in the last century to leave a foul taste in our mouths forever. It is, rather, to propose that government be viewed as an instrumentality of gifts, *pardons* (Fr.), graces unasked for, unearned, and unredeemable: To recognize that the highways and communication systems that government launches, builds, and maintains (including the internet); the dams, irrigation projects, electrical utilities, sewage, and water systems it administers; the safety from fire and crime it confers; the protections from foul food, dirty air and water, and impure drugs it promises; the medical advances whose research it funds; and the K–12 schools, junior colleges, and public universities it oversees, are gifts, and to be in the habit of sensing in them unpayable debts, presupposes a humility of spirit seemingly beyond the reach of the Christian Patriot. In their mind, "I built it myself!"

An attitude of ingratitude toward government is exercised in familiar ways: by a shrill insistence that one is "taxed enough already" and thus owes nothing more to society; through a hostility toward "jack-booted government thugs" who have the effrontery to trample on one's individual liberties; through an unrelenting, frequently foul-mouthed sniping at elected officials; and above all, through a vociferous refusal to consent to the idea that there is such a thing as a commonweal and that this collective good can and should be fairly distributed among the citizenry.

By the collective good, I not only have in mind the nation's gross economic product, her foodstuffs, shelter, clothing, medical care, electricity, communications and transportation facilities, educational resources, police forces, and fire crews. But beyond this are its tokens of honor, its scientific research output, and artistic creations: its music, painting, cinema, and dance. There are also the goods, so to speak, for which government exists in the first place: the opportunities for bona fide leisure, recreation, and spiritual growth. Finally, there is Earth—the air, water, and material resources without which none of the preceding are possible. The question is not, as Christian Patriots claim: *Is* there such a thing as a *bonum communum?*, an answer to which is so patently obvious as to barely deserve a response. It is, rather, how is this commonwealth to be allocated, to whom, and in what proportions? Should new tax and wage laws and banking and financial regulations be imposed on the rich? Or can distributive justice be achieved by inculcating in businesspeople a higher moral standard? Do providers of capital deserve what they get today— more than a third of the national income? Or should the far larger number of workers receive a greater proportion, as they did prior to the 1980s? Although precise figures are subject to debate, estimates are that in the early 1950s, the typical corporate CEO earned approximately twenty times more than their firm's average worker; at Fortune 500 companies today, the ratio ranges anywhere between 200:1 to 350:1. Is this equitable? If not, how should it be addressed? Resolving these questions civilly is the purpose of democracy, and government is the only agency capable of carrying out the public's decisions in a nondiscriminatory, relatively cost-effective way. One thing is for sure: To leave these decisions to the "invisible hand" of the market is to relinquish our responsibility as citizens to determine the kind of world we shall have (Pearlstein, 2013). And to express "hate" for the means by which the common good is determined and then disposed is to deny government the platform it needs to carry out its responsibilities in a legitimate way.

The impious "gorge" themselves "without making a return." "Quick to grasp, slow to give" (Lothario dei Segni [Pope Innocent III], 1969: book 2, secs. xiv, xvi), they pontificate about how a "free man cannot claim help from and cannot be charged to give help to another"; that one must use "all [their] powers exclusively for [their] own welfare"; that they have no duty toward others except respect, goodwill, and courtesy (Sumner, 1883: 24, 30); and that if the poor "are not sufficiently competitive to live, they die, and it is best they should die" (Herbert Spencer, quoted by Hofstadter, 1959: 41). *"Not my child, not my problem!"* is a life philosophy as puerile as it is niggardly and cruel.

Hypocrisy

States, the counties in them, and the conservative legislators from those counties with the most antigovernment voting records are among the largest beneficiaries of government-financed enterprises, including military installations and coal, petroleum, and agricultural subsidies (Gilson, 2012). Some call this "red-state socialism" after the color customarily given to regions and people with histories of support for Republican Party candidates. Others favor the phrase, "red/blue paradox." I prefer the word *hypocrisy*. However we en-frame it, Mississippi, Alaska, Louisiana, West Virginia, the Dakotas, Kentucky, and Virginia, all of which have reputations for far-right activism, receive upwards of $2 in federal benefits for every $1 they remit in taxes to Washington, DC. Their chief benefactors are the "blue" bastions of liberalism such as New Jersey, Connecticut, New Hampshire, Minnesota, Illinois, Delaware, California, New York, and Colorado. Among the many explanations for this paradox is that red states are chronically poor and predominantly rural, and their populations are comparatively ill-educated, whereas blue states are, in the main, prosperous, urban, and degreed.

It is important not to make too much of hypocrisy. After all, as sociologists have long noted, a distinguishing attribute of humanity everywhere *is* hypocrisy (from *hypokritēs*, a role player in ancient Greek drama). We are all "make-believe animals" who are never so truly ourselves than when we enact grand narratives (Loy, 2010: 34). True, "all the world is *not* a stage," Erving Goffman once wrote, but the ways by which it is *not* are difficult to discern (Goffman, 1959: 17–20, 22–4, 30–3, 56–9, 70–7). To accuse another of hypocrisy, then, may be tempting, but it is largely vacuous.

The charge of hypocrisy, however, usually involves more than just the accusation that another is putting on a show. It is, rather, that what they verbally convey about themselves, over which—Freudian slips notwithstanding—they have control, is inconsistent with the information they *give off*: the so-called body-talk, over which they have little or no control. In this expanded sense, hypocrisy is the basis of stock characterizations in theater and on the screen. Not the least of these is the ostensibly abstemious, antigay evangelical minister caught in *flagrante delicto* in the arms of his male lover from whom he has recently purchased cocaine or, less fictionally, the savvy pastor of TV who condemns adultery from the pulpit and then seduces his secretary after church. (When the pastor in question tried to justify his infidelity, he accused his wife of being "too large." She returned the insult by replying that he was "too small." Their very public divorce destroyed their multi-million-dollar media empire, bankrupted their massive real-estate holdings, and put an end to their political influence.)

This, then, is what I have in mind in saying that Christian Patriots are hypocrites: They are unwitting victims of their own puritanical pronouncements. Like "God's Bullies" everywhere (Young, 1982), in other words, they inflict on others what they are unable or unwilling to acknowledge in themselves. But, to repeat, no one has a monopoly on hypocrisy. For every "manly man" who takes up arms to defend the Prince of Peace, there is a liberal proponent of public education who secretly enrolls her children in an exclusive private academy.

Ideological Falsity

If an ideology can be shown to be "false," then assuming its proponents are rational, they will take it upon themselves to renounce it. This is a strategy technically known as "ideology critique" (Geuss, 1981). The idea is that instead of judging an ideology by an external standard to which its adherents may object, it uses that ideology's own stated purposes as a reference point for evaluation. If it can show that the ideology in question deludes its advocates or impedes them in the pursuit of their expressed interests, then it is "contradictory" and unworthy of rational support.

The ideology of Christian Dominionism is false in three respects, each of which I discuss next. First, it legitimizes "surplus" (unnecessarily gratuitous) inequality, harming the material interests of its proponents. Second, it mystifies corporate domination, making it difficult for Dominionists to understand why surplus inequality matters. Third, it undermines the institutions that make progressive social reform possible.

If it is not already clear, let me emphasize again that in the logic of ideology critique, the truth or falsity of an ideology is not assessed by its correspondence (or lack thereof) to empirical reality, as important as this may be in other respects. As pointed out earlier, Christian Patriots are able to assemble imposing bodies of data to support their contentions, even if what they occasionally cite lacks credibility. Indeed, hypotheses alleging that the brains of mass murderers are entrained by government ELF wave magnifiers, that lax gun laws positively correlate with gun safety, that ethnicity causes poverty, and so on, typically are posed in ways that render them virtually irrefutable. Nor does the falsity of Christian Dominionism have anything to do with allegations that its purveyors are ill-educated, semi-crazed, or socially estranged. To argue this way would merely replicate a standard move in the magical thinking characteristic of dogmatism. As we also noted earlier, Christian Patriots are *not* measurably less educated, more demented, or more alienated than the average American. On the contrary—possible authoritarian inclinations aside—they are relatively rational actors who are attempting to maximize their interests as they see them, given what they know about their situations, even if what they know is minimal or incorrect. To repeat, if Christian Dominionism is false, it is so because its policy program contradicts its professed end, which is to protect and enhance middle-class interests and values.

Gratuitous Inequality

The "Great Compression" of American riches lasted from 1937 to 1947. Since that time there has occurred a "Great Divergence" (Piketty & Saez, 2003;

Cassidy, 2014): The after-tax inequality of income and wealth has exploded. By 2011, the top 1 percent of American earners was taking home 22.5 percent of the nation's total income, a figure identical to that in 1928, just prior to the Great Depression.

The clearest measurement of income inequality, applicable to any political unit, is the Gini coefficient, the values of which vary between 0 (meaning perfect equality) and 1.0 (absolute inequality). In the mid-1970s, the pretax Gini coefficient for the United States was about 0.40. Since that time, it has increased more than 20 percent to approximately 0.49. The *after-tax* number is somewhat smaller than this but shows the same trajectory. Today, the United States ranks about sixtieth in terms of income inequality among the one hundred and fifty-three nations for which there are records, lagging behind Russia, Iran, Syria, Vietnam, Algeria, Croatia, India, Bangladesh, Korea, Iraq, Egypt, Pakistan, Ethiopia, and Afghanistan (Gini Index–Mundi, n.d.). Utah, Alaska, Wyoming, and New Hampshire are among the most income-egalitarian states; New York, Connecticut, Washington, DC, and Massachusetts are among the most unequal.

Growing inequality in America can be attributed to several factors. One is the unprecedented growth in pretax capital gains, interest earnings, rents, and dividends, as compared to stagnating wages and salaries since 1980. From 1980 to 2010, the top four hundred earners in America enjoyed an average income increase of 392 percent, while the bottom half of earners enjoyed less than a 10-percent increase. A second factor has been the precipitous decline in the marginal federal income tax rate on large fortunes, which, under the New Deal reached 90 percent. During the Reagan and Bush administrations, tax rates on the highest incomes fell from 70 percent to 15 percent; during that same period the top tax rate on ordinary wages and salaries remained at 35 percent. Coupled with this has been the growing practice of establishing nontaxable foundations and trusts to avoid taxes altogether, writing off donations to so-called charitable and educational groups, and secreting financial assets in offshore tax havens. Third has been an erosion of government transfer payments to the middle and lower classes: flat Social Security pensions, Medicare, unemployment, and Medicaid benefits, and the strangulation or elimination of various welfare programs.

As to the long-range causes of these factors, there is little consensus. Among the most plausible hypotheses are (1) a growing premium for skill-based "information" work and a corresponding lowering of demand for unskilled manual labor since 1980, (2) a failure of schools to prepare American youth to assume high-tech occupations, and (3) an increase in foreign manufacturing competition (due, in part, to American firms sending their productive apparatuses overseas to countries where labor costs are lower). Beyond these considerations are the halving of union membership as a proportion of the total labor force since 1960, an end to federal government infrastructure projects and, above all, the growing influence of the probusiness lobby in the nation's capital, which now spends nearly sixty times more to influence legislation and regulatory action than do public-interest and labor lobbyists combined. Finally, over the last generation, a corporate culture has emerged that valorizes private greed over common interests. As we will see momentarily, the ideology of Christian Dominionism has played a central role in this development.

Few Patriots deny the reality of growing inequality (for an exception, however, see Garrett, 2010). After all, many of them have been victimized by it. What they claim instead is that exposure of the fact is either "class warfare" (i.e., it is a Marxist claim and therefore ipso facto unfair, given that "America has no social classes")—that the wealthy use their excess to "make" jobs for "takers"—or that income disparities have little impact on the life chances of the disadvantaged, because poor American families have ample opportunities to advance themselves in the pecking order (Novak, 1981: 49).

In regard to this last point, Dominionists claim that it is not low income as such that bears on a person's life chances but the person's capacity to *consume* and that, given generous government transfer payments and the existence of barter-based mutual support systems in poor, immigrant neighborhoods, consumption problems are not nearly as severe as raw income numbers alone might suggest (Edsall, 1984).[1] Neutral government economists take issue with this assertion, saying that the maintenance of customary consumption levels has become increasingly challenging over the last three decades. From 1983 to 2007, the bottom 95 percent of Americans saw their average debt level double, from 60 cents for every dollar of income to $1.40. Contrary to Dominionist suspicions, the poor do not take out credit to purchase luxuries but to cover rent, school supplies, and cheap medical care (Congressional Budget Office, 2011: 4–5).

Christian Dominionism is in the neo-Calvinist tradition. Thus, it is not surprising that it offers a partially secularized theodicy (or justification) of inequality that derives from John Calvin's doctrine of Election. In brief, Calvin supposes that insofar as all human acts are tainted by Original Sin, then no amount of charity or churchgoing can guarantee salvation. This axiom, however, clashes with the gut-gnawing need people have for salvific reassurance. Over time, then, Calvinist conventicles devised a number of outward signs by which believers could discern their divine election. As Max Weber has shown (1958b), one of these signs is worldly prosperity. Specifically, while one can never *earn* salvation through "works," they might yet be assured of it if they are industrious, focused, sober, tightfisted and, other things being equal, rich. This eventually led to an equation—one that Calvin himself would likely never have endorsed[2]—between belief in personal sanctification and wealth, and the contrary proposition that poverty is an earthly sign of damnation.

From this theology come two popular American narratives, both of which have been absorbed into Christian Dominionism. The first—and like all horror stories, more compelling—is an anecdotal defamation of moochers and takers, the citizenry of what Ayn Rand calls the "ineptocracy." There is the story of the Cadillac-driving welfare mother, for instance, who exchanges food stamps or her own or her daughter's body for cash to purchase drugs; the strapping young buck who uses food stamps to purchase steak; the so-called 10 government contract workers always seen standing around on federal highway projects; the voluntarily idle surfer dude or indolent, alcohol-addled West Virginia mining family who live off Social Security disability payments. These are morality tales that have been repeated so often as to have assumed the status of unassailable legends. In the tautologically circular way described in Chapter 4, they reinforce what Dominionists always already know: The poor deserve what they get.

The second narrative extols the virtues of producers or job makers, the magnates of capitalism, and the joys of unfettered capitalist accumulation.

The Corporatist Apologia

As American wealth began its ineluctable concentration after the Civil War, a new kind of social organism came into being, the business corporation, and with it a new way to justify inequality: the legend of corporatism.

A corporation is an association established through a charter issued by a recognized authority—a church, a monarch, or a state—that permits it to regulate its internal affairs with a minimum of interference. The first Euro-American corporations were cities, followed by religious orders, universities, overseas colonies (such as Jamestown and Plymouth), professions, and voluntary organizations. With the appearance of joint stockholding companies in the nineteenth century, corporate charters began to be issued to organizations whose sole purpose was to make money. What followed was a series of Supreme Court decisions that erected a bulwark for profit making, using as their basis the Fourteenth Amendment of the Constitution (McCloskey, 1951). These culminated in *Santa Clara County v. Southern Pacific* (1886) and in *Pembina Consolidated Silver Co. v. Pennsylvania* (1888) wherein business corporations were conferred a status that, until that time, had been granted solely to human beings: personhood. Now, corporate charters could be spoken of metaphorically as birth certificates; that if properly nourished with capital, they could flourish; but if not, they might die (i.e., go bankrupt). Like people, they could enter into contracts, sue and be sued, be taxed, and be granted the rights of free speech (recently re-affirmed by *Citizens United v. Federal Election Commission* [2010]) and conscience [as in *Burwell v. Hobby Lobby*, 2014]). Details of these and related decisions were refined over the decades, allowing federal courts to reject the wisdom of state-legislated business regulations (e.g., *Chicago, Milwaukee & St. Paul RR v. Minnesota* [1890]) and to outlaw legally passed mandatory workday restrictions (*Lochner v. New York* [1905]).

As business corporations rose to prominence, a new kind of hero began to be written into the mythos of American preeminence: the upwardly mobile, middle-level corporate manager. His first incarnation was in the form of Ragged Dick, the central character in a widely read 100 + book series authored by Horatio Alger Jr. Gifted with an ethic of honesty, thrift, sobriety, and "open-faced, manly cheer," Ragged Dick is depicted as slowly ascending the corporate hierarchy into middle-class respectability, moving from streetwise bootblack to conscientious stock boy, and from there to lowly clerk, ending up as secretary to the chief executive officer.

In the Roaring Twenties, the simple-hearted Dick was superseded in popular literature by a more morally ambivalent character, one suitable to an age of decadent excess (Prothro, 1954): F. Scott Fitzgerald's *Great Gatsby*, the *nouveau riche* son of an eastern European immigrant farmer named Gatz, whose money comes from bootlegging. In the imagination of post–World War II America, a still slicker variation appeared on the literary scene: the engineer-scientist Howard Roark and capitalist adventurer John Galt, the major protagonists of Ayn Rand's *The Fountainhead* (1943) and her 1,200-page magnum opus, *Atlas Shrugged* (1957). Panned by critics at the time as "the second worst book of the last 1,000 years," *Atlas Shrugged* is said to have enjoyed American sales second only to the Bible (Walker, 1999: 295–6).

Rand was a germophobic, Dexadrine-quaffing, chain-smoking adulteress, haughty, conspiratorial, outspokenly proabortion, and contemptuous of the "bovine contentment" of family life (Walker, 1999: 113). Furthermore, following the inspiration of her literary mentor, Friedrich Nietzsche (Atlas Society, 2000), she viewed religious devotion as a "short-circuit of the mind." For all this, however, in what must rank as one of the great perversities of Christian moral theology—on a par with the concept of "holy war"—her philosophy of selfishness (technically known as *Objectivism*) has been eagerly incorporated into Christian Dominionism, transmogrifying in the process into one of the cardinal "virtues" (Rand, 1961). While naïve Dominionists continue to cling to Jesus' Golden Rule—see our earlier discussion of compassionate conservatism—Randroids, as they call themselves, mock them by donning "What would John Galt do?" bracelets.

For Galt, the operating rule of a life well lived is not "do unto others." It is "What's in it for me?" "One puts oneself above all and crushes everything in one's way to get the best for oneself. Fine!" Rand wrote near the end of her life (Walker, 1999: 230). Selfishness not only advances one's own ego, she claims but, through the unintended consequences of Adam Smith's magical "hand," every other ego as well. In a tendentious speech given to fellow industrialists gathered in Galt's Gulch (a fictional utopia in Ouray, Colorado, where they have fled from the "parasites" of the lowlands), Galt (i.e., Rand) enthuses about the role that selfishness plays in the story of human progress. "The root of all good," s/he concludes, explicitly contradicting biblical teaching (1 Tim. 6: 10) "is money." Or in words later memorialized by Gordon Gekko in the movie *Wall Street*, "Greed, for lack of a better word, is good!"

Alan Greenspan (whom Rand considered her "special pet") and Milton Friedman, both of whom rose to prominence during the Nixon-Reagan era, played seminal roles in the absorption of Objectivism into Christian fundamentalism by defending it against liberal critics. In his book-length retort to progressives, Friedman writes that "self-interest [egotism] is not myopic selfishness." On the contrary, "it is whatever it is that suits the participant in question, whatever it is they value" (Friedman & Friedman, 1980: 27). For one person, this might be fine art, for another a sculpted body, and for others fine food, or even charitable giving. Rand once argued that so long as charity entails no self-sacrifice on the donor's part, it is perfectly "rational" and in theory, at least, ethically acceptable (as applied to Christmastime giving, see Schwartz, 2014).[3]As for the corporate "person," its sole obligation to society "is to increase its profits": to augment the value of the stock held by its shareholders (Friedman, 1970).

Rand is largely responsible for the ridicule she endured over the years. For instance, the moniker she adopted for herself, "Rand"—at birth, she was Allisa Rosenbaum—is rumored to have been borrowed from the monetary unit of South Africa. "Galt," in turn, is said to be a Yiddish inflection of *Geld*, the German word for gold (Walker, 1999: 278–9, 288). Jeff Walker claims that Galt honors John Gal, who was an early spokesman for the National Association of Manufacturers and Rand's private attorney. Just as a dollar-sign flag waves over Galt's Gulch, so it is for members of the Rand cult.

The *meine Kämpfe* of Rand's heroes is presented in just the right tone to appeal to the romantic sensibilities of those for whom individual freedom is paramount, her primary audience: emotional adolescents of any age, struggling to free themselves from the cloying hold of their parents (who, according to Walker, are symbolized by "totalitarian collectivism") (Packer, 2011; cf. the case of libertarian multimillionaire Peter Thiel, 2009). First, like Ragged Dick, they are shown as rising from middling, if not abjectly poor, circumstances. Galt, for instance, is portrayed as the son of a garage mechanic; the central character in Rand's futuristic novella *Anthem* (1938), Equality 7-2521, is born to a street-sweeper. After Equality accidently stumbles across the long-forgotten pronoun for ego and then discovers his own, Rand has him rechristened as "The Conqueror." Second—here we are reminded of the socially mal-adept teenager who finds him- or herself excluded from the high school "in" group— he uses his brains to excel in science, math, and engineering. These provide the stage on which he will dramatize his singularity and liberate himself from the crowd. For Roark, this involves dynamiting a socialist-style high-rise housing project the design specifications of which betray his refined aesthetic. After defending himself in court against the herd-like, sycophantic standards of the masses, the jury finds him not guilty. Now, third, comes the sweet wine of revenge: The hero wins, weds, and beds "a woman for a man like Howard Roark": the boss's daughter, Dominique Francon; or in the case of Galt, Dagny Taggert. Rand describes Taggert as having rescued Galt from a bevy of socialist bureaucrats who are about to torture him for speaking on-air in favor of egotistic individualism. Like all government agents, she writes, bureaucrats claim to be acting altruistically but, in reality, are serving only themselves.

With the rise of the communitarian movement in the late 1960s, the enchantment of the Randroid hero began to fade. Sensing growing menace in the development, Lewis Powell, a noted business leader, penned a "Confidential Memorandum" to the U.S. Chamber of Commerce. In it he warns that the "free enterprise system" must take steps to defend itself against "new leftists and their supporters" who, he claims, have taken over college campuses, the liberal media, and the ministry (Powell, 1971). It will no longer be enough, he writes, for capitalists to engage in PR campaigns, fund charitable causes, and lobby government. To save themselves, they will have to confront the "disquieting forces" of dissent directly: monitor high school textbooks for "un-American" content; "visit" broadcasters and college presidents and demand "fairness," "openness," and "balance"; set up speakers' bureaus to pontificate about the "American system"; and "without undue pressure," encourage college trustees to give equal time to the "forgotten man" (a reference to the protagonist in William Graham Sumner's paean to egotism [1883]). In short, "the Ralph Naders" (a noted consumer-protection activist) and "the Herbert Marcuses"' (a prominent new-left social critic) "who openly seek destruction of the system" must be silenced. But negativism, Powell warns, will not be enough. Business leaders will also have to endow their own think tanks, staffed with "eminent scholars who believe in the American system," capable of issuing apologies for capitalism in ways that appeal to the masses.

Beginning with John Olin (chairman of Olin-Mathieson Chemical) and Richard Scaife (media billionaire and heir to the Mellon banking and oil fortune), and since then followed by a troop of mimics, Powell's recommendations have been taken to heart. Business magnates have devoted fortunes to underwriting the promotion of corporatism. One of the most fascinating products of this venture is a small book by Michael Novak: *Toward a Theology of the Corporation,* published by the American Enterprise Institute in 1981.

Novak writes that like Isaiah's suffering servant (Isa. 53:2–3) who sorrowfully, if stoically, endures mankind's rebuke, the corporation is "a much despised incarnation of God's presence in this world" and, like the suffering servant, it is desperately in need of a well-spoken advocate. Novak's argument hardly lives up to the promise of its title, but we can see in it an effort to elevate corporations out of the level of mere personhood into the stature of gods.

Corporations, Novak writes, exhibit seven (a number, he says, equal to the count of Roman Catholic sacraments) "signs of grace" (Novak, 1981: 37–43). For ease of presentation, I reduce them to five. First, by "unlocking" earth's riches, they "mirror" God's omnipotence. Second, by means of their chartered independence, they mirror God's "freedom from the state." Third, insofar as their internal workings can be adopted by any culture, they mirror God's transcendence. Fourth, by orchestrating the efforts of countless disparate souls into a single pursuit, they mirror God's unifying power. And fifth, they provide a milieu within which employees can "work out their salvation." This being the case, it follows that they are not just worthy of our grudging tolerance but deserve our pious devotion. We should *"regard it [the corporation, as] the fulfillment of a vocation from God and a way of cooperating in the completion of Creation as God intended it"* (Novak, 1981: 29; author's emphasis).

Novak is a Catholic but lambasts scholasticism (mentioned several times in the last chapter) for its "kindergartner's" understanding of commercial realities, for its moral "naivety," for its "ignorance" of history, and for its

"Constantinean" impulse to impose its outlook on society. What he finds particularly galling is scholasticism's failure to appreciate Ayn Rand's "self-evident" axiom that all human behavior "is based on rational self-interest" (Novak, 1981: 11).

The Coarsening of Life and Civic Disengagement

Oddly, there is one corporate "gift of grace" that Novak overlooks. It is that, like the God of the Old Testament, corporations are well along the path to making the world over after their own image and likeness (cf. Gen. 1: 26). Although the phrases used to describe this development may be new—"creative destruction" (Joseph Schumpeter) and "disruptive innovation" (Clayton Christensen)—the fact is not.[4] Already by the 1960s, corporate logic colonized the ordinary-life world to such a degree that it was already being spoken of as a commercial enterprise in all but name: a series of "swaps" between "players," who "brand" themselves by "body advertisements" (Goffman, 1979) to maximize their individual "payoffs" (Homans, 1961); "incentivize" had entered the common argot as a reference to how "operations" (i.e., behavioral "outputs") could be "managed" by "positive reinforcers" (food, sex, and especially money). And within a generation more, critics would be writing of "a new tyranny," the corporation, that threatened to "devour" the last vestiges of the "fragile and defenseless": the natural environment, considerations of ethics, feelings of compassion, the concept of human personhood, and ironically (the plausibility of) God (Pope Francis, quoted in Cassidy, 2013).

Today, theme-park visitors can pay to bypass queues awaiting carnival rides and for special treatment in the event they find themselves jailed. Individuals can pay for the opportunity to "sponsor" a public arena, a subway, a nature trail, or a greenway; for the right to affix their corporate logo to a public-school cafeteria table, a classroom locker, school bus, or fire engine; for entry into exclusive hunting grounds; for access to spare body parts, sperm, and eggs; for on-demand concierge medical care and seats at prestigious private colleges; and for the right to pollute the water and air (Sandel, 2012). Some economists have even proposed that the opportunity to immigrate to America be limited to those with the capacity to pay (Becker, 2005).

Dominionists laud the exercise of turning public goods into private commodities and then auctioning them off to the highest bidder, arguing that besides enhancing individual liberty, this "maximizes efficiency" by taking their distribution out of the hands of ideologically driven do-gooders. But as Michael Sandel points out, financial inducements have a tendency to "corrode" and "debase" the worth of human action. When people are paid to do what they otherwise might out of love, duty, or custom, the doing is not only made less satisfying; it becomes less likely. This is seen in blood donations and volunteer work, both of which decrease in frequency when paid for (Titmuss, 1971), and in the "stiff resistance" peasants mount against attempts to rationalize the workplace by promising them cash payments for increased productivity (Weber,

1958b: 57–60). (Because they need to do less to attain their traditional standard of living, their output decreases.) Likewise, religious commitment: The less that a church or synagogue asks of its members' time, energy, donations, and sacrifice, the *less* steadfast they become (Moss-Kanter, 1972). Contrary to the objectivist claim that human behavior is essentially egotistic, when it comes to *life as it is actually lived*, people seem driven less by hedonic calculation than they do by affection, duty, and tradition (Weber, 1964: 15–16).

When calls go out to "Starve the Beast!" public agencies go underfunded and the reliability of services deteriorates. Predictably, this spurs demands that they be run in a more businesslike way, most notably by cutting overhead expenses, which invariably means laying off staff. Revenue offices are downsized, bridges and paved roads deteriorate, prisons and security needs go unmet, and the quality of utility deliveries is compromised (water, sewage, pollution abatement, garbage disposal, and electricity). Supplemental nutrition programs for the poor are slashed, along with heating allowances and medical insurance subsidies. Regulations that limit potential corruptive connections between deposit banks and investment companies disappear, putting the nest eggs of middle-class savers at risk. Corporations are freed from having to pay fees to underwrite the enforcement of regulations that protect consumers from fraud. Access to museums and galleries, zoos, parks, and archives is jeopardized. Public broadcasting and medical laboratories set up to protect public health are put at risk. All of these lend credence to the myth that "government can't do anything right." Critics insist that it be put on a still stricter diet, that it be made smaller and even less proficient. What follows is a further decline in public services. This feeds back to evoke still greater distrust in government, cries for more budget cutting, in a vicious self-destructive cycle.

Like a noxious miasma, distrust in government leaks into other institutional realms: to mistrust of religious leaders, educators, and scientists, to medical doctors, military leaders, parents, and neighbors (Cass, 2013). We become wary of store clerks who swipe our credit cards, drivers with whom we share the road, and strangers whom we happen upon in our travels. Reports of lying and cheating become rampant. In response, firearms purchases go up and "castle laws" are passed. We enter into prenuptial contracts with our intendeds, closet ourselves in gated communities, and lock our doors at night. Civil deliberation about the good life, happiness, and justice "quietly drains away" (Sandel, 1996). What little remains becomes rancorous, uncompromising, and gridlocked. Whereas citizens in an earlier time might have believed they could influence the decisions affecting their lives, they now end up "bowling alone" (Putnam, 2001) or worse: They find themselves "alone together" (Turkle, 2012) in front of mobile screens, "communicating" with computer icons. Like teenage Japanese *hikikomori* (voluntary shut-ins), they barricade themselves in offices and bedrooms, resentful of intrusions. At the very moment that the fable of sovereign citizenship comes into prominence, in other words, its actualities become characterized by isolation, paralysis, and drift. Freedom devolves from a sense of shared responsibility for the nation as a whole into the individual capacity to make informed consumer choices. Overwhelmed by forces beyond our understanding and control, we undertake quests for consolation on the internet, and find it in the irrefutable verities of apocalyptic utopianism, in far-right fantasy with its satanic Conspiracy and whimsical Cure. As it turns out, however, the Cure further impoverishes civic life, making it that much more difficult to resist the penetration of corporate logic into ever more intimate spheres of the life-world. But this is another way of saying that it is "false." The Cure contradicts its stated purpose, which is to secure and advance the public interest.

Dominionism and the Destabilization of Civic Institutions

Besides voting, Americans historically have enjoyed many ways to "exercise the muscles of civic virtue" and keep themselves fit for public life (Skocpol, 1999a, 1999b). Among them are active participation in professional associations and religious communities, and involvement in such diffuse-focus, nonsectarian voluntary groups as the Elks Club, the Grange, and parent–teacher organizations. There are also countless informal gathering places that facilitate citizenship, such as coffeehouses, bookstores, farmer's markets, and community gardens. The following paragraphs briefly touch on four traditional sites of American civic engagement: labor unions, public schools, the commons, and the post office. My goal is to show how, as targets of Christian Dominionist hostility—which is to say, the Cure—each increasingly finds itself imperiled, putting at risk the concerns of those whom it claims to protect.

Labor Unions

It is difficult to exaggerate the role that labor unions have played in the building of America's middle class. According to labor historian Philip Dray (2010), without unions there would be no 40-hour workweek, no minimum wage guarantees, no occupational safety regulations or paid vacations, no unemployment benefits or Social Security.

Originally, labor unions were more than vehicles set up to negotiate favorable working terms for dues-paying members. By adapting the ancient guild system to the conditions of factory production, they also readied blue-collar workers to participate in modern society. They ran worker-owned consumer co-ops and credit agencies and funded social centers equipped with reading libraries, medical dispensaries, and funeral arrangers. They organized children's clubs and gymnasiums and sponsored continuing education programs, athletic leagues, orchestras, and marching bands. They held concerts, dances, plays, operas, and parades. Most salient for our purposes, they provided opportunities for members to practice the arts of citizenship: to network, take part in petition drives, and conduct protests and strikes; to debate the merits of public policy, barter with employers, run for office, keep financial records, and record meetings (for the example of hard-rock mining unions in the inner-mountain West, see Norlen, 1992). Viewed in this way, the collapse in union membership since the 1960s has had a profound and deleterious effect on American democracy.

This is not the place to speculate about the causes of de-unionization, apart from mentioning TV entertainment and the diversions from civic life afforded by amusement parks and movies. What is important is that Christian Patriots who consider unions (incorrectly) to be the vanguard of socialist revolution have been hard at work eliminating their last vestiges by outlawing collective bargaining rights for public officials and passing right-to-work laws. Ironically, "Reagan Democrats," as they are known, blue-collar retirees who have benefitted from past union activism, are sometimes in the forefront of these efforts. (When President Reagan crushed the air-traffic-control officer union after it went on strike for safer working conditions, he won the eternal devotion of the far-right.)

Right-to-work legislation exacerbates what economists call the "free-rider" phenomenon. That is to say, workers can continue to enjoy the benefits of union-negotiated contracts even if they themselves do not pay union dues. In this way, to borrow the language of Ayn Rand, they "maximize their egotistic interests." But this is so only initially, for in the long run the bargaining power of unions is undercut and, with this, a proletarian "class-*for*-itself," which earlier had controlled the price of labor by limiting its supply—a poor man's facsimile of a professional monopoly—is turned into a "class-*in*-itself," a fragmented aggregate of increasingly impoverished monads fighting each other in a job market controlled by corporations. As observed earlier, this is one of the prime causes of growing inequality in America since 1980.

Public Schools

Perhaps even more important than unions in the formation of American civic virtue have been public schools. Schools, of course, are first of all where young people are trained to assume jobs. But of equal importance for our purpose is the role schools play as trustees of national values. They provide safe zones where children are made aware of a social reality—America—that transcends their petty class, ethnic, sectarian, age, gender, and sexual differences. Much civic education takes place in the formal classroom setting where students are introduced to the Founders and memorize passages from the nation's definitive documents: the Preamble, the Bill of Rights, the Gettysburg Address, and so on. But the most important lessons in citizenship are taught incidentally, through involvement in such school activities as organizing and attending dances; participating in pageants that reenact notable events in a local community's imagined past; playing intra- and extramural sports; and engaging in extemporaneous, nonsupervised comingling (where students learn about bullying and civility); and, not least, through student body politicking: campaigning for office, keeping records, and managing pretend treasuries.

As we observed earlier, public schools and those who run them are under relentless attack by Christian Patriots (Ravitch, 2013). Their incessant belittling is partly due to the fact that American student proficiency scores in math and reading perennially lag behind those tallied by Finnish, Japanese, Chinese, and Korean children; partly because many public-school teachers are members of the quasi-professional National Education Association and American Federation of Teachers (which are cited by Patriots as the main reason for low achievement scores); and partly because public-school lesson plans touch on multiculturalism, Darwinism, sex education, and environmentalism, all of which challenge one or more tenets of Christian Dominionism.

Whatever its causes, the consequences of the Dominionist siege of public schools have been dramatic. They include calls to end teacher tenure, along with the unions that protect them (calls that are frequently accompanied by anecdotes of outrageous malfeasance); advocacy of criminal background checks for teachers and mandatory drug testing; merit-based raises to "incentivize" intra-school teacher competition; school funding cutbacks and the scuttling of bond measures; putting an end to automatic pay raises for teachers who earn master's degrees; hiring of noncertified paraprofessionals to replace state-certified instructors; farming out of public education to home schools, charter schools, and sectarian private schools (underwritten by tax subsidies and vouchers); and, finally, the introduction of massive enrollment online courses, which hold the promise of getting rid of the troublesome human factor (read *teachers*) altogether. These developments have been given enormous impetus by the diffusion of corporate accountancy principles into the classroom and the insistence that "hard data" (standardized test scores) be used to measure "school-based target acquisition" (teacher competency).

Gone unnoticed in these policy recommendations is that, while the proficiency of American students does appear to pale in comparison to that of foreigners, with notable exceptions the lowest student achievement scores of all occur in states and in school districts controlled by Dominionist legislatures and school boards (Mississippi, Louisiana, West Virginia, Alabama, South Carolina, etc.). In other words, the unwitting casualties of the siege of public education are the children and grandchildren of the Dominionists themselves.

The Commons

In the American West, no site of public involvement is more important than its public lands and forests, air and water resources, fisheries and wildlife. (For a reminder, see the prologue to this book.) The national commons comprise more than half the acreage in all the states west of the Mississippi River and much more than this in the Rocky Mountain region. In Utah, Nevada, and Idaho, the commons comprise 75 percent, 88 percent, and 70 percent of each state's total acreage, respectively; in Alaska, the percentage is 96.

The commons are where all Americans, regardless of difference, are granted the right, even if they don't always have the opportunity, to slow down, face the challenges of solitude and danger, and simply gape in wonder at nature's bounty. When not preserved for this purpose, they are managed by the federal government for grazing, timber, watershed protection, and mining.

Frederick Turner Jackson announced the "closing" of the frontier over a century ago, but enough of it still exists to nourish a myth of American difference, with its sometimes admittedly obnoxious pretensions of self-reliance, adventure, and irrepressible wildness. More prosaically, the commons provide space for citizenship training and practice. Here one can meet with others who value something larger than their insular workday, religious, and family lives—in parks, on trails, or while ascending a mountain scarp—and can work with them by offering public testimony, appealing official decisions, conducting policy research, staging demonstrations, devising nonprofit action groups, and organizing membership drives.

Speaking through the mouths of Dominionism's western cousins, the so-called "Sagebrush Rebels," Christian Patriots demand that the federal government "cede" the commons back to the 50 "sovereign states," who are said to have "temporarily loaned them" to the feds in the first place in exchange for what Patriots consider the questionable privileges of statehood. Because few western states have the financial wherewithal to manage the lands in question, plans are to sell them to timber barons, mining magnates, or cattle ranchers; auction them off to the wealthy for private hunting and fishing preserves; or outsource their management to private concessionaires. Reminiscent of the British enclosure, when the gentry barred peasants from lands (the commons) traditionally used for mowing, pasturing, hunting, and firewood, those unable to pay access fees would be denied entry. Not surprisingly, the interests of the native peoples who reside in proximity to the commons, the *real* "original owners," are routinely overlooked by Patriots.

Whenever objectivist (Randroidian) economic theory is applied to questions of public policy, the problem of the free-rider arises. In this case, it takes the form of "the tragedy of the commons" (Harden, 1968). According to Garrett Harden, who coined the phrase, if a commons is not protected by zoning laws or by some other coercive mechanism, then rational individuals in the pursuit of their selfish interests will degrade them to the detriment of all, including themselves. This has been thoroughly documented by countless cases of overgrazing, deforestation, fisheries depletion, air and water pollution, ocean acidification, and the extermination of various large and small animal species. According to Harden, appeals to moral restraint cannot solve the tragedy of the commons because, by means of the instrumentalist logic of the free-rider, altruistic behavior is "punished." That is, those who neglect to maximize their utilization of the resource in question will suffer the greatest "opportunity costs."

The Post Office

The Post Office Act of 1792 established cheap postal rates and guaranteed letter writers freedom from government surveillance. This, together with the construction of stagecoach post-roads, played an important role in uniting the republic. Most of the post offices were staffed part-time by federal employees, who in the decade of the 1830s constituted three-quarters of the total federal workforce. The cracker-barrel, pot-bellied stove conviviality of the post office is a subject of sentimental romance but, in many rural districts, it remains true: The post office *is* the social center of village life. Here locals can play at citizenship by deliberating over issues of the day.

Before 1792, slaves deemed trustworthy by their masters were assigned to transport the mails. Although this was done away with in the Deep South following a series of slave revolts (Boyd & Chen, n.d.), elsewhere it continued under various Republican administrations. After the Civil War, African Americans received appointments as postal clerks and carriers through a system of patronage. Following passage of the Pendleton Act in 1883, however, civil service examination scores replaced favoritism as the primary criterion for hiring. (Until World War I, federal law required that photos be attached to government job applications which, of course, allowed for discrimination. This practice was ended by Presidents Harding, Hoover, and Roosevelt.) By the 1960s, the Post Office Department (POD) was the single largest employer of educated African Americans in the country, providing job security, opportunities for career advancement, a pension, and one of the few pathways to middle-class respectability, outside the military and the black church.

In 1970, the POD union conducted a series of nationwide strikes for higher salaries. This, coupled with the association of the POD with African Americans and "big government," conspired to stoke the simmering coals of Dominionist rage across the Old Confederacy. In response, and as part of his "Southern strategy," President Nixon reorganized the POD into the United States Postal Service (USPS), turning it into a government-owned business corporation. Henceforth, it would have to support itself exclusively from sales on stamps and services.

During the age of "snail mail," the USPS enjoyed a competitive advantage over private delivery companies. With the advent of electronic mail, however, this advantage quickly grew into a burden; the USPS saw its revenue stream diminish. The burden became back-breaking when, in 2006, Congress mandated that the USPS prefund the health care costs and pensions of retirees 75 years into the future, the only federal agency for which this is required. To cover the new expenses, the USPS was forced to consolidate letter-processing centers, close rural post offices, and limit weekend deliveries, further compromising its competitive posture. Predictably, Dominionist ideologues recommended that the USPS henceforth be fully "privatized" (DeHaven, 2011). This, they promised, would enable it to downsize a staff of "questionable competence" (which, to this point, had been protected from elimination by "onerous" civil service regulations) and replace it with more compliant, *non*unionized staff of part-time carriers and clerks, who need not be given medical insurance or pensions. Apart from those who lose their jobs as a result, the ultimate victims are the housebound elderly and those who lack internet access, many of whom are enthusiastic Dominionists.

Conclusion

Hannah Arendt (1967 [1951]) attributes the rise of rightist fanaticism in Europe during the 1920s and 1930s to the catastrophe of World War I and the shattering of state authority that followed. As legal protections for minorities and refugees lost legitimacy, she writes, Jews, gypsies, Slavs, and sexual "inverts" found themselves facing the predations of various fascist mobs. The ways by which they had earlier conveyed their dignity as human beings—through marriage, home ownership, professional work, voting, and worship—were taken away, as soon thereafter were their lives.

Arendt goes on to argue (following Thomas Hobbes) that in the absence of a "Leviathan," a state apparatus powerful enough to "over-awe" and frighten the public into submission, there is little, if anything, to curb its appetites. What follows is a war of all against all: *Homo homini lupus*. Each citizen becomes a devouring wolf. For a "grotesque homunculi of the superman whose natural destiny is to rule the world" (Arendt, 1967 [1951]: 170), a tiny elite whose wealth and power obviate the need for state protection, this is fine and well but, for the masses, it means a "solitary" life, "poor, nasty, brutish, and short."

It is important that we not draw facile equivalences from broad likenesses— as pointed out earlier, to accuse the American far-right of being fascistic is both inaccurate and unfair—but if what Arendt says is even partly true, it is difficult not to be alarmed when we hear Christian Patriots prate about how the federal government is granting "special rights" to gays, "quotas" for unqualified blacks, and "amnesty" to undocumented Hispanics; how it is "coddling" poor women, the sick, and elderly and is turning indigents into "wards of the state." To be sure, these are not precisely the complaints once issued by European fascists, but they are near enough to cause us pause.

Arendt says that in addition to its aversion for the state, an indolent company of corrupt, incompetent clerks, the distinctive feature of postwar European ultra-rightism was its veneration of the People, a vibrant *"corpus separatum"* with its unique *Volkgeist* and God-given destiny. A parallel theme runs through Dominionism: Christian Reconstruction (CR), Christian Identity (CI), and the New Apostolic Reformation (NAR) all express disdain for government but, at the same time, they sing the praises of the folk. Having noted this, however, it should also be noted that there exists a striking difference between European-style fascism and Christian Dominionism: With the exception of CI, Dominionism is largely devoid of Judeophobia. Instead of going after Jews, Dominionists rail against such imaginary entities as the Hidden Hand, the Illuminati, and Force X. And yet it is also true (again, like European fascism) that Dominionism evinces what Arendt calls "Jew envy" (Arendt, 1967 [1951]: 241–3). By this she means mimicry of the narrative of the Chosen People. It attempts to plant its Volkish genealogies in faux-biblical soil. The three most telling examples of this are the Book of Mormon and its tale of Lehi and the tribe of Manasseh, who are said to have sailed to the Americas just prior to the fall of Jerusalem; CI's fable of the Lost Tribes of Israel, who allegedly trekked over the Caucasus mountains and ultimately arrived in this country; and the legend of America's pilgrim forefathers, whom legend has fleeing persecution at the hands of Pharaoh-like British kings to embark on a "divinely appointed mission" to spread the gospel of the Lord in the New World.

Resemblances or their lack to European fascism aside, like all extremisms, Dominionism harbors a penchant for violence. In May 2014, Christian Patriots announced the beginning of what they titled Operation American Spring. Modeled after the Arab Spring of 2 years earlier, it promised to draw some 30 million bikers, truckers, hunters, and militia to Washington, DC, to undertake "tyranny housecleaning," ousting and, if necessary, jailing the "criminal elitist members of the incumbent government led by that Kenyan usurper [Barack Obama]." When "a fluffy, cuddly lamb" (meaning, the federal government) "gets eaten by a mean old wolf" (presumably, a well-armed Patriot), said organizers, this "is not an illegal or immoral event." But one blogger warned, nor does it mean that the confrontation would be a "cakewalk." No. "It will be painful, and some people will die ... some of us will end up in a cell, and some may be injured" (Hamner, 2014). (For a photo of the dozen or so who eventually showed up for the event, see Zimet, 2014; for disappointment at its flop, see Chumley, 2014.)

There is no little irony in the fact that Christian Patriots profess faith in their *own* fluffy, cuddly lamb: the Lamb of God, Jesus Christ. And while this lamb urges them to "hate the sin," it also admonishes them to "love the sinner." It is likely this more than anything else that has so far kept most Patriots from acting out their fantasies in blood. The problem is that Jesus' call for mercy can and is so easily overridden by a deeper craving on the part of Patriots—for an enemy of the Left compared to which they can know themselves Right.

Notes

1 Thomas Edsall gained notoriety in 2009 for approving the PhD thesis of Jason Richwine at Harvard University. Richwine argues that the IQs of non-Cuban Hispanic immigrants to America are "permanently" inferior to those of their white hosts and therefore they should be discouraged from entering the country (Ward, 2013).

2 According to Richard Tawney, "the quality ... most sharply opposed to ... the Founder of the Christian Faith [Jesus] ... consists of the assumption that the attainment of riches is the supreme object of human endeavor and the final criterion of human success" (Tawney, 1926: 234–5).

3 Schwartz is a distinguished fellow at the Ayn Rand Institute.

4 In Chapter 1 of the *Communist Manifesto* (first published in 1848 and subsequently revised many times) Karl Marx writes: Corporate capitalism "drowns the most heavenly ecstasies of religious fervor, of chivalrous enthusiasm, of philistine sentimentalism, in the icy water of egotistic calculation," resolving "personal worth into exchange value, and in place of the numberless indefeasible chartered freedoms, set up that single, unconscionable freedom—Free Trade".

Interlude 8

Biblically Inspired Investing

Sean Hyman of Dallas, Texas, is a one-time Christian Dominionist pastor and a graduate in ministry from a "minor Bible college." He is also the formulator of what he titles "The Biblical Money Code" (Hyman, 2013), a set of teachings presumably borrowed from King Solomon, Jesus Christ, and St. Paul. Hyman claims that if subscribers follow the code, they will be able to "maximize their wealth accumulation" and thereby create the conditions for "sovereign individuality." To facilitate this, he sells memberships in an "exclusive" club that he describes as being composed of 26,000 affiliates worldwide and 300,000 readers. He also offers monthly advice on "Christian investments" in gold certificates, offshore trust funds, and e-commerce, as well as information on asset protection, tax avoidance, dual citizenship, and access to a "golden rolodex" of expert money managers.

The central idea of the Biblical Money Code is that the root of all evil is not money per se but the love of it. It follows, then, that if one "un-loves" money, profits can be earned that are both safe and ethical. By the "un-love" of money, Hyman means an attitude of detachment. The problem with the love of money, he says, is that it leads to greed and thus to imprudent investing. Or it results in the opposite, a reluctance to invest at all, living every day in poverty out of fear of being poor for one. The biblical rule, Hyman teaches, is to avoid risking everything out of greed or risking nothing at all and thereby "burying your talents" (an allusion to ancient Jewish currency) and being permanently impoverished. Instead, he urges his followers to be like Jesus of Nazareth, whom he describes as "a shrewd businessman." Jesus cast out from his presence the "wickedness" of both the avaricious rich and the fretful poor, because neither had faith in the Lord sufficient to grant them the courage to sell when others bought or buy when others sold. It is their fidelity to Christ, Hyman tells us, that explains the worldly success of such billionaires as Warren Buffett and Sir John Templeton.

8 Far-Right Fantasy 4

False Consciousness

Christian Dominionism is false in two ways. First, as just shown, its policies contradict what it purports to value. Second, and of equal importance, it is falsely *conscious*. That is, it mistakes its stories as natural facts, as if they are not stories at all but ontological truths. In doing so, Dominionism deludes its proponents about what their interests are and shrinks their political horizons, limiting what they imagine to be possible.

The technical term for false consciousness is *alienation*, which originally referred to how manufactured goods have the eerie quality of rebounding back to haunt their makers (Marx, 1999 [1844]). That is, they return to "deform their formers": hindering, poisoning, injuring and, in some cases, killing those who design and fabricate them. Originally, the concept was applied to steel goods, agricultural wares, and armaments, but the idea has since been generalized to encompass all cultural products, from languages and legal systems, to art forms, religions, and folkways (Berger & Luckmann, 1967).

The crucial event in the happening of alienation is forgetfulness. Those who author the world, so to say, lose sight of their responsibility for it and end up attributing it to a source outside themselves: to a god, to fate, or to DNA. Christian Dominionism offers countless examples of this. One is its conviction that the Bible and the Constitution are not human works at all but God's. Another is Michael Novak's bizarre assertion that business corporations "complete Creation as God intended it" (Novak, 1981: 29). Still another is Dominionism's conviction that the bourgeois (Ayn Randian) ego is an irreducible natural fact. (In reality, as historians of consciousness have long known, it is a culturally contingent *arti*fact [Neumann, 1973 {1954}]). The case of alienating forgetfulness I want to focus on here, however, is the Dominionist certainty that the qualities of its enemies are given in the nature of things themselves.

Nothing is more pivotal to the sense of Christian Patriot identity than knowledge of what they are *not*—namely, Them. To some Patriots, Them is a jihadist, secretly working behind the scenes to impose Shari'a law on liberty-loving Americans. For others, like Jonah Goldberg (2007), Them is a "liberal fascist" such as Woodrow Wilson, Franklin Roosevelt, or Hillary Clinton. In the mind of Iowa Congressman Steve King, Them is an undocumented immigrant with "calves the size of cantaloupes" due to hauling "75 pounds of marijuana across the desert" as a "drug mule" (Milbank, 2013). And the list goes on. There are butch-cut "femen" and "femi-Nazis" who are said to "sexually mutilate people." The Covenant, Sword and the Arm of the Lord (n.d.) describes them as "sodomite homosexuals waiting in their lusts rape," "negro beasts of the field … [whose] cannibalistic fervor shall cause them to eat the dead and the living," and "seed of Satan Jews who sacrifice people in darkness." Most worrisome of all are "city-living … 'do-gooders' who've fought for the 'rights' of these groups." For more than a few Patriots, these visages give themselves to consciousness as a unitary specter called, simply, Evil.

In premodern cosmology, evil is experienced as an ethereal principle, Ahriman, Satan, Mara, or Shiva; and it is dealt with in a manner appropriate to the spirit world, through ritual appeasement and offerings. In the modern world, however, where the gods are largely "dead," even in the everyday dealings of reputed believers, evil is de-sacralized. It is experienced as a material thing, an all-powerful, omniscient *human* malevolence housed in big government or carried to our shores by aliens who intend our doom: a horror movie come to life.

A human carrier of evil is undoubtedly a ghastly thing, but a world without one is worse, for at least with a human evil, bad things are dependable. The ills that befall us can be said to happen for a reason. Were there no evil-doers, the world would be rudderless. It would have no foundation, no direction, no direct*or*. Our misfortunes would have to be attributed to accident, blunder, or chance. But this would be unbearable, because it would force us to face our existential precariousness, our bottomless vulnerability and impermanence, which is to say, our death.

In the imagination of the far-right, evil-doers are rumored to emerge at night from caves or fortress-like buildings (like the Bilderberg Hotel or the Skull and Bones Club at Yale University), from dark forests (Bohemian Grove), or from fetid-smelling slums—the dregs (*Dreck,* Ger. = feces) or "bowels" of the underworld. Like crows, they speak the language of "caw-caw," *kakka*, shit, and legend has them residing amidst garbage-eating animals. Each totem in the crypto-zoology of the far-right is associated with a specific villain: 'coons with black people, dogs with gays, cats with witches, pigs with Jews, and (bureauc) rats with feds. Like the Mormon elders once accused of presiding over degraded delights in the parlors of the temple seraglio, or the priests and nuns said to commit terrible debaucheries in tunnels beneath parish churches, the evil-doer stands for Death, the cosmic killer, who is forever plotting to destroy us.

With the advent of modern medicine, sickness metaphors have inserted themselves in extremist oratory. The enemy of the far-right becomes a microbe or a cancer or, more frightening still, a disease vector, a carrier of hepatitis C (as is said of Mexican immigrants), typhoid fever (the Irish), tuberculosis (Russian Jews), bubonic plague (the Chinese), influenza (the Spanish), or hemorrhagic fevers (black Africans). In either case, "bio-security" measures are called for: "ethnic cleansing," the decontamination of alien property by fire and "surgical strikes," or efforts at boundary management—quarantines, barbed-wire fences, infrared scanners, and troop deployments.

The point I want to emphasize is that while these and related objects of detestation present themselves to Patriot consciousness as self-sufficient, autonomous beings, in reality they are devised from raw materials that Patriots have "cast apart" from themselves. That is to say, the Patriot enemy is its own project, its own collective projec*tion*. It is an outcome of the joint transference of the Patriots' *own* vanity, envy, rage, gluttony, greed, lust, and laziness onto an individual or group "out there" who can now be treated, eliminated, or expulsed. What proportion of Patriot transference is unconscious and what proportion is attributable to the cynical manipulations of politicians, preachers, and pundits is a separate question. Whatever the case, Patriots forget their role in the making of the monsters against whom they fight, which is another way of saying they are participants in political-military magic. By reforming, exorcising, or killing the symbol of death, they can pretend again and again to escape the most intolerable thing of all, their "greatest ownmost possibility," to quote Martin Heidegger (1962: 284), their death. This explains their "collective effervescence" (as Emile Durkheim [1954] calls it) when they learn of victory, for victory means "We are saved from Death!" It also explains why those offered up for the Patriot cause are honored as heroes: "They have died that we might live!"

The construction of the Patriot enemy follows a long-traveled four-step path: labeling, satanization, embedment, and sacrifice (Aho, 2011: 40–4).

- *Labeling.* By *labeling* is meant the coining of and imposition on a person or group of a slanderous title: "wop," "mick," "fag," "pinhead," "Commie-pig," "mooch," "fascist," "freeloader," etc. Although the characteristics of the defamed will naturally vary depending on historical circumstances, they must always have two qualities. First, they must be similar enough to Patriots as to be able to receive their projection (or, to say it technically, so that Patriots can see something of themselves in them). Second, they must be different enough from Patriots in skin color, eye shape, height, physiognomy, language, faith, desire, and/or behavior as to allow them to serve as *escapegoats*, to be able carry away from Patriots their own unassimilated rot and murderous-nous. Given that no one can actually avoid his or her own decline and death, of course, the affixing of defamatory labels is entirely fantastical. But Patriots lose sight of this, forget it in the momentary ecstasy of being able to identify "once and for all" who is behind the world's ills: "*It is Them!*"
- *Satanization* (Juergensmeyer, 2003) refers to the elaboration by Patriots of legends that explain why the labeled are, as supposed, carriers of death. Nowadays such myths are drawn from a combination of theology (It's because they harbor the Devil), biology (The evil is in their genes), pop-psychology (They have acquired a "culture of death"), or pop-sociology (Due to rapid social change, they've lost their "moral compass"). Typically,

these accounts are accompanied by anecdotes that detail the evil-doers' complicity in one or more primal crimes. These often involve violations of the orifices—the mouths, anuses, and/or genitals—of children or women that validate the label in the circular manner recounted in Chapter 4: How do we know they are evil? Because look what they've done. But how do we know they did it? Well, because they're evil. Whether the defamed admit to the libel or not is all the same. Indeed in a Kafkaesque way, the fervency of their denials often confirms their guilt. ("If they aren't guilty, then why are they so defensive?") However this may be, the crucial point to note about satanization is that it rhetorically absolves Patriots of their role—helps them forget their part—in the making of the enemy. The enemy's diabolism is invariably *the enemy's* fault. We are but innocent victims.

- *Embedment.*   When the libels and myths are instilled in the minds and hearts of children by Patriot parents, teachers, and peers, they come to be mistaken by those children as natural facts. That is, their actuality as social artifacts is (once more) forgotten or, more to the point, never learned. This is easier than it appears, for children are not present when the labels are first devised, not there when mythmakers compose their atrocity tales. Instead, they receive them as if they always already existed. As we saw earlier, it is not the years of formal education alone that determine why a child comes to despise a particular other. Rather, it is through content of the lessons they learn and/or the authoritarian pedagogy by which those lessons are instilled.

- *Sacrifice.*   The culminating step in diabolization is the "irrevocable act" (Fanon, 1963): the expulsion, imprisonment, beating, or slaying of the evil-doer. In the act of cleansing the republic of the American *anathema*, Patriots come to recognize, "re-know," its cultural *thema*, the values and institutions that make it exceptional and favored among nations. To be sure, this is a kind remembering (as opposed to a *dis*membering), for by means of it, Patriots are reunited on the basis of their shared hatred. But at a deeper level, the irrevocable act entails a profound *mis*-remembering. This is because, once again, Patriots forget, they overlook the fact that the villain being sacrificed is only an idol, a fetish of their own invention. This blindness reinforces the conviction of their blamelessness and amplifies their cruelty.

The cure, so to say, for any species of political fanaticism—right-wing or left—can be found only by reversing this four-step process. In other words, the actors in question must re-appropriate to themselves what they have heretofore jointly projected outward onto the other. To say it differently, they must "learn to live with the Devil" (Batchelor, 2004), to masticate, swallow, and reintegrate into themselves their own vileness, the existential fact that they are in decay and moving inexorably toward death. This can be momentarily denied but, in the end, there is no goat large enough to inveigle their escape.

Unfortunately, re-appropriation cannot be accomplished by the head alone. If that were possible, then readings in peace studies and multiculturalism would suffice. Instead, re-appropriation presupposes a conversion of the heart, and it is precisely here where the greatest challenge of Patriot forgetfulness becomes evident. For all their prating about salvation, many Patriots appear to have yet to undergo its precondition: "*a circumcision of the heart*" (Rom. 2:29).

St. Paul contrasts a wounding of the heart with genital circumcision, the ritual signifier of male entry into the Jewish community. According to Paul, a surgical cutting of the penis "means nothing" (1 Cor. 7:18–19). And as for those who "disturb" you about it, he prays that "the knife slips" and the *mohel* ends up slicing himself (Gal. 15:12). Rather, what is required, he says, is a painful realization of *my own* culpability, sin, and error, perhaps analogous to Jacob's awakening at Peniel (Gen. 32:26–32).

Jacob is a man with whom a Christian Patriot might well identify, an "extremely rich" owner of flocks, camels, asses, oxen, and slaves. The problem is that he has obtained his fortune partly through trickery and fraud (Gen. 25:29–34, 27:1–36, 30:25–43). Thus, he harbors a guilty conscience and, in a manner familiar to all of us, he unconsciously projects this guilt onto his victims, accusing *them* of fakery, fearing *their* revenge. "Greatly afraid of his wronged step-brother, Esau," Jacob tries to assuage him with flattery and gifts. These having failed, he takes his anxiety to bed, whereat he commences to "wrestle" with an "angel." In the course of the struggle, he is stricken in the sciatic nerve by the shocking realization that the enemy is not out there after all but right here in his devious heart. It is at this moment that he is rechristened and becomes the patriarch of Israel ("God contends" or "struggle with God" may be more literal meanings). Or, to use a favorite Patriot image, he is crowned a hero.

Naturally, there are multiple ways to read the story of Jacob, but one of the most compelling concerns the mistake made when we equate "holy war" (or "jihad") with skirmish against an external foe. To a truly circumcised Christian, the real holy war is a neverending, sweat-inducing *internal* struggle against the temptations of righteousness. When fought well, all the putative divisions that have heretofore blocked our path, between moochers and makers, producers and takers, between the "white and delightsome" and the "dark and loathsome," between the proponents of life and those of choice, between the Axis of Evil and the Alliance of the Free, collapse. They dissipate like fog on a spring morning. "There are no more distinctions between Jew and Greek, slave and free, male and female, but all of you are one" (Gal. 3:26–8). This is the lesson that Christian Patriots seem to have forgotten.

Moral forgetfulness is predicated on "the silence of others who for one reason or another indulge" it (Sharp, 1998: 135), which takes us back to the echo-chamber communication systems emblematic of the far-right. Their danger is not merely that they generate nonscientific certainties, which is true enough, but that they nurture prejudices and in this way prepare its audiences psychologically to commit detestable deeds in good conscience.

To gain clarity about our own insidiousness, "we need an honest, objective mirror," says Daryl Sharp. For the religiously inclined, this may involve something on the lines of private, anonymous confession to a priest, with a premium placed on a prior, detailed examination of conscience. A more secularized constituency, on the other hand, may favor one of a variety of depth psychologies: Freudian, Jungian, Adlerian, or the like. A still more promising venue may be a public tribunal of truth and reconciliation of the sort employed in post-apartheid South Africa during the middle 1990s (Villa-Vincencio & Doxtader, 2003). Here, perpetrators of violence (on both sides) confessed their crimes to those whom they had tormented in exchange for amnesty. Although cynics criticized them for inflaming an already volatile situation, evidence suggests that on the contrary, the hearings helped defuse hatreds by weakening the adhesive on the labels enemies had earlier fastened to one another, undermining the power of their mutually vilifying myths, and allowing them to see, perhaps for the first time, their shared humanity. Archbishop Desmond Tutu, who witnessed several tribunals, described them as profoundly touching and moving, as "something spiritual, even sacramental."

The exact way to self-knowledge, of course, takes us beyond our immediate concerns. What is important to acknowledge at this point is that "it is not enough to hate your enemy. You have to understand how the two of you bring each other to deep completion" (Don Delillo in Loy, 2010: 65). In other words, to deal effectively with the problem of loathing, we need to focus less on the wrongness of Them and more on the smugness of Us, to unsparingly critique again and again our surprised "Who me?" innocence and realize that we could be the enemy.

Epilogue

A Latter-Day Fortress

In 2012, a cohort of self-described Christian survivalists from northern Idaho announced formation of an "exit strategy" from the "firestorm" they prophesied was about to engulf the nation: a constitutionally correct, biblically sanctified community known as "the Citadel" (Citadel.com). "Establishment Republicans," said the advertising brochure, were discouraged from applying for membership, along with Marxists, liberals, and non-Christians (Citadel spokespeople consider themselves to be "religious separatists," not racial separatists [SurvivalBlog.com]). The literary inspiration for the Citadel is Ayn Rand's fabled mountain refuge for the 1 percent, Galt's Gulch; its architectural model is the medieval fortress of Rothenburg ob der Tauber in Germany.

Those accepted for membership into the Citadel are given the title "Pioneers." Pioneers are required to come equipped with and be proficient in the use of "the American icon of liberty," the gun. None are granted title to their lots but "lease" them for a monthly fee from a corporation. Although the corporation's directors say that the Federal Reserve System is the cause of the impending firestorm alluded to earlier, lessees are told that "FRNs" (Federal Reserve notes) are acceptable legal tender, as are credit cards and PayPal entries. Restrictive covenants require that Citadel housing be constructed from poured concrete. Pioneers, however, are granted the "liberty" to choose their own facades and color schemes.

Plans are for the Citadel to encompass several thousand backwoods acres, enough to accommodate 3,500 to 7,000 families. They will be housed behind by a low outer wall and a second, higher internal wall with guard towers (that contain condominium units). Inside these two walls, different neighborhoods will be sealed off in such a way as to provide clear gunfire sightlines in the event of an invasion. Each neighborhood in turn will have its own aesthetic: log cabin, ranch style, colonial, and so on. In addition to the standard accoutrements of circa 1950s small-town America with its farmer's market, church steeples, walkways, parks, and banks (that issue gold and silver coins), the Citadel will have bomb shelters, and its major employer will be a firearms factory, the III Arms Company. The Citadel will also have boarding schools that "educate not indoctrinate," an interactive firearms museum, "one of the finest, most comprehensive libraries in the nation," "quaint" bed and breakfast inns, an

RV park, and a "high end" hotel for tourists, for the idea is that the Citadel serve as a "premier" vacation destination, along the lines of Disneyland. In other words, it is intended as a Christian Patriot theme park, a profit-making simulacrum of a past that never was, a case study in sentimental nostalgia.

The first "beachhead" of the Citadel, a showcase of housing designs, has already been erected on a pine-treed mountaintop. Citizens from the surrounding towns have responded with a mixture of Chamber of Commerce–like pride, fascination, and (with memories of the one-time *Brüders Schweigen* still resonant) terror. Citadel spokespeople have warned county fathers that if they "fail to offer suitable incentives" for them to stay, they will relocate elsewhere within what they call the "American Redoubt" (whose borders are identical to the five-state Pacific Northwest White Aryan Bastion once advertised by the Aryan Nations Church), preferably, in Wyoming or Montana.

Appendix

American Right-Wing-Implicated Fatalities from 1980 to 2015

What follows is a conservative list of American right-wing related fatalities, including suicides and activist-initiated police killings, since late December 1979. The list excludes state executions of convicted right-wing terrorists (such as Frank Spisak Jr.) as well as police slayings of unarmed, poor minority people, although some of these appear to have been motivated partly by far-right sentiments.

Women have long been feared by men and occasionally hated (Lederer, 1968). What is new, at least in my experience, is political gynocide, the killing of women for ideological reasons. The clearest documented example of this, not mentioned in the following list because it occurred in Canada, is Marc Lépine's shooting to death of 14 female engineering students in Montreal, Dec. 6, 1989. In his suicide note, Lépine wrote that "feminists have always ruined my life" (Fox & Levin, 2005: 229). He had compiled a hit-list of nineteen other "radical feminists" whose lives he was forced to spare, he wrote, owing to "lack of time." The closest American approximation to this concerns mass murderer "Jo Jo" Hennard (see list, Oct. 16, 1991). Hennard was enraged by a recent Supreme Court nomination hearing and by his belief that the male nominee in question had been sexually harassed by a female underling. He accused feminists of causing the decline of civilization and had earlier filed a civil rights complaint with the local FBI against women of the world, claiming they are "treacherous vipers" (Fox & Levin, 2005: 232–3).

The list that follows does not count death threats made against government officials, nonfatal assassination attempts, or nonfatal assaults or shootings of homosexuals, immigrants, or other minorities. It omits nonfatal bombings of gay bars, government facilities, and abortion clinics, and cases in which the victim(s) later killed themselves (e.g., the Mexican American teenager who was beaten and sodomized with a patio umbrella pole by local skinheads at a lawn party, underwent 30 surgeries, and subsequently took his own life). Finally, it does not include incidents in which the perpetrator(s) in question had no known neo-Nazi, Klan, or related affiliations. This includes the killers of gay college student Mathew Shepherd, in Laramie, WY (Oct. 6, 1998), and Jared Loughner, who shot to death five individuals and a federal judge, before critically wounding a U.S. Congresswoman in Phoenix, AZ (Jan. 8, 2011).

While there is evidence in both cases that the assailants were influenced by popular hate media, they were not known members of hate groups.

More difficult to classify are racist skinhead gang murders, which are estimated to have totaled more than 50 from 1987 to 2001 (Zeskind, 2009: 344). Many of these, however, turn out to have been intragroup or intergang rivalry killings (such as that of skinhead leader David Lynch, who was fatally wounded on March 3, 2011, and Jeff Hall, a noted neo-Nazi, who was shot to death by his young son several months later). There have also been occasional murders by skinheads of their own parents (cf. Bryan and David Freeman, Feb. 27, 1995), as well as random street attacks on the homeless or on otherwise compromised victims (such as the African American woman killed by Walter Dille Jr., in 2007 during a botched carjacking). Only those skinhead attacks that appear to have been ideologically motivated are listed here.

Vile words are the subject of this book, and they are, of course, distinguishable from violent acts, but they are not entirely separable. When hostile, dehumanizing rhetoric is coupled with other factors, the likelihood of bloodshed goes up. Among these additional factors are easy access to firearms and explosives, the availability of a human target (due to the target's isolation or physical vulnerability), permissive gun laws, structured segregation from target populations, and cultural norms that recommend violence as a solution to personal slights or imagined injustices. (For a detailed consideration of these and related factors citing cross-cultural examples, see Levin and Rabrenovic [2004] .)

For further information on these incidents, see *Facts on File*, "Terror from the Right" by the Southern Poverty Law Center (http://www.splcenter.org/get-informed/publications/terror-from-the-right), and local newspaper articles for the relevant incidents.

Date	Place	Perpetrators and Orientation	Fatalities
Nov. 1979	Greensboro, NC	Neo-Nazi and KKK activists	5
Sept. 1980	New York	Joseph Christopher, neo-Nazi	7
1976–80	Salt Lake City, UT, etc.	Joseph P. Franklin, neo-Nazi and KKK	13[a]
Mar. 1981	Alabama	James Knowles, Henry Hays, United Klans	2
1982	Cleveland, OH	Frank Spisak, Jr., neo-Nazi, antigay	3
1982	Oroville, CA	"Red" Warthan, neo-Nazi	1
1982	Winder, GA	John McMillan, KKK	1[b]
1982	Arkansas	Ralph Snell, Covenant, Sword and the Arm of the Lord	2
Feb. 13, 1983	Medina, ND	Kahl family, Posse Comitatus	2
June 3, 1983	Walnut Ridge, AK	Gordon Kahl, Posse Comitatus	2[b]
1984	Kootenai County, ID	*Brüders Schweigen*	1
June 18, 1984	Denver, CO	*Brüders Schweigen*	1
July 18, 1984	San Ysidro, CA	James Huberty, survivalist, anti-immigrant[d]	22[b]
Oct. 1984	Cairo, NE	Arthur Kirk, Posse Comitatus	1[b]
Dec. 8, 1984	Whidbey Island, WA	Robert Mathews, *Brüders Schweigen*	1[b]
Apr. 1985	Boise, ID	Eugene Kinerk, Aryan Nations	1[c]
Apr. 15, 1985	Arkansas	David Tate, Aryan Nations	1
Summer 1985	Rulo, NE	Michael Ryan, Tim Haverkamp, Christian Identity	2
Dec. 24, 1985	Seattle, WA	David Rice, anti-Semite	4

Date	Place	Perpetrators and Orientation	Fatalities
May 16, 1986	Cokeville, WY	David and Doris Young, racists[e]	2[c]
Jan. 7, 1987	Shelby, NC	Probable White Patriot Party, antigay	5
1987	Chicago, IL	Jonathan Hayes, Aryan supremacist	1
1987	Bonner County, IA	Robert Pires, The Order Strike Force II	1
Jan. 1988	Marion, UT	Adam Swapp, antigovernment	1
Nov. 1988	Portland, OR	East Side White Pride, anti-immigrant	1
Jan. 7, 1989	Stockton, CA	"General" Patrick Purdy, white supremacist	6[f]
1991	Ft. Worth, TX	William Brodsky, racist skinhead	1
May 1991	Jacksonville, FL	Church of the Creator, neo-Nazi	1
Oct. 16, 1991	Killeen, TX	"Jo Jo" Hennard, misogynist	23
Aug. 21–31, 1992	Ruby Ridge, ID	Weaver family, Aryan Nations	2 (2[b])
Mar. 10, 1993	Pensacola, FL	Michael Griffin, antiabortion	1
Dec. 30, 1994	Brookline, MA	John Salvi, antiabortion	2
Feb. 1, 1995	Tilly, AR	Chevi and Cheyne Kehoe, Aryan People's Republic	4
Apr. 19, 1995	Oklahoma City, OK	Timothy McVeigh, Terry Nichols, antigovernment	168
Oct. 9, 1995	Hyder, AZ	Sons of Gestapo	1
Dec. 7, 1995	Fayetteville, AK	James Burmeister, Randy Meadows, neo-Nazi	2
Jan. 1996	Ohio	Aryan Republican Army	1[c]
Apr. 12, 1996	Jackson, MS	Larry Shoemake, neo-Nazi	1
July 27, 1996	Atlanta, GA	Eric Rudolph, Army of God (see also Jan. 29, 1998)	1

Date	Place	Perpetrators and Orientation	Fatalities
Dec. 1996	Denver, CO	Nathan Thill, neo-Nazi, anti-immigrant	1
July 24, 1997	Chelan, WA	Jason Bush, anti-immigrant (see also June 12, 2009)	1
Jan. 29, 1998	Birmingham, AL	Army of God, antiabortion	1
May 29, 1998	Cortez, CO	Alan Pilon, Robert Mason, Jason McVean, antigovernment	3[c]
June 7, 1998	Jasper, TX	John King et al., KKK	1
July 4, 1998	Las Vegas, NV	Ross Hack, racist skinhead	2
Oct. 23, 1998	Amherst, NY	James Kopp, antiabortion	1
July 1, 1999	Redding, CA	Benjamin Williams, James Williams, Christian Identity	3[c]
July 2, 1999	Illinois, IN	Benjamin Smith, Church of the Creator (neo-Nazi)	3[c]
July 20, 1999	Happy Valley, CA	Matthew Williams, antigay	2
Aug. 10, 1999	Los Angeles, CA	Buford Furrow, Aryan Nations	1
Nov. 23, 1999	Elkhart, IN	Alex Witmer, Jason Powell, Aryan Brotherhood	1
Apr. 28, 2000	Pittsburg, PA	Richard Baumhammers, Free Market Party	5
Aug. 2001	Sampson County, NC	Church of the National Knights of the KKK	1
Sept. 15, 2001	Dallas, TX	Mark Stroman, Aryan Brotherhood, anti-Muslim	2
Dec. 11, 2001	Culver City, CA	David Rubin, Earl Krugel, JDL[g] (anti-Muslim)	1[c]
Feb. 2, 2003	New Bedford, MA	Jacob Robida, antigay	1
Feb.–Mar. 2003	New York City	Larme Price, anti-immigrant	5
July 2003	Michigan	Scott Woodring, Michigan Militia	2[b]
Aug. 2003	Boston, MA	Joseph Druce, antigay, anti-Semite	2

Date	Place	Perpetrators and Orientation	Fatalities
Jan. 9, 2004	Dateland, AZ	Anti-immigrant skinheads	1
May 24, 2004	Tulsa, OK	Wade Lay, Christopher Lay, antigovernment	1
June 15, 2006	Yonkers, NY	Anti-immigrant skinheads	1
June 25, 2007	Salt Lake City, UT	Curtis Allgier, white supremacist	1
July 12, 2008	Shenandoah, PA	Anti-immigrant skinheads	1
July 27, 2008	Knoxville, TN	Jim Adkisson, antigay	2
Dec. 7, 2008	Queens, NY	Anti-immigrant skinheads	1
Jan. 21, 2009	Brockton, MA	Keith Luke, antigovernment, racist	2
Feb. 27, 2009	Miramar Beach, FL	Dannie Roy Baker, anti-immigrant	2
Apr. 4, 2009	Pittsburg, PA	Richard Poplawski, racist, anti-Semite	3
Apr. 25, 2009	Okaloosa County, FL	Joshua Cartwright, antigovernment	2
May 31, 2009	Wichita, KS	Scott Roeder, antiabortion	1
June 10, 2009	Washington, DC	James von Brunn, neo-Nazi, antigovernment	1
June 12, 2009	Arivaca, AZ	Shawna Forde, Minutemen, anti-immigrant	2
Oct. 2009	Phoenix, AZ	Travis Ricci and Araron Schmidt, racist skinheads	1
Oct. 31, 2009	Seattle, WA	Christopher Monfort, antigovernment	1
Feb. 18, 2010	Austin, TX	Joseph Stack, antigovernment	3[c]
Mar. 4, 2010	Washington, DC	John Bedell, antigovernment	1[b]
May 6, 2010	Phoenix, AZ	Gary Kelly, anti-immigrant	1
May 20, 2010	West Memphis, AR	Joseph/Jerry Kane, antigovernment	4[b]

Date	Place	Perpetrators and Orientation	Fatalities
Jun. 11, 2010	Arizona	Federation for Anti-immigrant Reform	1
Aug. 21, 2010	Baltimore, MD	Jermaine Holley, anti-immigrant	1
Jan. 2011	Cooperstown, ND	Daniel Wacht, racist skinhead	1
June 26, 2011	Jackson, MS	Ten-member teenage racist gang	1
July 18, 2011	Summit, NJ	Anti-immigrant skinheads	1
Sept. 2011	Pacific Northwest	David "Joey" Pederson, Aryan Death Squad	4
Dec. 5, 2011	Long County, GA	Issac Aguigui, the Family, antigovernment	2
Jan. 1, 2012	Rainier National Park, WA	Benjamin Barsins, antigovernment survivalist	2[c]
Jan. 26, 30, 2013	Paradise Valley, AZ	Michael Crane, antigovernment	3
May 2, 2012	Gilbert, AZ	Jason Ready, U.S. Border Guard, neo-Nazi[h]	5[c]
Aug. 6, 2012	Oak Creek, WI	Wade Page, Hammerskin Nation, racist	7[i]
Aug. 16, 2012	New Orleans, LA	Brian/Terry Smith et al., antigovernment	2
Mar. 19, 2013	Colorado, TX	Evan Ebel, 211 Crew (racist skinhead)	4[j]
July 2013	Jonesville, SC	Jeremy and Christine Moody, skinheads	2[k]
Nov. 1, 2013	San Diego, CA	Paul Ciancia, antigovernment	1
Apr. 13, 2014	Kansas City, MO	"Francis Cross," White Patriot Party (neo-Nazi)	3
June 6, 2014	Cummings, GA	Dennis Marx, antigovernment	1[b]
June 8, 2014	Las Vegas, NV	Jerad and Amanda Miller, antigovernment	5[b,]
Sept. 12, 2014	Blooming Grove, PA	Eric Frein, antigovernment survivalist	1
Nov. 28, 2014	Austin, TX	Larry McQuilliams, antigovernment, anti-immigrant	1[b]

Date	Place	Perpetrators and Orientation	Fatalities
Feb. 10, 2015	Orlando, FL	Joseph Paffen, Sovereign Citizen	1[b]
Feb. 10, 2015	Chapel Hill, NC	Craig Hicks, anti-Muslim	3
Feb. 27, 2015	Tallahasse, FL	Curtis Holley, Sovereign Citizen	2[b]
Mar. 19, 2015	Mesa, AZ	Ryan Giroux, racist skinhead	1
June 17, 2015	Charleston, SC	Dylann Roof, Council of Conservative Citizens, racist	9
June 18, 2015	Tonasket, WA	James Faire, Sovereign Citizen	1

Notes

a Murders for which perpetrator was indicted or to which he confessed.

b Includes perpetrator's death by police.

c Includes perpetrator's suicide.

d There is evidence that Huberty subscribed to the Mid-American Aryan Nations. Most of his victims were Hispanic.

e The Youngs took a grade school hostage to extort ransom from Congress for the founding of a racially pure utopian society. While there are indications that David was a member of a Posse Comitatus unit, authorities consider his ties "uncertain."

f School massacre with five Southeast Asian victims, followed by assailant's suicide.

g Jewish Defense League.

h U.S. Border Guard is a private militia.

i Murder of six American Sikh worshippers, followed by assailant's suicide.

j After Ebel was killed in a shootout, police found a hit-list on Ebel's body with the names of more than twenty public officials, one of whom he had already murdered.

k The victims were a registered sex offender and his wife.

References

Acocella, Joan (2013). "What the Hell." *The New Yorker*, May 27: 82–5.

Activist Post (Sept. 4, 2013). *NorCal County Votes to Secede, Create New State "Jefferson"* (consulted Sept. 9, 2013). At: http://www.activistpost.com/2013/09/norcal-county-votes-to-secede-create.html

Adorno, Theodor, Frenkl-Brunswik, Else, Levinson, Daniel J. and Sanford, Nevitt. (1950). *The Authoritarian Personality*. New York, NY: Harper.

Aho, James (1990). *The Politics of Righteousness*. Seattle, WA: University of Washington Press.

Aho, James (1994). *This Thing of Darkness*. Seattle, WA: University of Washington Press.

Aho, James (1998). *The Things of the World: A Social Phenomenology*. Westport, CT: Praeger.

Aho, James (1999). "White Man as a Social Construct." *European Legacy* 4: 62–72.

Aho, James (2005). *Confession and Bookkeeping*. Albany, NY: State University of New York Press.

Aho, James (2006). "The Danse Macabre." *Sociological Spectrum* 26: 387–403.

Aho, James (2011). *Sociological Trespasses: Interrogating Sin and Flesh*. Lanham, MD: Lexington Books.

Alexander, Michelle (2012). *The New Jim Crow*. New York, NY: The New Press.

Alman, Ashley (2013). *Larry Klayman Tells Obama to "Put the Quran Down" at Veterans Rally* (consulted Oct. 15, 2013). At: http://www.huffingtonpost.com/2013/10/13/larry-klayman-obama-quran_n_4094589.html

Altemeyer, Bob (1988). *Enemies of Freedom*. San Francisco, CA: Jossey-Bass.

Andersen, Rosanna (2014). "Tea Party." *Idaho State Journal*, Jan. 28, p. A6.

Arendt, Hannah (1967 [1951]). *The Origins of Totalitarianism*. Cleveland, OH: The World Publishing Co.

Armstrong, Karen (2000). *The Battle for God*. New York, NY: Alfred Knopf.

Aronson, Elliott, and Patnoe, Shelley (1997). *The Jigsaw Classroom*. New York, NY: Longman.

Atlas Society (2000). *Nietzsche and Ayn Rand*. At: http://www.atlassociety.org/Nietzsche-and-ayn-rand

Augustine, St. (1960). *Confessions of St. Augustine*, trans. by John Ryan. Garden City, NY: Doubleday & Co.

Bailey, Juanita (2013). "Earl Column." *Idaho State Journal*, Aug. 15, p. A6.

Baker, C. B. (1985). "Soviet Weather Mayhem." *Youth Action News*, Nov.

Bamford, James (2008). *The Shadow Factory*. New York, NY: Doubleday.

Barkun, Michael (1996). *Religion and the Racist Right*. Chapel Hill, NC: University of North Carolina Press.

Barna, George (2008). *Survey Reveals the Life Christians Desire* (consulted Jan. 12, 2013). At: http://www.barna.org/barna-update/article/18-congregations/29-survey-reveals-life-christians-desire

Barron, Bruce (1992). *Heaven on Earth?* Grand Rapids, MI: Zondervan.

Barton, David (2011). *The Founding Fathers and Slavery* (consulted Oct. 14, 2011). At: http://www.wallbuilders.com/libissuesarticles.asp?id=122

Batchelor, Stephen (2004). *Living with the Devil*. New York, NY: Riverhead Books.

Becker, Gary (2005). *Sell the Right to Immigrate* (consulted June 8, 2013). At: http://www.becker-posnerblog.com/2005/02/sell-the-right-to-immigrate-becker.html

Becker, Ernest (1975). *Escape from Evil*. New York, NY: Free Press.

Beckman, Martin "Red," and Benson, William (1985). *The Law That Never Was*. South Holland, IL: Constitutional Research Associates.

Bennet, John C. (1842). *History of the Saints; Or, An Expose of Joe Smith and Mormonism*. Boston: Leland & Whiting.

Berger, Peter, and Luckmann, Thomas (1967). *The Social Construction of Reality*. New York, NY: Doubleday-Anchor.

Berman, Marshall (1988). *All That Is Solid Melts into the Air*. New York, NY: Penguin.

Blee, Kathleen (2002). *Inside Organized Racism*. Berkeley, CA: University of California Press.

Bobo, Lawrence, and Bobo, Fred (1989). "Education and Political Tolerance." *Public Opinion Quarterly* 53: 547–59.

Bobo, Lawrence, Kluegel, James, and Smith, Ryan (1997). "Laissez-Faire Racism: The Crystallization of a Kinder, Gentler, Anti-Black Ideology," in Steven Tuch and Jack Martin (eds.), *Racial Attitudes in the 1990s* (pp. 15–44). Westport, CT: Praeger.

Bonillo-Silva, Eduardo (2003). *Racism without Racists*. Lanham, MD: Rowman & Littlefield.

Bowe, John (2010). *Bound for America* (consulted Jan. 29, 2014). At: http://www.motherjones.com/politics/2010/05/immigration-law-indentured-servitude

Boyd, Gregory (2007). *Myth of a Christian Nation*. Grand Rapids, MI: Zondervan.

Boyd, Deanna, and Chen, Kendra (n.d.). *The History and Experience of African Americans in America's Post Service* (consulted Nov. 11, 2013). At: http://www.postalmuseum.si.edu/africanamericans/

Brantley, Max (2012). *Loy Mauch Update: The Republican Rep is on Record on Slavery, Too* (consulted Aug. 7, 2015). At: http://www.arktimes.com/ArkansasBlog/archives/2012/10/06/loy-mauch-update-the-republican-rep-is-on-record-on-slavery-too

British Centre for Science Education (2007). *In Extremis: Rousas Rushdoony and his Connections* (consulted Sept. 20, 2011). At: http://www.bcseweb.org.uk/index.php/Main/RousasRushdoony

Brown, Tim (2013). *Obama Eligibility Attorney ... Sets Date for Revolution to End Obama's "Reign of Terror"* (consulted Oct. 15, 2013). At: http://freedomoutpost.com/2013/09/obama-eligibility-attorney-larry-klayman-sets-date-for-revolution-to-end-obamas-reign-of-terror/

Buchanan, Pat (2008). *A Brief for Whitey* (consulted Sept. 5, 2014). At: http://www.buchanan.org/blog/pjb-a-brief-for-whitey.969

Burghart, Devin (2014). *Status of the Tea Party Movement: Part Two* (consulted Jan. 27, 2014). At: http://www.IREHR.org/issue-areas/tea-party-nationalism

Campbell, J. B. (2011). *The Military Solution* (consulted Mar. 17, 2013). At: http://www.JBCampbellextremismonline.com

Camus, Albert (1956 [1947]). *The Rebel*, trans. by Anthony Bower. New York, NY: Vintage.

Capehart, Jonathan (2013). *The Irrational Fear of President Obama* (consulted Oct. 16, 2013). At: http://www.washingtonpost.com/blogs/post-partisan/wp/2013/10/16/the-irrational-fear-of-president-obama/

Cass, Connie (2013). *Poll: Americans Don't Trust One Ano*ther (consulted Dec. 4, 2013). At: http://www.usatoday.com/story/news/nation/2013/11/30/poll-americans-dont-trust-one-another/3792179/

Cassidy, John (2013). *Pope Francis's Challenge to Global Capitalism.* (consulted May 5, 2014). At: http://www.newyorker.com/news/john-cassidy/pope-franciss-challenge-to-global-capitalism

Cassidy, John (2014). "Forces of Divergence." *The New Yorker*, March 31: 69–73.

Celock, John (2012). *Jon Hubbard, Arkansas Legislator, Says Slavery May "Have Been a Blessing" in New Book* (consulted May 14, 2013). At: http://www.huffingtonpost.com/2012/10/05/jon-hubbard-arkansas-slavery-book_n_1943661.html

Chalmers, David (1981 [1965]). *Hooded Americanism*. New York, NY: Franklin Watts.

Cherry, Conrad (ed.) (1998). *God's New Israel*. Chapel Hill, NC: University of North Carolina Press.

Chumley, Cheryl (2014). *Operation American Spring Falls Flat* (consulted May 17, 2014). At: http://www.washingtontimes.com/news/2014/may/16/operation-american-spring-falls-flat-very-disappoi/

Clapp, Rodney (1987). "Democracy as Heresy." *Christianity Today* 31 (3): 17–23.

Clarkson, Frederick (1997). *Eternal Hostility*. Monroe, ME: Common Courage.

Cohn, Norman (1967). *Warrant for Genocide*. New York, NY: Oxford University Press.

Cohn, Norman (1975). *Europe's Inner Demons*. New York: Basic Books.

Collins, Randall (1982). *Sociological Insight*. New York, NY: Oxford University Press.

Congressional Budget Office (2011). *Trends in the Distribution of Household Income between 1979 and 2007* (consulted Oct. 23, 2012). At: http://www.cbo.gov/publication/42729

Corcoran, James (1996). *Bitter Harvest*. Boulder, CO: Westview Press.

Covenant, Sword and the Arm of the Lord (CSA) (n.d.). *Prepare War.* Pontiac, MO: CSA Bookstore.

Crawford, Jarah (1984). *Last Battle Cry*. Middlebury, VT: Jann.

Daily Beast (2014). *Utah Man Gives Up Gay Marriage Hunger Strik*e (consulted Jan. 7, 2014). At: http://www.thedailybeast.com/articles/2014/01/06/utah-man-gives-up-gay-marriage-hunger-strike.html

Daily Kos (2009). *Rep. Paul Broun Uses "Holy Water" against Obama* (consulted Oct. 13, 2014). At: http://www.dailykos.com/story/2009/01/15/684419/-Rep-Paul-Broun-uses-Holy-Water-against-Obama#

Daugherty, Ron (2013). "The Obituary for the U.S." *Idaho State Journal*, July 24, p. A6.

DeHaven, Tad (2011). *Toward A Solvent U.S. Postal System* (consulted Nov. 11, 2013). At: http://www.forbes.com/sites/realspin/2011/10/10/toward-a-solvent-u-s-postal-system/

Delillo, Don (1985). *White Noise*. New York, NY: Viking.

Diamond, Sara (1995). *Roads to Dominion*. New York, NY: Guilford.

Donovan, Lauren (2013). *Tiny North Dakota Town Stunned to Learn of White Supremacist's Plans* (consulted Aug. 25, 2012). At: http://bismarcktribune.com/

news/local/tiny-north-dakota-town-stunned-to-learn-of-white-supremacist/article_f21e5568-0bf5-11e3-bbd5-0019bb2963f4.html

Dorrien, Gary (2009). *Social Ethics in the Making*. Malden, MA: Wiley-Blackwell.

Dray, Philip (2010). *There's Power in a Union*. New York, NY: Doubleday.

Drudge, Matt (2013). *Poll: 29 % of Registered Voters Believe Armed Revolution Might be Necessary in Next Few Years* (consulted May 2, 2013). At: http://www.drudgereportarchives.net/article.php?ID = 4133498

Durkheim, Emile (1954). *The Elementary Forms of Religious Life*, trans. by J. W. Swain. Glencoe, IL: Free Press.

Dyer, Joel (1997). *Harvest of Rage*. Boulder, CO: Westview Press.

Earl, Lance (2013a). "A Declaration of War." *Idaho State Journal*, May 6, p. A6.

Earl, Lance (2013b). "As President, I Will … " *Idaho State Journal*, Sept. 15, p. C1.

Earl, Lance (2013c). "Reply to a Coward." *Idaho State Journal*, May 27, p. A6.

Earl, Lance (2013d). "The Things I Know." *Idaho State Journal*, Apr. 28, p. A6.

Earl, Lance (2014). "Letter-to-the Editor." *Idaho State Journal*, Feb. 13, p A6..

Edsall, Thomas (1984). "The Hidden Prosperity of the 1970s." *Public Interest* Fall: 37–61.

Emry, Sheldon (1981). *Bible Law on Money*. Phoenix, AZ: Lord's Covenant Church.

Emry, Sheldon (1984). *Billion$ for Bankers*. Phoenix, AZ: Lord's Covenant Church.

Ewing, Heidi, and Grady, Rachel (2006). *Jesus Camp* [video] (consulted Dec. 2, 2011). At: http://www.youtube.com/watch?v=6RNfL61VWCE

Fanon, Frantz (1963). *Wretched of the Earth*, trans. by C. Farrington. New York, NY: Grove Press.

Farias, Victor (1989). *Heidegger and Nazism*, trans. by Paul Burrell, ed. by Joseph Margolis and Tom Rockmore. Philadelphia, PA: Temple University Press.

Fay, Brian (1996). *Contemporary Philosophy of Social Science*. Hoboken, NJ: Wiley-Blackwell.

Fischer, Bryan (2011a). *Islam and the First Amendment* (consulted Jan. 4, 2012). At: http://www.afa.net/Blogs/BlogPost.aspx?id

Fischer, Bryan (2011b). *Muslim Immigration to the US is 'Toxic Cancer'* (consulted Jan. 4, 2012). At: http://talkingpointsmemo.com/muckraker/bryan-fischer-muslim-immigration-to-the-u-s-is-a-toxic-cancer

Flynn, Kevin, and Gerhardt, Gary (1990). *The Silent Brotherhood*. New York, NY: Signet.

Forest, James (ed.) (2006). *The Making of a Terrorist, Volume 1: Recruitment*. Westport, CT: Praeger Security International.

Fox, James, and Levin, Jack (2005). *Extreme Killing*. Thousand Oaks, CA: Sage.

Fraud (n.d.). *Federal Reserve Fraud and the "Invisible Government"* (consulted Nov. 16, 2011). At: http://www.healthfreedom.info/Federal_Research_Fraud.htm

Friedman, Milton (1970). "The Social Responsibility of Business Is to Increase Its Profits." *New York Times Magazine*, Sept. 13.

Friedman, Milton, and Friedman, Rose (1980). *Free to Choose*. New York, NY: Harcourt Brace Jovanovich.

Fuller, Jaime (2014). *Everything You Need to Know about the Long Fight between Cliven Bundy and the Federal Government* (consulted Apr. 16, 2014). At:http://www.washingtonpost.com/news/the-fix/wp/2014/04/15/everything-you-need-to-know-about-the-long-fight-between-cliven-bundy-and-the-federal-government/

Gardner, Amy (2009). *Va. Candidate McDonnell Says Views Changed Since He Wrote Thesis* (consulted Sept. 10, 2014). At: http://www.washingtonpost.com/wp-dyn/content/article/2009/08/29/AR2009082902434.html

Garrett, Thomas (2010). *U.S. Income Inequality: It's Not So Bad* (consulted Oct. 12, 2013). At: https://www.stlouisfed.org/Publications/Inside-The-Vault/Spring-2010/US-Income-Inequality-Its-Not-So-Bad

Geuss, Raymond (1981). *The Idea of a Critical Theory.* Cambridge: Cambridge University Press.

Gilbert, Keith (1986). "Affidavit and Genocide Convention Complaint of Keith Gilbert to the United Nations." Notarized mimeograph, Boise, ID, Oct. 21.

Gilson, Dave (2012). *Most Red States Take More Money from Washington than They Put in* (consulted Aug. 15, 2013). At: http://www.motherjones.com/politics/2011/11/states-federal-taxes-spending-charts-maps

Gini Index–Mundi (n.d.). *Countries Ranked by GINI Index–Mundi* (consulted Sept. 13, 2013). At: http://www.indexmundi.com/facts/indicators/SI.POV.GINI/rankings

Goffman, Erving (1959). *The Presentation of Self in Everyday Life.* New York: Doubleday-Anchor.

Goffman, Erving (1979). *Gender Advertisements.* New York, NY: Harper & Row.

Goldberg, Jonah (2007). *Liberal Fascism: The Secret History of the American Left.* New York, NY: Doubleday.

Goldberg, Michelle (2007). *Kingdom Coming.* New York, NY: Vintage.

Grann, David (1999). *Where W. Got Compassion* (consulted Feb. 14, 2011). At: http://www.nytimes.com/1999/09/12/magazine/where-w-got-compassion.html?pagewanted=all&src=pm

Greenberg, Brad (2008). *Racism Colors Judicial Bid* (consulted Jan. 29, 2014). At: http://www.jewishjournal.com/los_angeles/article/racism_colors_judicial_bid_20080528/

Gregor, A. James (2006). *The Search for Neofascism.* New York, NY: Cambridge University Press.

Gregory, David (1988). "Catholic Labor Theory and the Transformation of Work." *Washington and Lee Law Review* 119: 119–57.

Griffin, Susan (1992). *A Chorus of Stones.* New York, NY: Doubleday.

Grimstead, Jay (n.d.). *Coalition on Revival Web Page* (consulted Dec. 23, 2011). At: http://www.reformation.net/

Gross, Terry (2011). *A Leading Figure in the New Apostolic Reformation* [video interview] (consulted Oct. 5, 2012). At: http://www.npr.org/2011/10/03/140946482/apostolic-leader-weighs-religions-role-in-politics

Grosz, Stephen (2013). *The Examined Life.* New York, NY: Norton & Co., Inc.

Guinness, Os (1993). *Dining with the Devil.* Grand Rapids, MI: Baker Book House.

Gusfield, Joseph (1980 [1963]). *Symbolic Crusade.* Westport, CT: Greenwood Press.

Hall-Jamieson, Kathleen, and Cappella, Joseph (2008). *Echo Chamber: Rush Limbaugh and the Conservative Media Establishment.* New York, NY: Oxford University Press.

Hamilton, Richard (1982). *Who Voted for Hitler?* Princeton, NJ: Princeton University Press.

Hamner, Suzanne (2014). *Operation American Spring: General and Colonel Call for A Massive March on Washington* (consulted Aug. 7, 2015). At: http://www.freedomoutpost.com/2014/01/operation-American-Spring

Harden, Garrett (1968). "The Tragedy of the Commons." *Science,* 162 (3859): 1243–8.

Harnden, Toby (2009). *Barack Obama Faces 30 Death Threats a Day* (consulted Mar. 12, 2012). At: http://www.telegraph.co.uk/news/worldnews/barackobama/5967942/Barack-Obama-faces-30-death-threats-a-day-stretching-US-Secret-Service.html

Hartz, Louis (1955). *Liberal Tradition in America*. New York, NY: Harcourt, Brace.

Hay, Malcolm (1981). *The Roots of Christian Anti-Semitism*. New York, NY: Anti-Defamation League of B'nai B'rith.

Hedges, Chris (2006). *American Fascists: The Christian Right and the War on America*. New York, NY: Free Press.

Heidegger, Martin (1962). *Being and Time*, trans. by J. Macquarrie and E. Robinson. New York: Harper & Row.

Heidegger, Martin (1995). *The Fundamental Concepts of Metaphysics*, trans. by W. McNeil. Bloomington, IN: Indiana University Press.

Hofstadter, Richard (1959). *Social Darwinism in American Thought,* rev. ed. New York, NY: George Brazillier.

Hofstadter, Richard (1963). *The Paranoid Style in American Politics and Other Essays*. Cambridge, MA: Harvard University Press.

Hofstadter, Richard (1964). "Pseudo-Conservatism Revisited," in Daniel Bell (ed.), *The Radical Right* (pp. 97–103). New York, NY: Doubleday-Anchor.

Homans, George (1961). *Social Behavior*. New York, NY: Harcourt, Brace & World.

Hyman, Sean (2013). *The Biblical Money Code* (consulted Aug. 10, 2013). At: http://www.w3.newsmax.com/.../video_money_codeb.cfm?...code...

Ingersoll, Julie (2011). *Dominion Theology, Christian Reconstructionism, and the New Apostolic Reformation* (consulted Feb. 21, 2011). At: http://religiondispatches.org/dominion-theology-christian-reconstructionism-and-the-new-apostolic-reformation/

Jacobs, Cindy (2011). *Birds Dying Because of DADT Repeal* [video] (consulted Mar. 8, 2011). At: http://www.youtube.com/watch?v=17WGTvPHGg

Jeffness, The (2013). *Oklahoma Tornado Proven False Flag Conspiracy* (consulted May 22, 2013). At: http://beforeitsnews.com/alternative/2013/05/oklahoma-tornado-proven-false-flag-conspiracy-2657410.html

Jensen, Tom (2009). *Obama's December Standing* (consulted June 24, 2014). At: http://publicpolicypolling.blogspot.co.uk/2009/12/obamas-december-standing.html

Johnson, Luke (2013). *Ron Johnson: Obamacare 'Greatest Assault on Freedam in our Lifetime'* (consulted June 9, 2014). At: http://www.huffingtonpost.com/2013/01/28/ron-johnson-obamacare_n_2567993.html

Johnson, William (1985). *The Pace Amendment to the Constitution*. Los Angeles, CA: Johnson, Pace, Simmons & Fennell.

Johnstone, Ronald (2004). *Religion in Society*, 7th ed. Upper Saddle River, NJ: Pearson/Prentice-Hall.

Jones, Alex (2009). *Bohemian Grove* (consulted Dec. 31, 2013). At: http://www.youtube.com/watch?v=FpKdSvwYsrE

Juergensmeyer, Mark (2003). *Terror in the Mind of God*. Berkeley, CA: University of California Press.

Kimmel, Michael (2013a). *America's Angriest White Men* (consulted Sept. 5, 2014). At: http://www.salon.com/2013/11/17/americas_angriest_white_men_up_close_with_racism_rage_and_southern_supremacy/

Kimmel, Michael (2013b). *Angry White Men*. New York, NY: Nation Books.

Kornhauser, William (1959). *The Politics of Mass Society*. New York, NY: Free Press.

Kuo, David (2005). *Please, Keep Faith* (consulted Apr. 4, 2014). At: http://www.beliefnet.com/News/Politics/2005/02/Please-Keep-Faith.aspx

Labi, Nadya (2014). "Rogue Element: How an Anti-Government Militia Grew on a US Army Base." *The New Yorker* May 26: 50–61.

Larsen, Richard (2013a). "Dismantling Dollar's Status." *Idaho State Journal*, July 21, p. C1.

Larsen, Richard (2013b). "Quiet Rage Building Across the Nation." *Idaho State Journal*, Dec. 8, p. C1.

Larson, Neal (2014). "The Lessons of Arlington." *Idaho State Journal*, May 25, p. C1.

Lederer, Wolfgang (1968). *The Fear of Women*. New York, NY: Harcourt Brace Jovanovich.

Levin, Jack, and Rabrenovic, Gordana (2004). *Why We Hate*. Amherst, NY: Prometheus.

Levine, Bruce (2012). *Will the Young Rise Up and Fight Their Indentured Servitude to the Student Loan Industry?* (consulted Jan. 29, 2014). At: http://www.alternet.org/story/153879/will_the_young_rise_up_and_fight_their_indentured_servitude_to_the_student_loan_industry

Levy, Ken (2013). "Extreme Statements Made at Gun Show." *Idaho State Journal*, Feb. 7, p. A3.

Lindsey, Hal (1970). *The Late, Great Planet Earth*. Grand Rapids, MI: Zondervan.

Lipset, Seymour M. (1960). "'Fascism': Left, Right, and Center," in S. M. Lipset (ed.), *Political Man* (pp. 131–76). New York, NY: Doubleday.

Lipset, Seymour M., and Raab, Earl (1970). *The Politics of Unreason*. New York, NY: Harper & Row.

Lipset, Seymour M., and Raab, Earl (1981). "The Election and the Evangelicals." *Commentary* 15: 25–32.

Lizza, Ryan (2011). "Leap of Faith." *The New Yorker*, Aug. 15: 54–63.

Lofland, John (1977). "Becoming a World-Saver Revisited." *American Behavioral Scientist* 20: 805–18.

Lofland, John, and Skonvod, Norman (1981). "Conversion Motifs." *Journal for the Scientific Study of Religion* 20: 373–85.

Lofland, John, and Stark, Rodney (1965). "Becoming a World-Saver: A Theory of Conversion to a Deviant Perspective." *American Sociological Review* 30: 862–75.

López, Ian Haney (2014). *Dog Whistle Politics*. New York, NY: Oxford University Press.

Lothario dei Segni (1969). *On the Misery of the Human Condition*, trans. by Margaret Mary Dietz, ed. by Donald Howard. New York, NY: Bobbs.

Lott, John (2010). *More Guns Less Crime*, 3rd ed. Chicago, IL: University of Chicago Press.

Loy, David (2010). *The World Is Made of Stories*. Somerville, MA: Wisdom Publications.

MacDonald, Andrew (1980). *The Turner Diaries*. Washington, DC: National Alliance.

Mallon, Thomas (2013). "Less Said: A Biographer Speaks Up for Calvin Coolidge." *The New Yorker*, March 11: 66–71.

Marimow, Ann, and Hermann, Peter (2013). *Navy Yard Shooter Aaron Alexis Driven by Delusions* (consulted Sept. 25, 2013). At: https://www.washingtonpost.com/local/crime/fbi-police-detail-shooting-navy-yard-shooting/2013/09/25/ee321abe-2600-11e3-b3e9-d97fb087acd6_story.html

Marx, Karl (1972[1848]). "The Communist Manifesto," in Robert Tucker (ed.), *The Marx–Engels Reader*. New York: W.W. Norton & Co.

Marx, Karl (1999 [1844]). "Estranged Labor," in Charles Lemert (ed.), *Social Theory*. Boulder, CO: Westview.

Mauss, Armand (1968). "Mormon Semitism and Anti-Semitism." *Sociological Analysis* 29: 11–27.

Mazza, Ed (2014). *Tea Party Candidate Says It's OK to Stone Gays to Death* (consulted June 5, 2014). At: http://www.huffingtonpost.com/2014/06/11/scott-esk-stoning-gays_n_5486678.html

McCalmont, Lucy (2014). *Rep. Mo Brooks: Dems Wage War on Whites* (consulted Sept. 3, 2014). At: http://www.politico.com/story/2014/08/mo-brooks-war-on-whites-109703

McCloskey, Herbert (1967). "Personality and Attitude Correlates of Foreign Policy Orientation," in James N. Rosenau (ed.), *Domestic Sources of Foreign Policy* (pp. 51–110). New York, NY: Free Press.

McCloskey, Robert (1951). *American Conservatism in the Age of Enterprise*. Cambridge, MA: Harvard University Press.

McCoy, Terrence (2014). "Glenn Beck Sued for Defamation after Calling Victim of Boston Marathon Bombings the 'Money Man' behind Attack ," *Washington Post*, April 1.

McDowell, Stephen (2003). *The Bible, Slavery, and America's Founders* (consulted Dec. 18, 2011). At: http://www.wallbuilders.com/liissuesarticles.asp?id=120

McKinley Jr., James (2010). *Texas Conservatives Win Curriculum Change* (consulted Mar. 14, 2010). At: http://www.nytimes.com/2010/03/13/education/13texas.html

Menand, Louis (2013). "How the Deal Went Down." *The New Yorker*, March 4: 69–74.

Milbank, Dana (2013). "Rep. Steve King's Rotten Tomatoes." *Washington Post*, July 24.

Miller, Alice (1984). *For Your Own Good*, trans. by Hildegarde and Hunter Hannum. New York, NY: Farrar, Straus, Giroux.

Miller, Alice (n.d.). *Adolf Hitler: How Could a Monster Succeed in Blinding a Nation?* (consulted Mar. 29, 2013). At: http://www.natural child.org/alice_Miller/adolf_Hitler.html

Miller, Lisa (2013). *NRA Convention Vendor Removes Bleeding Obama Target* (consulted June 25, 2014). At: http://www.huffingtonpost.com/2013/05/06/nra-convention-obama-target_n_3223158.html

Mills, C. Wright (1940). "Situated Actions and the Vocabulary of Motives." *American Sociological Review* 5: 904–13.

Momenteller, Bob (1998). *Mena Arkansas: Drugs, Money and Murder* (consulted Apr. 23, 2012). At: http://www.etherzone.com/1998/reich3.html

Monk, Maria (1999 [1836]). "Awful Disclosures of the Hotel Dieu Nunnery," in Nancy Schultz (ed.), *Veil of Fear*. West Lafayette, IN: Purdue University Press.

Moss-Kanter, Rosabeth (1972). *Commitment and Community*. Cambridge, MA: Harvard University Press.

Mosse, George (1980). *Masses and Man: Nationalist and Fascist Perceptions of Reality*. New York, NY: H. Fertig.

National Public Radio (2010). *Growth of Militia Groups 'Astounding'* (consulted Mar. 12, 2013). At: http://www.npr.org/templates/story/story.php?storyId=125361348

Nelson, Benjamin (1949). *The Idea of Usury*. Princeton, NJ: Princeton University Press.

Neumann, Erich (1973 [1954]). *The Origins and History of Consciousness*. Princeton, NJ: Princeton University Press.

Nisbet, Robert (1953). *The Quest for Community*. New York, NY: Harper & Bros.

Noonan Jr., John (1957). *The Scholastic Analysis of Usury*. Cambridge, MA: Harvard University Press.

Norlen, Art (1992). *Death of a Proud Union*. Cataldo, ID: Tamarack Publishing.

Norquist, Grover (n.d.). *Grover Norquist Quotes* (consulted Mar. 26, 2013). At: http://www.brainyquote.com/quotes/authors/g/grover_norquist.html

North, Gary (n.d.a). *The Bible Mandates Free Market Capitalism* (consulted Nov. 11, 2011). At: http://www.garynorth.com/public/department57.cfm

North, Gary (n.d.b). *The Dominion Covenant: Genesis* (consulted Nov. 8, 2011). At: http://www.garynorth.com/public/472.cfm

North, Gary (n.d.c). *Taxation in the Bible* (consulted Oct. 26, 2011). At: http://www.garynorth.com/public/2315.cfm

North, Gary (n.d.d). *Usury, Interest, and Loans* (consulted Mar. 10, 2012). At:http://www.garynorth.com/public/4007.cfm

Novak, Michael (1981). *Toward a Theology of the Corporation*. Washington, DC: American Enterprise Institute.

Now the End Begins (2009–2014). *13 Similarities between Obama and Hitler* (consulted Jan. 1, 2014). At: http://www.nowtheendbegins.com/pages/obama/obama-and-hitler-similarities.htm

Oberschall, Anthony (1973). *Social Conflict and Social Movements*. Englewood Cliffs, NJ: Prentice-Hall.

O'Donnell, Michael (2014). "ISU Instructor Shoots Himself in the Foot," *Idaho State Journal*, Sept. 3, p. A1.

Olasky, Marvin (1996). *Renewing American Compassion*. New York, NY: Free Press.

Olasky, Marvin (2000). *Compassionate Conservatism*. New York, NY: Free Press.

Oliner, Samuel, and Oliner, Pearl (1988). *The Altruistic Personality*. New York, NY: Free Press.

Orwell, George (1944). *What Is Fascism?* (consulted Jan. 21, 2014). At: http://orwell.ru/library/articles/As_I_Please/english/efasc

Packer, George (2011). "No Death, No Taxes." *The New Yorker*, Nov. 28: 44–57.

Packer, George (2013). *The Unwinding: An Inner History of the New America*. New York, NY: Farrar, Strauss & Giroux.

Parker, Christopher, and Barreto, Matt (2013). *Change They Can't Believe In*. Princeton, NJ: Princeton University Press.

Pearlstein, Steven (2013). *Is Capitalism Moral?* (consulted Oct. 18, 2013). At: https://www.washingtonpost.com/opinions/is-capitalism-moral/2013/03/15/a9ed66d4-868b-11e2-999e-5f8e0410cb9d_story.html

Perlstein, Rick (2007). "Christian Empire." *New York Times*, Jan. 7.

Peters, Peter (1992). *Death Penalty for Homosexuals Is Prescribed in the Bible*. LaPorte, CO: Scriptures for America.

Peters, Peter (1994). *Strength of a Hero*. LaPorte, CO: Scriptures for America.

Pew Forum (2008). *US Religious Landscape Survey* (consulted Jan, 13, 2013). At: http://www.pewforum.org/files/2008/06/report2-religious-landscape-study-full.pdf

Pieper, Josef (1966 [1954]). *The Four Cardinal Virtues*. Notre Dame, IN: Notre Dame University Press.

Piketty, Thomas, and Saez, Emmanuel (2003). "Income Inequality in the United States: 1913–1998." *Quarterly Journal of Economics* 118: 1–39. Update to 2007 at: http://www.emlab.berkeley.edu/users/saez

Pitcavage, Mark (1996). *Every Man A King* (consulted Dec. 5, 2013). At: http://archive.adl.org/mwd/freemen.html

Popper, Karl (1965). "Science: Conjectures and Refutations," in *Conjectures and Refutations* (pp. 33–65). New York, NY: Basic Books.

Popper, Karl (1995 [1945]). *The Open Society and Its Enemies*. New York: NY: Routledge.

Posner, Sarah (2013). *Bush's Director of Faith-Based Initiatives Praises Liberal Successor* (consulted Apr. 4, 2014). At: http://www.salon.com/2013/02/05/former_bush_director_of_faith_based_initiative_extols_liberal_successor_partne/

Powell, Lewis (1971). *Confidential Memorandum: Attack on American Free Enterprise System* (consulted June 15, 2012). At: http://www.law.wlu.edu/powellarchives/page.asp?pageid=1251

Prince, Erik (2014). *Civilian Warriors*. New York, NY: Portfolio Trade.

Pronger, Brian (2002). *Body Fascism*. Toronto, Canada: University of Toronto Press.

Prothro, James (1954). *The Dollar Decade*. Baton Rouge, LA: Louisiana State University Press.

Public Policy Polling (2013). *Democrats and Republicans Differ in Conspiracy Theory Beliefs* (consulted Apr. 5, 2013). At:http://www.publicpolicypolling.com/main/2013/04/democrats-and-republicans-differ-on-conspiracy-theory-beliefs.html

Putnam, Robert (2001). *Bowling Alone*. New York, NY: Touchstone Books.

Rand, Ayn (1961). *The Virtue of Selfishness*. New York, NY: New American Library.

Ravitch, Diane (2013). *Reign of Error*. New York, NY: Knopf.

Reuters (2012). *Norway Killer - 'Insane' diagnosis "Worse than Death"* (consulted Aug. 28, 2015). At: http://uk.reuters.com/article/2012/04/04/uk-norway-breivik-idUKBRE8330GN20120404

Richardson, James, and Stewart, Mary (1983). "Conversion Process Models and the Jesus Movement," in James Richardson (ed.), *Conversion Careers*. Beverly Hills, CA: Sage.

Ridgeway, James (1996). *Blood in the Face*. New York, NY: Basic Books.

Roover, Raymond de (1958). "The Concept of the Just Price." *Journal of Economic History* 18: 418–34.

Rushdoony, Rousas (1973). *The Institutes of Biblical Law*. Nutley, NJ: Craig.

Ryan, John A. (1971 [1906]). *A Living Wage*. New York, NY: Arno.

Sandel, Michael (1996). *Democracy's Discontent*. Cambridge, MA: Harvard University Press.

Sandel, Michael (2012). *What Money Can't Buy*. New York, NY: Farrar, Straus & Giroux.

Schaeffer, Francis (1981). *A Christian Manifesto*. Westchester, IL: Crossway.

Schaeffer, Frank (2008). *Crazy for God*. Cambridge, MA: Da Capo Press.

Schlesinger Jr., Arthur (1986). *Cycles in American History*. Boston, MA: Houghton Mifflin.

Schlesinger Sr., Arthur (1965). "Extremism in American Politics." *Saturday Review*, Nov. 17: 21–5.

Schwartz, Peter (2014). *Objecting to the "Season of Giving"* (consulted Dec. 20, 2014). At: https://www.washingtonpost.com/opinions/objecting-to-the-season-of-giving/2014/12/19/f2ecb6a4-7fdc-11e4-9f38-95a187e4c1f7_story.html

Selznick, Gertrude, and Steinberg, Stephen (1969). *The Tenacity of Prejudice*. New York, NY: Harper Torchbooks.

Sharp, Daryl (1998). *Jungian Psychology Unplugged*. Toronto, Canada: Inner City Books.

Sheehi, Stephen (2011). *Islamophobia*. Atlanta, GA: Clarity Press.

Sherman, Gabriel (2014). *The Loudest Voice in the Room*. New York, NY: Random House.

Simmel, Georg (1977). *The Problems of the Philosophy of History*, trans. by Guy Oakes. New York, NY: Free Press.

Simpson, John (1983). "Moral Issues and Status Politics," in Robert Liebman and Robert Wuthnow (eds.), *The New Christian Right* (pp. 187–205). New York, NY: Aldine.

Skocpol, Theda (1999a). "Advocates without Members," in Theda Skocpol and Morris Fiorina (eds.), *Civil Engagement in American Democracy* (pp. 461–509). Washington, DC: Brookings Institution.

Skocpol, Theda (1999b). "How Americans Became Civic," in Theda Skocpol and Morris Fiorina (eds.), *Civil Engagement in American Democracy* (pp. 27–80). Washington, DC: Brookings Institution.

Snow, David, Zurcher Jr., Louis, and Ekland-Olson, Sheldon (1980). "Social Networks and Social Movements." *American Sociological Review* 45: 787–801.

Southern Poverty Law Cente (2011). *Pop Singing Gaede Twins Renounce Racism* (consulted Aug. 30, 2013). At: https://www.splcenter.org/fighting-hate/intelligence-report/2011/pop-singing-gaede-twins-renounce-racism

Southern Poverty Law Center (n.d.). *April Gaede* (consulted Aug. 29, 2013). At: https://www.splcenter.org/fighting-hate/extremist-files/individual/april-gaede

Staff (2014). "State Senate OKs Guns on Campus." *Idaho State Journal*, Feb. 19, p. A1

Stock, Catherine (1996). *Rural Radicals*. Ithaca, NY: Cornell University Press.

Stolberg, Sheryl, and McIntire, Mike (2013). *A Federal Budget Crisis Months in the Planning* (consulted Oct. 9, 2013). At: http://www.nytimes.com/2013/10/06/us/a-federal-budget-crisis-months-in-the-planning.html?_r=0

Stouffer, Samuel (1966). *Communism, Conformity and Civil Liberties*. New York, NY: John Wiley.

Strauss, Daniel (2014). *Ben Carson: No, I'm Not Sorry I Compared U.S. to Nazi Germany* (consulted Nov. 4, 2014). At: http://www.TPM.com

Sumner, William Graham (1883). *What Social Classes Owe to Each Other*. New York, NY: Harper & Bros.

Tabachnick, Rachel (2011). *Rushdoony's Theocratic Libertarianism at Work* (consulted Sept. 15, 2011). At: http://www.Talk2action.org/story/2011/3/15/142615/800

Tawney, Richard (1926). *Religion and the Rise of Capitalism*. New York, NY: Harcourt, Brace & Co.

Tea Party (2012). *Secession Petitions Flood White House Website* (consulted May 6, 2014). At: http://www.teaparty.org/citizens-in-four-more-states-file-petitions-to-secede-from-united-states-15670/

Thiel, Peter (2009). *Education of a Libertarian* (consulted July 13, 2010). At: http://www.cato-unbound.org/2009/04/13/peter-thiel/education-libertarian

Titmuss, Richard (1971). *The Gift Relationship*. New York, NY: Pantheon.

Turkle, Sherry (2012). *Alone Together*. New York, NY: Basic Books.

Van Ausdale, Debra, and Feagin, Joe (2001). *The First R: How Children Learn Race and Racism*. Lanham, MD: Rowman & Littlefield.

Villa-Vincencio, Charles, and Doxtader, Erik (eds.) (2003). *The Provocations of Amnesty*. Trenton, NJ: Africa World Press.

von Hayek, Friedrich A. (1976). *Mirage of Social Justice*. Chicago, IL: University of Chicago Press.

von Hayek, Friedrich A. (1994). *The Road to Serfdom*. Chicago, IL: University of Chicago Press.

Wagner, C. Peter (2011). *Spiritual Warfare Strategy*. Shippensburg, PA: Destiny Image.

Wagner, Ulrich, and Zwick, Andreas (2006) "The Relation of Formal Education to Ethnic Prejudice." *European Journal of Social Psychology* 25: 41–56.

Walker, Jeff (1999). *The Ayn Rand Cult*. Chicago, IL: Open Court.

Wallis, Roy (1982). "Network and Clockwork." *Sociology* 15: 102–7.

Ward, Jon (2013). *Jason Richwine Dissertation on Low Hispanic IQ Puts Heritage on Defensive* (consulted Dec. 30, 2013). At: http://www.huffingtonpost.com/2013/05/08/jason-richwine-dissertation_n_3240168.html

Weber, Max (1958a). "Politics as a Vocation," in Hans Gerth and C. Wright Mills (eds.), *From Max Weber* (pp. 77–128). New York, NY: Oxford University Press.

Weber, Max (1958b). *The Protestant Ethic and the Spirit of Capitalism*, trans. by Talcott Parsons. New York, NY: Scribner.

Weber, Max (1964). *Theory of Social and Economic Organization*, trans. by Talcott Parsons. New York, NY: Scribner.

Weyrich, Paul (1999). *Paul Weyrich Letter* (consulted Mar. 14, 1999). At: http://www.rfcnet.org/archives/weyrich.htm,

Wilder, Forest (2011). *Rick Perry's Army of God* (consulted Oct. 23, 2011). At: http://http://www.texasobserver.org/rick-perrys-army-of-god/

Williamson, Vanessa, Skocpol, Theda, and Coggin, John (2011). "The Tea Party and the Remaking of Republican Conservatism." *Perspectives on Politics*, March (9): 25–43.

Willis, Oliver (2013). *Alex Jones Explains How Government 'Weather Weapon' Could Have Been Behind Oklahoma Tornado* (consulted May 23, 2013). At: http://mediamatters.org/blog/2013/05/21/alex-jones-explains-how-government-weather-weap/194167

Wilson, Bruce (2011). *David Barton's Plan for Biblical Slavery for America?* (consulted Dec. 20, 2011). At: http://archives.politicususa.com/2011/04/09/david-barton%E2%80%99s-plan-for-biblical-slavery-for-america.html

Wolf, Naomi (2007a). *The End of America*. White River Junction, VT: Chelsea Green Publishing Co.

Wolf, Naomi (2007b). *Fascist America, in 10 Easy Steps* (consulted Jan. 16, 2014). At: http://www.theguardian.com/world/2007/apr/24/usa.comment

Wolfinger, Raymond et al. (1964). "America's Radical Right," in David Apter (ed.), *Ideology and Discontent* (pp. 262–93). New York, NY: Free Press.

Young, Perry Deane (1982). *God's Bullies*. New York, NY: Holt, Rinehart & Winston.

Yurica, Katherine (2004). *Dominionist Bill Limits the Supreme Court's Jurisdiction* (consulted Jan. 7, 2011). At: http://www.yuricareport.com/Dominionism/ConstitutionRestorationAct.htm

Zeskind, Leonard (2009). *Blood and Politics*. New York, NY: Farrar, Straus & Giroux.

Zimet, Abbey (2014). *Operation American Spring ...* (consulted May 15, 2014). At: http://www.CommonDreams.org

Zuesse, Eric (2013). *Final Proof the Tea Party Was Founded as a Bogus AstroTurf Movement* (consulted Jan. 28, 2014). At: http://www.huffingtonpost.com/eric-zuesse/final-proof-the-tea-party_b_4136722.html

Index